Richard Cantillon

Richard Cantillon

Pioneer of Economic Theory

Anthony Brewer

London and New York

First published 1992
by Routledge
11 New Fetter Lane, London EC4P 4EE

Simultaneously published in the USA and Canada
by Routledge
a division of Routledge, Chapman and Hall, Inc.
29 West 35th Street, New York, NY 10001

© 1992 Anthony Brewer

Typeset in 10pt Palatino by University of Bristol Printing Unit
from the author's Postscript files

Printed and bound in Great Britain by
Mackays of Chatham PLC, Chatham, Kent

All rights reserved. No part of this book may be reprinted
or reproduced or utilized in any form or by any electronic,
mechanical, or other means, now known or hereafter
invented, including photocopying and recording, or in any
information storage or retrieval system, without permission
in writing from the publishers.

British Library Cataloguing in Publication Data
Brewer, Anthony, *1942–*
    Richard Cantillon : pioneer of economic theory.
    I. Title
    330.092

    ISBN 0–415–07577–7

Library of Congress Cataloging-in-Publication Data
Brewer, Anthony, 1942–
    Richard Cantillon : pioneer of economic theory / Anthony Brewer.
       p.   cm.
    Includes bibliographical references (p.   ) and index.
    ISBN 0–415–07577–7
    1. Cantillon, Richard, d. 1734. 2. Economists—France—Biography.
I. Title.
HB105.C3B74   1992
330'.092—dc20
[B]   91–36458
                                                                     CIP

To Janet, Robert, and David

Contents

Preface ix

1. **Introduction** 1
   1.1 Cantillon's life 1
   1.2 The *Essai sur la nature du commerce en général* 9
   1.3 Outline of the book 13

Part I: Cantillon's Economics

2. **The Economic and Social Framework** 19
   2.1 Human society 19
   2.2 Villages and cities 22
   2.3 The system as a whole 24
   2.4 The location of activities 29
   2.5 The economics of Arcadia 32

3. **Population** 36
   3.1 Births, deaths, and marriages 37
   3.2 Population and land 38
   3.3 The occupational structure 41
   3.4 Population and policy 42
   3.5 The theory of population in context 46

4. **Incomes** 49
   4.1 Entrepreneurs and hired men 50
   4.2 Wages 52
   4.3 Profits and interest 54

5. **The Land Theory of Value** 61
   5.1 Market prices 62
   5.2 Intrinsic value 63
   5.3 The 'par' between land and labour 65
   5.4 Heterogeneous land 68
   Appendix: a formal model of land values 70

6. **Money, Prices, and the Trade Balance** 75
   6.1 The circulation of money 76
   6.2 The velocity of circulation 80
   6.3 Money and the price level 83

vii

	6.4 Balance of payments adjustment	84
	6.5 Money and interest rates	91
	6.6 Augmentation and diminution	92
	Appendix: the value of monetary metals	95

7. **Banking and Exchange Rates** — 98
   - 7.1 Transfers of money — 98
   - 7.2 Exchange rates and the trade balance — 100
   - 7.3 Fractional reserve banking — 102
   - 7.4 National banks — 103

8. **Trade and Trade Policy** — 105
   - 8.1 The case for the market — 106
   - 8.2 Trade policy and population — 108
   - 8.3 Policy and the trade balance — 113
   - 8.4 Cantillon and mercantilism — 118

Part II: Cantillon's Place in the History of Economics

9. **Cantillon and his Predecessors** — 123
   - 9.1 Petty — 125
   - 9.2 Locke — 137
   - 9.3 Law — 146
   - 9.4 Cantillon and his predecessors — 157

10. **Cantillon and his Successors** — 158
    - 10.1 Quesnay and the Physiocrats — 159
    - 10.2 Steuart — 175
    - 10.3 Classical economics — 183

11. **Conclusion** — 195

Bibliography — 197

Index — 205

Preface

I first read Cantillon's *Essai sur la nature du commerce en général* out of duty – I was trying to cover some of the background to classical economics, and Cantillon was on the list of 'predecessors of Adam Smith'. Within a few pages I recognized a real theorist, of a really quite modern kind. Cantillon used simplifying assumptions to get to the heart of a problem, as modern theorists do. He explicitly refused to discuss what the aims of policy should be, and confined himself to analysing how any given aims should be secured; in other words, he was doing what would now be called positive economics, without using the term. Above all, he had a clear vision of the economy as an interrelated system and a strikingly consistent analysis of how the system worked. I thought then, and I still think now, that Cantillon has been seriously underrated by the majority of historians of economics. In the eighteenth century, only Turgot was his equal as a theorist. (Adam Smith had more influence, of course, but that is a different issue.)

This book is a study of Cantillon as an economic theorist. It would, of course, be possible to write about him from various different angles – to say more about the context, or about policy issues, and so on. In my view, it is his achievement as a theorist that marks him out as a significant figure in the history of economics, so I shall concentrate on his theory. To understand his work, however, it is necessary to know just a little about the world he was writing about, just as it helps to know a little about (say) the GATT or the IMF when reading modern work on international economics. I will therefore try to provide a bare minimum of background. What I will not do is to patronize Cantillon by judging him by some imaginary eighteenth century standards. He deserves to be judged by the same standards of rigour and coherence as any modern writer.

A study of Cantillon's economics is necessarily a study of his only surviving work, the *Essai sur la nature du commerce en général*. For brevity, I refer to it as the *Essai* throughout. It is not clear whether it was originally written in French or English, but the surviving text is in French. The standard translation, by Higgs, is based on an eighteenth century version of parts of the *Essai* published by one Malachi

Postlethwayt. I have modernized spelling and punctuation – since we have to use a translation, it might as well be a translation into modern English. I have also used the word 'entrepreneur', where it appears in the French, rather than the eighteenth century, but now archaic, English translation 'undertaker'.

Parts of the book are based on papers I have already published in *History of Political Economy*: 'Cantillon and the land theory of value' (1988), 'Cantillon and mercantilism' (1988), and 'Petty and Cantillon' (1992).

I would like to thank Mark Blaug for helpful comments, Renée Prendergast for changing my mind on Cantillon's profit theory, Alan Jarvis and Helen Gray of Routledge for editorial advice and encouragement, and Janet Brewer for help and support throughout. The errors are mine.

1

Introduction

Richard Cantillon was a key figure in the early development of economics. He was one of the first to see the economy as a single inter-connected system and to try to explain how it worked, and the first to present a coherent theory of prices and income distribution. He made major contributions to monetary theory and to the theory of balance of payments adjustment. The Physiocrats, writing only a few years after the (delayed) publication of Cantillon's one surviving work, the *Essai sur la nature du commerce en général*, took many of their ideas very directly from it. Adam Smith probably learnt from Cantillon's *Essai*, as well as from the Physiocrats. There is thus a direct line of intellectual descent from Cantillon's *Essai* to Smith's *Inquiry into the Nature and Causes of the Wealth of Nations*, and to modern economics.

1.1 CANTILLON'S LIFE

Cantillon's *Essai sur la nature du commerce en général* (1755, referred to below as *Essai*) was not published until many years after his death, and it soon sank back into obscurity. Cantillon was, in any case, a rather secretive man, and little was known about him. The *Essai* was not rediscovered until the late nineteenth century, when its importance slowly came to be recognized through Jevons' article of 1881, Higgs' translation and biographical essay of 1931, and Spengler's article of 1954. Various bits of biographical information about Cantillon were unearthed, over the years, by historians of economics, but it was not until the excellent biography by Murphy was published in 1986 that a reasonably rounded picture of this enigmatic figure emerged. Some gaps remain; we still do not know for sure exactly when or where Cantillon was born, and Murphy casts some doubt on the generally accepted account of his death.[1]

Cantillon came from an Anglo-Norman family, long established as landlords in Kerry, in the west of Ireland. They lost their lands after the Cromwellian invasion of Ireland in the 1650s, but may have returned as tenant farmers in the 1670s. Ironically, Cantillon's most important predecessor as an economist, William Petty, was attached to the British army and was responsible for surveying confiscated lands, including, presumably, those confiscated from the Cantillons.

Murphy (1986) thinks that Cantillon was probably born in the 1680s, at Ballyronan in County Kerry, Ireland; Walsh (1987) says that he was born in 1697 (which is hard to square with the fact that he was in a position of responsibility in 1711). The name Richard seems to have been popular in the family – several Richard Cantillons appear in the story. I shall refer to the economist as Cantillon, *tout court*, to distinguish him from others. He was certainly in France by 1708, when he took French nationality. If he did this on reaching his majority at the age of 21, he must have been born in 1687. It was said that he 'never wore shoes before he came to Paris' (Murphy, 1986: 26), so he was presumably not well off, though he had valuable banking connections in London and Paris through relatives.

In 1711 he was working for the British government as clerk to the assistant Paymaster General in Spain, channelling payments to British prisoners of war. This early venture is an example of the international scope of Cantillon's career; for the remainder of his life he moved between European capitals, particularly London and Paris, as his business interests dictated. In the climactic year of 1720, for example, he was in London, Paris, and Amsterdam within a period of a month, at a time when travelling between these cities must have been considerably more difficult and more time consuming than travelling between (say) London, Tokyo, and New York in modern times.

In Cantillon's day, the Atlantic seaboard of Europe was emerging as the heart of an extensive trading system that

---

[1] The account of Cantillon's life presented in this section depends very heavily on Murphy's work; where no reference is given for any particular point, Murphy is the source.

stretched (literally) around the world. London, Paris, and Amsterdam were the most important centres of trade and finance. The main opportunities to make really substantial profits were to be found in international trade and finance, and in operations involving government debt, because most everyday production and trade was carried out locally, on a very small scale. Precisely because long distance trade was still very costly and risky, it required substantial capital and promised large gains.

There was intense rivalry between the Netherlands, France, and Britain. Of these, the Netherlands was, of course, the smallest and poorest in resources, but it had dominated the trade of the region in the seventeenth century, and was still, perhaps, the most prosperous and most technically advanced. Cantillon thought its day was done; a small country can only succeed 'by accidents', so 'no minister can restore the republics of Venice and Holland to the brilliant situation from which they have fallen' (*Essai*: 195).

France had the largest population and the largest land area, but was hampered by relatively archaic institutions. France's size was not an unmixed blessing; Braudel (1990: 458–9) says that France was 'doomed by its sheer size'. Land transport was slow and costly, so economic advance was heavily concentrated in areas with good access to the sea, which ruled out a lot of France.

London, the third of the great cities of Western Europe, was displacing Amsterdam as the world's entrepôt, the centre of shipping and trade. Britain, with greater resources than the Netherlands, better ports than France, and a social system which encouraged enterprise, was emerging as the new hub of the European economy. France, however, was still the most important military power. Louis XIV's attempt to dominate Western Europe led to a series of wars, and hence to opportunities for alert financiers. It also left the major states of Western Europe heavily burdened with debt and open to innovative attempts to manage the debt more effectively and to reduce the burden of interest payments.

Cantillon acted as agent in Spain for James Brydges, Paymaster General, who profited from the war on a massive scale, became successively Earl of Carnarvon and Duke of Chandos, and ended up as one of the most wealthy and powerful men in England. As his trusted agent, and soon his friend, Cantillon made important contacts. Not much later, when he was back in Paris, he took the self-exiled Bolingbroke, chief minister of England until his fall and flight, into his house; a striking measure of how far he had come in a very few years.

Returning to Paris in 1714, Cantillon was associated with the banking business of a relative (also called Richard Cantillon, but distinguished by his French title, the Chevalier Cantillon) and in 1716 he got backing from Brydges, now Earl of Carnarvon, and bought his relative out. The business had already come close to failure, and the Chevalier went bankrupt soon after, though Cantillon paid off all his debts within a year. At the time of the takeover, the bank cannot have been worth much, since the price put on it was trivial, so Cantillon started his career as a banker with very little but his wits. He soon built the business up, using his London contacts, contacts in Holland found for him by Carnarvon, and contacts with Irish merchants in Bordeaux and Nantes. Cantillon's connections in Bordeaux must also have been helpful in the wine trade, another side to his business.

Banking then was, of course, very different from banking now: a private banker like Cantillon did not take deposits from the general public, as retail banks do now. A major part of his business was the transfer of money from one place to another. Banks still do this, of course, but it has become a routine activity. In the early eighteenth century, physically shifting money from one place to another was very expensive and risky. As Cantillon explained in the *Essai*, the alternative was to find offsetting payments due in the two centres involved, so someone in London who needed to make a payment in Paris could pay a London banker, and have the money paid out in Paris, while a payment from Paris to London was cancelled off against it. The key to this business was (and is) for a banker to have branches in different centres or, more usually, correspondents in other centres. Even so, there were considerable risks, because of the time it took to get messages from one place to another, but the returns were correspondingly high. Success depended on contacts (with other bankers and with potential clients), and on skill. Cantillon had both, after his experience as Brydges' agent in Spain.

Banking was a very international business; money transfers within a single country were important but, relatively speaking, international transfers, and the financing of international trade, were much more important than they are now. Cantillon's business was international from the start, because his comparative advantage was in his excellent connections in London and Paris.

The next phase in his life was tied up with the extraordinary career of John Law. Law was a Scot, from a family of goldsmiths and bankers in Edinburgh. His father died while he was still young, leaving him a moderate sum of money which he proceeded to squander in London. He killed a man in a duel, and had to flee from England in 1695, wandering around Europe for much of the rest of his life. He seems to have supported himself mainly as a professional gambler. He developed a set of ideas about economic policy, set out in a short book, *Money and Trade Considered* (1705), and in a series of proposals addressed to various European leaders (collected in Law, 1934).[1]

After a long series of rebuffs, Law finally won the confidence of the French Regent.[2] His basic idea was that resources were underutilized because of a lack of circulating money. In itself, this was not a new idea; merchants had been complaining of scarcity of money for centuries, rather as farmers are never satisfied with the weather. The school of writers now called 'mercantilists', who dominated debate on the subject, had generally aimed to alleviate the (alleged) scarcity by ensuring a positive balance of payments, and hence an inflow of (metallic) money from abroad.

Law wanted to short-circuit this process by establishing some sort of national bank, and issuing notes. Even this was not wholly new. What was new was that Law established himself, by degrees, as the chief minister of France, and set about carrying out his scheme. A substantial part of Cantillon's *Essai* was devoted to showing why schemes like Law's could not work (see chapters 6 and 7 below); the details of the scheme are not relevant here; what matters is that it gave Cantillon his chance to make a great deal of money.

Law was able to set up a General Bank in 1716, but found that the French state was burdened with massive debts, and therefore massive interest payments, as a result of Louis XIV's

---

[1] The best source for the fascinating story of Law's life is Hyde (1969); also Bordo (1987), Deane (1989: 39-48), and Murphy (1991). On Law and Cantillon, see Murphy (1984, 1986).
[2] Louis XIV had died, leaving a child as king.

wars. This overhang of debt obstructed his plans to raise money for his bank. His next move was to copy the South Sea Company in England (which had been in existence for some years, in a fairly undramatic way). His company, which went under several names but was generally called the Mississippi Company, offered to take over government debt, at a reduced interest rate, in return for monopoly privileges in France's American territories, which stretched up the Mississippi river, but were almost completely undeveloped. To start with, shares were issued in exchange for government securities; later they were sold direct to the public, on easy terms, with a relatively small initial payment to encourage demand. In the early stages, individuals were willing to buy the shares because of exaggerated expectations of gain from the company's concessions in the French colonies.

A classic speculative boom soon developed, with people willing to pay unrealistically high prices for the shares, on the expectation of still further price increases. The shares, with a nominal value of 500 livres tournois (l.t.), were initially sold for an effective price of about 150 l.t. and ultimately reached a high of about 10,000. Those who bought early made colossal gains, as France was gripped by speculative fever. Law was able to maintain the boom for a time by manipulating monetary policy through his control of French government policy and through his bank, which had become, effectively, a central bank.

Cantillon was closely involved with these events. He was introduced to Law at an early stage, and was soon acting as banker and agent for Law in the latter's private dealings. He went into partnership with Law to buy land in the Mississippi region, and to send an expedition out to settle it (this venture came to nothing in the end). Most important, he bought shares early and sold at a large profit, thinking that the scheme was unsound and was bound to fail. Law thought highly of Cantillon to start with, then turned against him, and at one point threatened to imprison him. When Law's plans were going sour, he asked Cantillon to return as his deputy (and thus, effectively, as deputy prime minister of France) but the writing was on the wall, and Cantillon had no wish to be involved. Whether he ever had any faith in Law's scheme is doubtful, but he recognized an opportunity when he saw one.

The fortune that Cantillon made in the first phases of the Mississippi Company boom was only the beginning. The shares of the South Sea Company in England started to rise, as the speculative fever spread from Paris, and as the South Sea Company started to copy some of Law's methods. Soon, a speculative boom was raging in London, and Cantillon took advantage of it, as he had in Paris.

A third opportunity presented itself when Law, in effect, tried to raise the international value of the French livre, while at the same time trying to hold interest rates down. In the early eighteenth century, coins were of gold or silver, and often circulated outside their country of origin. Both France and England had a money of account, used for fixing prices and debts, which was not an actual coin: in England the pound sterling, in France the livre tournois. It was thus possible to change the value of coins in terms of the money of account. The notes issued by Law's bank, and the shares of his company, were denominated in livres tournois. He planned to devalue coins, and hence to raise the value of the livre tournois in terms of metal and of other currencies, as part of his plan to demonetize metals and go over to a wholly note based money. The idea was that people would choose to hold notes when they knew that specie was going to lose value.

Many believed Law could do it. Cantillon did not. He speculated against Law, by lending livres in Paris to be repaid in London in sterling. Cantillon's judgement was right, and he made another large profit, at least on paper, but he was left with the problem of collecting his debts from people who had lost a lot of money, and who blamed him for it. He was also assessed for a very large sum in tax in France, where the collapse of Law's schemes was followed by heavy retrospective taxes on those thought to have gained excessively. Even so, he was now a very rich and well known man, who mixed in the highest circles.

In the last decade of his life he was enmeshed in lawsuits, principally with Lady Mary Herbert, her lover, Joseph Gage, and their families and associates. They had borrowed from Cantillon to buy Mississippi stock, when it was riding high, (or, in the case of several relatives, had guaranteed the debts of others of the clan) and had lost heavily when the price fell. They now hoped to recoup their losses by claiming that Cantillon had defrauded them. The principal allegation was that he had taken Mississippi stock as collateral, had sold it when the price was high, and then demanded more collateral as the price fell. In effect, they accused him of having used their shares to short the market. Cantillon was even arrested and imprisoned (though only for a few hours), on criminal charges of having stolen the disputed shares. Murphy has examined the evidence, and finds Cantillon probably not guilty of the charges.

As the affair dragged on it became ever more bizarre, with accusations and counter-accusations of murder plots, involving a weird gallery of characters (including a spy and a bigamist – Cantillon's life was nothing if not colourful). There was also a separate (and less frenzied) series of disputes involving Cantillon and Law, who was back in England in the early 1720s, almost penniless, after a spell in exile in Venice. (Law left London in 1725, and died in Venice in 1729.)

In 1734, Cantillon's house in London was burnt to the ground, and a body, which was assumed to be his, was found in the ashes. Exactly what happened that night remains a mystery. First reports suggested a simple accident; Cantillon had been reading in bed, and had set fire to it. Doubts soon arose about this account, and several of Cantillon's servants were tried for murder, accused of having killed him and then ransacked the house and set fire to it to cover up the crime. Different witnesses at the trial told wildly conflicting stories, and the accused were acquitted. Suspicion remained about a cook, one Joseph Denier, who had been dismissed ten days before the fire after working for Cantillon for eleven years; he fled the country and could not be brought to trial.

Murphy discusses a further possibility, that the fire may have been deliberately set by Cantillon himself, and that the body, which was never positively identified, was not that of Cantillon. (Bodies, it seems, were not hard to get hold of for dissection.) On this hypothesis, Cantillon staged his own death in order to escape the lawsuits in which he was embroiled. The main evidence for this story is that a mysterious person, the 'Chevalier de Louvigny', turned up in the Dutch colony of Surinam immediately after Cantillon's apparent death, carrying a number of documents relating to Cantillon, as well as a considerable quantity of money and valuables. This individual was pursued but not apprehended; he abandoned the documents, which is how they were identified. He must presumably have been either the murderer or Cantillon himself. If the murderer, why would he carry these valueless but incriminating papers?

Murphy points out that there are discrepancies in the hypothesis that Cantillon was murdered: why, for example, did he withdraw a huge quantity of money on the day before his apparent death (allegedly £10,000, more money than even quite prosperous people would handle in a lifetime)? On the other hand, given that he did, might this not be the motive for murder? There is little hope that the truth will ever be known.

1.2 THE *ESSAI SUR LA NATURE DU COMMERCE EN GÉNÉRAL*

Dramatic though Cantillon's life was, he is remembered now as an economist, the author of the *Essai sur la nature du commerce en général*. There is evidence, both from his correspondence and from reports at the time of his death, that he wrote much more, starting as early as 1718 (see Murphy, 1986: 50), but only the *Essai* seems to have survived the fire in his house on the night of his death (though there is always a chance that more might turn up, preserved in an obscure archive somewhere, since Cantillon certainly sent copies of some of his writings to friends; that is how the *Essai* was rescued). What survives is a version in French, which circulated in manuscript in France for many years before it was finally published in 1755. Internal evidence suggests that it was composed around 1730 (Murphy, 1986: 246).

Which language it was originally written in is unclear; the published version was described as a translation from the English, but that proves nothing, because it was common to claim that a book had been published abroad, in order to evade the French censorship system.[1] Even if it was originally written in English, the translation could well have been done by Cantillon himself. There was originally a 'supplement', containing empirical data and numerical calculations, which Cantillon referred to frequently in the text of the *Essai*, but it is now lost.

---

[1] One Malachi Postlethwayt quoted extensively from the *Essai* (without acknowledgment) in a number of works (1749, 1751, 1755, 1757), some of which were published, in English, *before* the publication of the *Essai* in France. He clearly had access to a copy which has since been lost, possibly an English original written by Cantillon. There is no way of knowing.

In any case, the *Essai* is a work of genius, and it was undoubtedly written by Cantillon. His style is so simple and clear that it does not matter much whether the text that survives is a translation or the original; the author's intention comes across unmistakably in virtually every passage.

The subject of the book is economics. There was no generally accepted name for the subject at the time: 'commerce' or 'trade' was the best word available, so an essay on 'trade in general' was an essay on economic principles. The *Essai* deals with the topics which you would expect to be discussed in any modern textbook of economics: production, the allocation of resources between different uses, the generation and distribution of incomes, the location of different economic activities, the role of money, the effects of changes in the money stock and in monetary institutions, foreign trade, the balance of payments, and so on. It was the first systematic treatment of economic principles of a sort a modern economist would recognize.

It is primarily a work of theory. Cantillon was careful to set out his argument in general terms, without relying on specific cases, events, or countries, except as illustrations. Where he needed them to make the point, he constructed even more abstract and simplified models to focus on a particular problem; some of the key arguments of part one are presented in a model of a single isolated estate, treated as if it were a self-sufficient economy.

Even the more 'applied' material of parts two and three is set out in general terms; there are some fairly long discussions of specific cases (augmentations and diminutions of the French currency, shortages of silver currency in Britain, when the ratio of the gold and silver prices got out of line with the free market ratio, and so on), but they serve to show that Cantillon's more general theory can be adapted to deal with these special cases. In his own words: 'I confine myself always to the simple views of commerce lest I should complicate my subject, which is too much encumbered by the multiplicity of facts which relate to it' (*Essai*: 265).

The *Essai* is divided into three parts, the first dealing with a closed and essentially non-monetary economy, the second with the determinants of price levels and competitiveness in an open, monetary economy, and the third with more technical aspects of monetary policy, with exchange rates, banking, and the like. (This last part, obviously, deals with issues raised by Law's system, though Law is not mentioned by name anywhere in the *Essai*.) In short, Cantillon started with a simplified, and thus unrealistic, model, and added complications one at a time, just as a modern theorist would.

Cantillon's basic model, set out in part one of the *Essai*, is unique, in that he treated land as the only genuinely scarce resource. Population adjusts to the demand for labour, so unlimited amounts of labour are available (given time) at real wages governed by social custom. Labour can be treated as if it were a produced intermediate good. To put it very simply: labour is always available, so long as enough land is allocated to growing the necessary food, and to providing the other necessities of life.

Cantillon recognized that his model, with land as the only scarce resource, implies a land theory of value; the cost of anything can be reduced to the land needed, directly and indirectly, to produce it, including the land needed to support the labour force. Cantillon did recognize the need for capital investment in production, but he did not treat capital scarcity as a constraint on total output. In effect, he (implicitly) assumed that enough saving would always be forthcoming when there is a demand for the product. As a result, it is no surprise to find that he had no real theory of profit; this is perhaps the main weakness in his theory.

No other significant economist has ever constructed a model quite like this. Before Cantillon's time, most economic writing concentrated on trade or on monetary issues, with no very clear idea of how the economy as a whole worked. The main exception was William Petty, who is frequently said to be Cantillon's main intellectual ancestor. Petty, however, argued that land was abundant and labour scarce, a view diametrically opposed to Cantillon's (and one which makes it very difficult to see how land could command a rent, as Petty knew it did). Cantillon's immediate successors, the Physiocrats, took over much of his analytical apparatus, while arguing that agriculture in France (the only case they were interested in) was producing well below its true potential. Capital investment was needed to raise agricultural output, and increased demand and higher prices were needed to induce investment. They did, it is true, retain Cantillon's view that the surplus over labour costs accrues to the landlord as rent, but this is inconsistent with their treatment of capital, not land, as scarce. Among these early pioneers of economic theory, only Cantillon had a consistent model linking resource supplies, value, and distribution.

The second part of the *Essai* is about money. Cantillon insisted that money had to have 'intrinsic value'. He took over the quantity theory of money, which he found in Locke, and developed it. His main contribution was to insist that an increase in the money supply could only affect prices through its effect on the demand for goods, an effect which would be felt differently, at least to start with, depending on the way the extra money reached the economy. In particular, printing extra banknotes would lead either to the bank failing, or to an artificial boom vulnerable to a sudden loss of confidence. This was clearly intended as a criticism of Law's system and Law's theories.

On the other hand, a balance of trade surplus would bring in extra money, drive up prices, and eventually reverse itself. This is the 'specie-flow' mechanism, which Cantillon was one of the first to recognize. He thought, however, that price increases would take quite a long time to come through, because the money would enter the system as extra profits in the hands of merchants and export producers, who were likely to hoard the money initially, to invest later. Since prices would be slow to rise, the process could last some time. Even when prices had increased, Cantillon held that a country could sustain a high price level with balanced trade for some considerable time, provided it was based on real competitive strength in manufacturing, since competing manufactures in low cost centres would take a long time to become well enough established to be an effective threat.

This was one component of his mercantilist attitude to economic policy. 'Mercantilism' is not easy to define, and some have denied that such a thing ever existed. There can be no doubt, however, that the great majority of writers on trade in the seventeenth and early eighteenth centuries, especially in Britain, were anxious to maintain a positive balance of trade in order to increase the money stock, or the stock of precious metals, and that they sought to do so by promoting exports, and discouraging imports, of manufactures. It is convenient to have a term, 'mercantilism', to describe this common view.

Cantillon accepted mercantilist policy prescriptions, but not because of any naive identification of money with wealth. He thought that a relatively high price level could be maintained for a considerable length of time, during which the terms of trade would be favourable. He particularly stressed the benefits in terms of power and military strength; with a high price level, it would be possible to raise more money in taxes, and hence to maintain larger armies (recruited, presumably, where wages and prices were lower). He also argued that a state which exported manufactures, and used the proceeds to import food and raw materials, would be able to maintain a larger population than its territory would otherwise support, with gains in political and military power.

The final part of the *Essai* starts with a very important chapter, on foreign trade, but the rest of part three deals mainly with relatively technical matters of banking practice, along with a fairly thorough discussion of exchange markets and exchange rates. The chapters on banking are clearly designed, at least in part, to refute Law's policies and the theories they were based on.

1.3 OUTLINE OF THE BOOK

This study of Cantillon's economics is divided into two parts. In part I, I set out Cantillon's theory, with only a minimum of references to his predecessors and successors. In part II, I set his work in the context of the history of economic ideas from the late seventeenth to the late eighteenth centuries, from Petty to Adam Smith. I have adopted this plan because I want to emphasize the internal coherence of Cantillon's theory, which is best done by examining it in its own right, without digressions to discuss whether particular parts of it came from Petty, or from some other source, and without giving it marks out of ten for anticipating, or failing to anticipate, later developments.

Land and land ownership play a central role in Cantillon's economics. In chapter 2, I describe Cantillon's picture of the economic system. Significantly, his chapter titled 'of human societies' is devoted to arguing that the ownership of land is bound to be unequal, creating two primary classes, the landowners and the rest. The people who cultivate the land live in villages distributed over the face of the land, but landowners live in cities, or at least spend a large part of their incomes there. The flow of payments between city and country was the key to Cantillon's treatment of the circulation of money.

The size of the population, dealt with in chapter 3, depends on the number of people the land can support, and on the way the land is used. If there are many horses, for example, land must be used to feed horses rather than people, and the population must be below its theoretical maximum. (Almost) everyone wants to marry, and have children, but they will not do so unless they can afford to bring up their children in what they regard as a suitable style. Incomes, therefore, are determined by social custom, not by the bare physical requirements of subsistence, as in later versions of the otherwise similar 'Malthusian' account of population.

Chapter 4 deals with incomes. The general level of wages is governed by social custom, which controls the birth rate, and thus the supply of labour (in the very long run). Wage differentials must compensate for differences in risk, training costs, and the like, because of mobility of labour between occupations. The surplus over the cost of production of agricultural goods, including labour costs at socially determined levels, accrues to landlords as rent. The final section of chapter 4 examines Cantillon's rather puzzling treatment of profit and interest.

Chapter 5 covers Cantillon's account of the determinants of market prices, his explanation of the adjustment of current market prices towards 'intrinsic values', and his land theory of value. With land as the only scarce resource, the prices of goods depend on the amount of land needed to produce them, including the land needed to support the labour force.

In parts two and three of the *Essai*, Cantillon introduced money into the story. Chapter 6 deals with his account of the circulation of money, of the determinants of the velocity of circulation, and of the effects of monetary changes on the price level. Money, in his time, was based on gold and silver (mainly silver). Broadly speaking, Europe could only obtain these metals by importing them from the Americas or elsewhere. Monetary theory and the theory of the balance of payments were thus inextricably linked; Cantillon made substantial contributions to the theory of balance of payments adjustment, the specie-flow mechanism, and to the theory of money and prices. The last two sections of chapter 6, together with chapter 7, summarize Cantillon's analysis of some more technical monetary issues – augmentation and diminution of the currency, exchange rates and transfers of money, banks and banking, and so on. Many of them are connected with the lessons of Law's system.

Chapter 8, the final chapter of part I, examines Cantillon's treatment of international trade and trade policy. There is, on the face of it, a paradox here, in that Cantillon was clearly a direct ancestor of the Physiocrats, of Adam Smith, and of classical economics, in matters of economic theory, but his policy views were very much in the 'mercantilist' tradition of his contemporaries, which Smith and his followers rejected as no more than error and special pleading. I shall argue that there is no conflict between Cantillon's basic theory and his policy views. He reached different conclusions from those of the classical economists because his assumptions, both about the facts of the case and about the aims of policy, were different from theirs.

In part II of this book, I set Cantillon in the context of the history of economic theories from the late seventeenth to the late eighteenth century. Chapter 9 deals with his predecessors. Cantillon has often been linked with Petty, as part of the main line of descent which led to classical economics. Marx, for example, described Petty as the first classical economist. I shall argue that Cantillon took very little from Petty, and that he completely remade the little that he did take. Petty's system (in so far as his work is coherent enough to be called a system) was quite different from Cantillon's, because Petty explicitly and repeatedly insisted that land was not scarce, while for Cantillon land scarcity was fundamental. Locke probably taught Cantillon rather more than Petty did, at least in monetary economics, though again Cantillon went far beyond his mentor. Law is also worth considering, not because Cantillon took much from him (what they shared mainly derived from Locke), but because several sections of Cantillon's *Essai* may have been intended as implicit criticisms of Law.

Finally, in chapter 10, I examine Cantillon's legacy to his immediate successors. The most immediate and most important links connect Cantillon with Quesnay and his followers, the 'Physiocrats', who developed their theory in the decade or so after the eventual publication of the *Essai*, and who undoubtedly based much of their analysis on what they learned from Cantillon. Their work has been the subject of a great deal of research and debate, but it remains rather difficult to interpret, probably because of its internal contradictions and inconsistencies. In brief, Quesnay noted that French agriculture was far less productive than agriculture in England, but he took most of the tools of analysis which he used to discuss this problem from Cantillon, who had assumed that the land was fully used. The two best known elements of Quesnay's economics – the *Tableau Economique*, and the idea that only agriculture is truly productive – were both based very closely on Cantillon's theory, though it is unlikely that Cantillon would have approved of the uses Quesnay made of them.

James Steuart was also (almost certainly) influenced by Cantillon, though he may not have played much of a part in transmitting Cantillon's ideas to later generations of economists, because his work was so completely eclipsed by Adam Smith's *Wealth of Nations*, and because he used only the most superficial features of Cantillon's theory. Like the Physiocrats, he thought that the land was underused, so his basic framework was very different from Cantillon's. The main feature of his *Inquiry into the Principles of Political Oeconomy* was his lack of faith in the market mechanism, and his insistence that the economy had to be actively managed by a 'statesman'. Cantillon did support a variety of interventionist policies, which may have misled Steuart into thinking that they were on the same side, but Cantillon understood the strengths of the market very well, and was careful to argue, in each case, that intervention was needed because there was some policy objective at stake that individual consumers could not be expected to take account of, such as military strength.

Cantillon's influence on Turgot and Smith, the founders of the classical tradition in economics, was less direct than his influence on Quesnay and Steuart, but I will argue that he did have a significant effect on their thinking, either directly or through the Physiocrats. Smith, of course, was a major influence on almost every serious writer on economic issues for a generation or two – it was primarily through his influence on Smith that Cantillon's ideas, stripped of their most distinctive features, became part of the mainstream of economics.

Part I

Cantillon's Economics

2

The Economic and Social Framework

It is easy, at a first reading, to dismiss the opening pages of the *Essai* as mere throat-clearing by Cantillon: a rather trite definition of wealth, a couple of pages of rather odd remarks on the history of land ownership, and a few apparently irrelevant and descriptive 'chapters' (only a page or two each) on villages, towns, and the like. On a second reading their purpose is clear: they set out a vision of what an economy is like, in almost the simplest possible terms (there is an even simpler model later: the whole economy reduced to a single isolated estate). Everything that follows is based on this simple, apparently naive, beginning.

2.1 HUMAN SOCIETY

The first chapter of the *Essai*, only a third of a page long and titled 'On Wealth', is straightforward enough. The first paragraph introduces the theme.

> The land is the source or matter from whence all wealth is produced. The labour of man is the form which produces it: and wealth itself is nothing but the maintenance, conveniencies, and superfluities of life. (*Essai*: 3)

Cantillon's definition of wealth as 'the maintenance, conveniencies, and superfluities of life' is enough to acquit him of the charge Adam Smith levelled against the mercantilists, of confusing money, or precious metals, with wealth. This is important, because Cantillon recommended policies which are now thought of as mercantilist; Cantillon's 'mercantilism' will be discussed in chapter 8.

That the land is the source of wealth, and labour produces it, was almost a cliché at the time. Compare, for example, Petty: 'Labour is the father and active principle of wealth, as lands are the mother' (Petty, 1662: 68). Significantly though, Cantillon gave land the pride of place, in the very first sentence. Unlike modern economists, Cantillon did not equate 'land' with natural resources in general; 'Rivers and Seas' are mentioned separately. 'But these Seas and Rivers belong to the adjacent lands or are common to all' (*Essai*: 3); the important thing about land, as Cantillon saw it, is that it can be owned by someone. The second chapter of the *Essai* deals with the ownership of land, before labour comes into the picture. The following few chapters, on villages, towns, and so on, deal with the way people get their living, directly or indirectly, from the land, and with the geographical pattern of settlement.

Taken as a whole, the first six chapters show how land and labour are brought together, with land, and the owners of land, firmly at the centre. There is no mention of capital as a factor in the production of wealth, alongside labour and land. Cantillon did not wholly overlook the need for investment, but he did not see it as a problem. His most direct successors, the Physiocrats, thought in terms of an economy which performed well below potential, because of a lack of capital investment. Cantillon did not.

The key to Cantillon's vision of the economic system is to be found in the second chapter of the *Essai*, 'Of Human Societies'. Few modern readers would expect to find a chapter with such a title devoted almost entirely to the issue of land ownership, but for Cantillon, land ownership was the basis of society. Someone has to own the land: 'If however we suppose that the land belongs to no one in particular, it is not easy to conceive how a society of men can be formed there' (*Essai*: 7).

He took full, transferable, private ownership of land for granted; indeed, he could not conceive of a human society without it. There is no hint here of any notion of feudal ownership (despite a passing reference to the origins of land ownership in France, which he saw as the result of conquest, followed by redistribution of the land by a conquering prince – presumably the king of the Franks – who divided it between his officers). Feudal ownership was not transferable, was tied to military duties, and so on. In a feudal system, peasants were tied to the land, but had rights to it, and the relation between landowner and tenant (lord and serf) was governed by an intricate set of laws and customs, defining the rights and duties of both parties. It is true that the feudal superior, in practice, had most of the rights, and was well placed to enforce them, but feudal ownership was still very different from the unfettered ownership Cantillon took for granted. In Cantillon's account, the landowner is free to do whatever he wants with his land.[1]

Note also that Cantillon did not claim any particular moral legitimacy for the ownership of land: 'It does not appear that providence has given the right of the possession of land to one man preferably to another: the most ancient titles are founded on violence and conquest' (*Essai*: 31). His own family, after all, had acquired their lands in the Norman conquest of Ireland, and had lost them to the soldiers of the invading Cromwellian army.

The main point of the chapter was to argue that

> in what way soever a society of men is formed the ownership of the land they inhabit will necessarily belong to a small number among them. (*Essai*: 3)

The population is necessarily divided into landowners and non-landowners. Since ownership is normally based on conquest, it usually starts off very unequal. Even if ownership were equally distributed, it would soon become unequal, because some have more children to divide their inheritance between, while some are 'lazy, prodigal or sickly' (*Essai*: 5), and are compelled to sell out to the frugal and industrious. The owner of an estate 'will employ upon it the labour of those who having no land of their own are compelled to offer him their labour in order to live' (*Essai*: 5).

The chapter on land ownership ('On Human Society') also,

---

[1] In fact, there were significant relics of feudalism in France, and a few even in England, in Cantillon's time. Here, as elsewhere, he simplified. In particular, the French cultivator was subject to a bewildering series of exactions: rent, taxes, tithes, seigneurial dues, and so on (Goubert, 1973). To treat all of these as rent, accruing to the landowner, was a significant act of abstraction.

very briefly, covers income distribution and resource allocation, introducing themes which will be dealt with at greater length later:

> each owner will manage the land himself or let it to one or more farmers: . . . it is essential that the farmers and labourers should have a living whether they cultivate the land for the owner or for a farmer. The overplus of the land is at the disposition of the owner. . . . As to the use to which the land should be put, the first necessity is to employ part of it for the maintenance and food of those who work upon it and make it productive: the rest depends principally upon the humour and fashion of living of the prince, the lords and the owner . . . if they delight in horses, pasture is needed, and so on. (*Essai*: 7)

The basic theme emerges very clearly here. The land is the starting point. The owners of the land control its use. Part of the produce of the land is needed to support those who work to produce it, but Cantillon assumed that there was no real choice over the composition of this part of output. The rest of output is the 'overplus' or, in language which has become popular since, the 'surplus', and is available to the landlord in whatever form takes his fancy. The tastes of the landlord govern the composition of the disposable part of output, and thus the allocation of land between different uses, the employment of labour, and so on.

2.2 VILLAGES AND CITIES

The basic unit in Cantillon's society is a village. Labourers are needed to cultivate the land, and they must live close to their work, so there must be villages dispersed over the land, for the farmers and farm workers to live in, together with the artisans (farriers, wheelwrights, and the like) who serve their immediate practical needs. The size of each village depends on the number of workers needed to work the territory (*Essai*: 9), plus the artisans needed to provide for them. If the landlords choose to live on or near their lands (instead of living in some distant city), they add to local demand, and thus to local population, since they employ servants and tradesmen. Note the implicit assumption that the land is fully used, which is reinforced only a few pages further on: 'if the village continue in the same situation as regards employment, and derives its living from cultivating the same portion of land, it will not increase in population in a thousand years' (*Essai*: 23). At least as far as agriculture is concerned, Cantillon's model was basically static.

Market towns exist because there are economies of scale in buying and selling. If buyers and sellers are concentrated in a single place, both sides can compare prices and qualities of goods on sale, which they could not if merchants went around scattered villages. Market towns, then, exist to serve the villages of a given territory, just as the villages exist to work a specific area of land. They are also the natural place for more specialized crafts which serve a wider area than a single village. Towns are the next step in a hierarchy of settlements, based on the villages, and hence on the area and characteristics of the land. Fertile areas are more densely populated, with more and larger villages, more trade, and larger market towns, because there is more business to transact, while less fertile areas are less densely populated.

Cities have a different role in Cantillon's (idealized) world. While towns are part of the 'working' part of the system, meeting the functional needs of cultivation and of the cultivators, cities are part of the 'luxury' sector (though they do not produce luxuries alone). Cities are where landlords spend their rents, gathering together 'to enjoy agreeable society' (*Essai*: 15). Landlords' spending supports a great variety of servants, artisans and traders ('bakers, butchers, brewers, wine merchants, manufacturers of all kinds'; *Essai*: 15), and they, in turn, spend their incomes (in part) on each other's products and services. In reality, of course, cities were often centres of foreign trade and of export manufacture, as well, but Cantillon ruled that out 'so as not to complicate our subject' (*Essai*: 17). Cities are not tied directly to the land in the way that villages and market towns are; they can be fixed in some 'pleasant spot' (*Essai*: 15), but they still owe their living to the land, and their size depends on the rents that are spent there, and thus on the surplus produced by the lands owned by the landlords who live in the city.

Capital cities, centres of spending by the king or prince, his courtiers, government functionaries, and so on, depend on the surplus of the lands of the kingdom, just as other cities do, but on a larger scale. Should the king move his capital, the new capital will become great at the expense of the city it has displaced (*Essai*: 17). Cantillon's example was St Petersburg, though he could equally have pointed to the example of Versailles, which was established in a spot the king thought 'pleasant'. The palace of Versailles, together with all its associated buildings, grew until they housed some 20,000 people, the size of a very respectable city at the time, even though the main functions of government were still carried out in Paris. To picture Cantillon's world, remember that market towns of the time might have no more than a few hundred inhabitants, and many 'cities' were not much larger.

The population of each village depends on the labour needed, directly and indirectly, to cultivate the land. Similarly, the populations of towns and cities depend on the opportunities for employment, and these opportunities derive ultimately from the revenues produced in agriculture. Each trade proportions itself to the demand for it:

> It often happens that labourers and handicraftsmen have not enough employment when there are too many of them to share the business. It happens also that they are deprived of work by accidents and by variations in demand, or that they are overburdened with work according to circumstances. Be that as it may, when they have no work they quit the villages, towns or cities where they live in such numbers that those who remain are always proportioned to the employment which suffices to maintain them; when there is a continuous increase of work there is gain to be made and enough others arrive to share in it. (*Essai*: 25)

Total population, too, adjusts to the demand for labour; Cantillon's population theory will be discussed fully in chapter 3.

2.3 THE SYSTEM AS A WHOLE

At two crucial points in his analysis, Cantillon used an example of a single, self-sufficient estate, to allow him to describe a complete economy in the simplest possible terms. It appears first in his discussion of the 'par' between labour and land, the basis of his land theory of value (discussed in chapter 5 below). It reappears in his discussion of the allocation of land between different uses, which is designed to show that the market reflects landowners' preferences, just as if they controlled the use of land directly. The analysis of the isolated estate (Cantillon's equivalent of Robinson Crusoe) provides the clearest statement of how he saw resources being allocated between different uses. It is a development of the argument sketched very briefly in the chapter 'On Human Societies', which has been discussed already.

> If the owner of a large estate (which I wish to consider here as if there were no other in the world) has it cultivated himself he will follow his fancy in the use to which he will put it. (1) He will necessarily use part of it for corn to feed the labourers, mechanics and overseers who work for him, another part to feed the cattle, sheep and other animals necessary for their clothing and food or other commodities according to the way in which he wishes to maintain them. (2) He will turn part of the land into parks, gardens, fruit trees or vines as he feels inclined and into meadows for the horses he will use for his pleasure, etc. (*Essai*: 59)

This compelling image of a life of rustic simplicity is the key to Cantillon's vision of how all economies, however complex, have to work. If consumers want, say, wine, then land has to be allocated to growing the grapes, and people have to tend the vines, make the wine, and so on; they in turn have to be fed, clothed, and provided with all they need. That much is true in a complex market economy or on an isolated estate, but on the estate the highly visible hand of the landowner does the allocating. The idea may have been suggested to Cantillon by thinking about the problems of building up an estate in undeveloped colonial territories. After all, he was an investor in a projected development in the territories of the Mississippi Company. The plan was, of course, to produce goods for export, to earn money and make profits to send back to France, but the estate still had to rely on its own resources to a very considerable extent. Cantillon spoke casually of slavery and of the employment of free men, as alternative forms of labour, as they were in the Americas at that time. Alternatively, he may have got the idea by observing the relatively self-sufficient life of some of the large estates in Europe at the time. Later in the eighteenth century, for example, on the Esterhazy estate, the owner did not have to go out to listen to music because he had his own orchestra and his own resident conductor and composer, a man called Haydn.

In a market system, of course, it is not so easy to see the link between consumers' 'fancy' and its consequences for the allocation of resources.[1] Cantillon's next step was to invite the reader to imagine a decentralization of decision making on his imaginary isolated estate. The owner could decide to rent the land to those who had previously been employed as overseers, and leave them to manage the process of production, thus allowing him to 'avoid so much care and trouble'. Prices could be set at a level which would allow each individual the same living standard as before, while the landowner would only have to collect the rent and buy the things he wants in the market. The overseers now become independent entrepreneurs.[2]

If the landlord consumes the same things as before (his 'fancy' has not changed), and if all the entrepreneurs and wage workers have the same living standards as they did when they were directly employed by the owner, then outputs, employment, and land use must be the same as before. The market can thus duplicate the results of centralized decision making, save the owner the trouble of organizing everything and at the same time provide better motivation for the now independent producers. This claim mattered to Cantillon in two ways. First, it shows that there is no need for centralized control: it provides a case for *laissez-faire*. He did not stress this point, presumably because he thought that there was a case for fairly detailed government intervention in an open economy (his 'mercantilist' case for state intervention in foreign trade will be discussed in chapter 8). Second, he claimed, it shows that the market duplicates the results of control *by the landowner*, so supporting his claim that it is the choices of landowners that govern the allocation of resources.

If there is excess supply of any good, its price falls, resources shift out of producing it, and so on. Prices adjust

---

[1] 'Fancy' is Cantillon's word for what would now be called 'preferences'.
[2] 'Entrepreneur' is rendered as 'undertaker' in Higgs' English translation, following the usage of the early eighteenth century. Since 'entrepreneur' is the term now generally used in economics, I shall use it in preference to 'undertaker'.

until they cover costs and yield a normal income to the producer.[1] In equilibrium, the result will be the same as it would have been if the landlord set the prices, or if he had controlled the whole estate himself. By extension, in a full blown market economy, with many landlords, the choices they make collectively, by deciding how to spend their rents, govern the allocation of resources.

Can this argument be sustained? Cantillon presented it very plausibly, but he fell far short of providing a formal proof (cf. Bowley, 1973). It is clear that additional assumptions are needed, assumptions that Cantillon evidently took for granted (it is hard to think that he was not aware of them, or at least that he would not have recognized them if they had been put to him). First, the market can only provide different rewards to different people if they carry out different jobs. It cannot give a higher reward to a faithful old retainer, and less to one who had offended the landowner, as a landlord who kept direct control could. Second, the pattern of relative rewards for different tasks can no longer be set by the landlord. Wage determination will be discussed in the next section; suffice it to say here that Cantillon seems to have assumed a level of wages in absolute terms, and a pattern of relative wages, determined partly by real economic factors (training costs, and the like) and partly by social convention. His argument, at least in its simple form, rests on the assumption that landowners who control their estates directly would choose a level and pattern of rewards identical to that set by the market.

In order to sustain his claim that:

> the fancies, the fashions and the modes of living of the prince, and especially of the landowners, determine the use to which land is put in a state and cause the variations in the market prices of all things (*Essai*: 59; chapter title),

he also needed to assume either that the consumption patterns of non-landlords were fixed in some way, leaving no scope for effective choices by anyone other than the landlords, or that the choices made by non-landlords were governed by the landlords' choices.

The consumption patterns of the mass of the population

---

[1] Cantillon's price theory will be discussed more fully in chapter 4.

could be taken as given, governed by the same social conventions which determine wage levels: 'Labourers and mechanics who live from day to day change their mode of living only from necessity' (*Essai*: 63). This cannot be a matter of physical necessity, of wages reduced to such a level that there is only one set of purchases that allows a bare subsistence, since Cantillon recognized that wages differed greatly between different areas: wages in parts of England were vastly higher than those in southern France (*Essai*: 37–9). If, however, it represents a minimum that is *socially* acceptable, it is reasonable to think of the composition of spending as fixed by convention.

However, Cantillon faced a major problem in dealing with the consumption of better-off farmers, merchants, and so on, as he himself recognized. These people clearly had enough income to follow their own 'fancies'. His response was fairly weak: 'they take as their model the lords and owners of the land' (*Essai*: 63), and imitate them, so the choices of the landlords still dominate through emulation. This is clearly a rather weak spot in Cantillon's case. It is part of a wider problem for Cantillon's land-centred economics: the treatment of capital and profit. To allow capital and profit an independent role alongside land and rent would have undermined his whole theoretical framework, and he was not prepared to take such a drastic step.[1]

Cantillon's model of the isolated estate as a representation of the system as a whole has been interpreted in a number of different ways. From one point of view, perhaps the most important feature of the analysis is the way the market responds to consumers' demands (though only the landlords are in a position to exercise any real choice). Cantillon was the first to state the doctrine of consumer sovereignty (Bowman, 1951: 4).

A complementary view is that of Walsh and Gram (1980: 21–2) and Walsh (1987: 319), who call Cantillon's isolated estate a 'planned economy'; on this view, Cantillon's argument that the market yields the same results as direct control by the owner, parallels modern discussions of the choice between central planning and the market.

Tribe (1978), by contrast, has claimed that there was no

---

[1] The treatment of capital and profit will be discussed further in the next chapter.

such thing as 'economics' in the seventeenth and early eighteenth centuries. One of the main justifications he offers for this extraordinary assertion is that the writers of this period conceived of the state as a royal household (Tribe, 1978: 81). Cantillon's account of an isolated estate seems, on the face of it, to be a striking confirmation of this argument.[1] Indeed, Cantillon's discussion of economic policy often fits Tribe's description rather well, because it was implicitly directed to a 'prince' or ruler, who might be expected to think of the state as if it were his private property. What matters, however, is that Cantillon had a consistent and sophisticated model of the workings of a market economy, and that he had good theoretical reasons for using the isolated estate as a starting point. In his model, land was the only scarce resource, so ownership of the land inevitably had a special role.

2.4 THE LOCATION OF ACTIVITIES

Cantillon's analysis of the isolated estate served as an image of the system as a whole; a market system is a single estate writ large. His discussion of villages and towns in the early chapters of the *Essai*, however, points to one difference between a single estate and a full scale economy; the larger system is spread out over more space. There is a further development of this theme in a much later section of the *Essai*, dealing with differences in relative prices and in price levels in different regions, and with the location of economic activities (*Essai*: 149–59). This part of Cantillon's argument was postponed to part two of the *Essai* because it is cast in terms of money price levels – money only comes into the story in part two – but the argument really depends on transport costs, not on money prices, and it seems more logical to deal with it here. It is worth remarking, incidentally, that locational issues have been underplayed by many economists, though Smith's discussion of rents in urban fringe areas is an honourable exception. Cantillon's treatment of the economics of location, brief though it was, could have been a valuable

---

[1] Though one could ask what is wrong with treating the state in this way; it was in many ways an appropriate image of the world as it was at the time.

start if it had been followed up by his successors. Instead, location became a German speciality (Blaug, 1979), owing little to Cantillon.[1]

Villages and market towns are necessarily dispersed over the land. Landlords, on the other hand, often live in cities rather than on their estates, especially in the capital city, and a substantial urban population exists to supply them with the things they need. Cities make their living mainly from landlords' spending, and only to a lesser extent by producing manufactured goods for sale to the rural sector. Cantillon chose to focus on the relation between the capital city and the countryside, effectively ignoring lesser cities in this part of his story.[2] Foreign trade can also be ignored at this stage in the argument.

Transport was costly in the early eighteenth century. For example, Cantillon reported that 'the carriage of wine from Burgundy to Paris often costs more than the wine itself costs in Burgundy' (*Essai*: 75). Food prices must therefore be higher in the capital than they are in the country, to cover transport costs, while the prices of urban goods must be higher in the country. Transport of food and raw materials was typically much more expensive, per unit of value, than transport of manufactured goods (manufactured goods, after all, are raw materials with value added to them by manufacture).

In Cantillon's picture, there was a flow of rents and taxes from all regions of the countryside to the capital, and a corresponding flow of food and raw materials to support the urban population and to provide materials for urban manufactures. There had to be a corresponding gradient of food prices across the whole country, with prices lower in places further from the capital. There might, one could argue, be a similar, but inverted, gradient of manufactured goods' prices, but it would be less pronounced, and might be altogether absent or reversed if country areas drew their manufactures from nearby cities where food prices, and thus money wages, were lower.

The point is that there is a one way flow of goods from the country to the capital, corresponding to payments of taxes and rents by country people. Landowners from remote areas

---

[1] See Hebert (1981) on Cantillon's contribution to spatial economics.
[2] In both England and France at the time, the capital was very much larger than any other city (as it still is).

find that their rents, in money terms, are lower than those of better placed estates. If they choose to live at the capital, they have to pay the high prices found in the capital when they spend their relatively low rent incomes. The surplus of their estates, in real terms, may be as large as any if measured on the spot, but it is eaten up by transport costs in the process of transferring it to the capital. 'Remoteness' must, of course, be measured in terms of transport costs, not linear distances; access to the sea or to river transport would reduce transport costs dramatically, but in regions with no good access to water transport, 'it is astonishing how scarce money is there' (*Essai*: 157).

Since transport costs differ for different goods, there will not be a single price gradient, but a different gradient for each good; higher transport costs per unit of distance, relative to the unit value of the product at its point of origin, mean a steeper gradient of prices. Relative prices of agricultural products will therefore vary systematically with distance from the capital. Incentives to use the land for different products will vary with relative prices, so land use will depend systematically on distance from the capital, 'the market prices of the capital serving as a standard for the farmers to employ the land for such or such a purpose' (*Essai*: 155). Goods with high transport costs will be produced 'near' the capital (where proximity is measured in terms of transport costs – 'near' means physically close to the capital, or close to ports from which products can be shipped to the capital). It is easy to see here the germ of von Thunen's later (and presumably independent) model of the concentric rings of activity surrounding a city (cf. Hebert, 1981).

One immediate policy conclusion that Cantillon deduced from this analysis was that manufactures should be set up in remote areas, since production costs will be low (wages are low where food prices are low), and transport costs are relatively low for (some) manufactures (*Essai*: 155). This is clearly a direct application of the argument about the location of agricultural activities summarized above – since manufactured goods have relatively low transport costs per unit of value, they should be produced far from the capital.

It is, however, interesting to ask why Cantillon should have shown such an evident lack of faith in the effectiveness of the market. Why should the market not ensure that manufactures are located in the least cost locations? (Cantillon had no such doubts in the case of agriculture.) New manufactures, he said, need 'encouragement and capital' and:

> When these manufactures are set up perfection is not at once attained. If some other province have them better or cheaper or owing to the vicinity of the capital or the convenience of a sea or river communication have their transport considerably facilitated, the manufactures in question will have no success. (*Essai*: 155)

He repeatedly stressed the difficulties of setting up new manufactures – this barrier to locational mobility of manufacturing activities played a key role in some of his arguments about economic policy (see chapter 8). Briefly, it seems that he thought of skills as difficult to transfer, as they undoubtedly were at the time, so an infant industry[1] takes a long time to become established.

2.5 THE ECONOMICS OF ARCADIA

It is rather odd that a banker and financier, who spent his life, and made his fortune, in the constantly changing, intensely urban, and international world of the financial markets, should present such an Arcadian vision,[2] a picture of an essentially unchanging world dominated by the land (and the landowners). Murphy has suggested that Cantillon's apparently backward looking view of the world may have been influenced by nostalgia for the life of his Anglo-Irish land owning ancestors or, perhaps, by discussions with the conservative statesman and theorist Bolingbroke, who shared his house in Paris for a time (Murphy, 1986: 48–9, 253–4). It is also worth pointing out that Cantillon made and preserved his money mainly by taking a very sceptical attitude to Law's financial schemes. His conviction that monetary events could have few real long term effects served him well.

Was the world of the early eighteenth century really like Cantillon's model? Agriculture was certainly by far the largest sector of the economy, in both Britain and France. Indeed, the

---

[1] Cantillon did not use this term, but it is clearly what he meant.
[2] According to *Brewer's Dictionary of Phrase and Fable*, Arcadia was a byword for pastoral simplicity and rustic bliss.

odd thing is that Cantillon's estimates of the size of the agricultural and non-agricultural sectors seem, if anything, to understate the predominance of agriculture in the economy, as judged by the best modern estimates. At one point (*Essai*: 87), he referred to 'a long calculation worked out in the supplement' showing that 25 adults could produce enough to support 100 people. If 50 per cent of the population were available for work, this would mean another 25 would be free to engage in non-subsistence activities, as producers of luxuries, soldiers, or anything else. If agriculture is assumed to produce mainly non-luxuries, and if it accounts for only a part (perhaps by far the largest part) of the half of the labour force engaged in producing necessaries, this makes agricultural workers something like half the labour force.

At another point he wrote: 'It is generally calculated that one half the inhabitants of a kingdom subsist and make their abode in cities, and the other half live in the country' (*Essai*: 45). This serves as the basis for an account of flows of goods and payments between city and country, very similar in its implications to the calculation referred to above.[1]

Most modern commentators estimate the urban fraction of the population in Cantillon's time as far less than a half. For example, Bairoch estimates that the urban population was only 12 per cent of the total in Europe in 1800, with figures for different countries ranging from 9 per cent for Germany to 37 per cent for the untypical case of the Netherlands (Bairoch, 1985; cf. Braudel, 1990: 415–18, 445, 447).

It might just be possible to rescue Cantillon's estimates (though it seems unlikely), for example by assuming that he was counting all non-agricultural activities as (notionally) urban, and that he drew the boundary between agriculture and the rest of the economy rather narrowly. Many non-agricultural activities like building, making and repairing farm implements, making simple cloth and clothing, and the like, were carried out in close association with agriculture, and are doubtless included in many estimates of the size of the agricultural sector. In any case, it is clear that he cannot be accused of overstating the relative scale of agriculture. The

---

[1] Cantillon's account of flows of payments between town and country was developed further in the course of his analysis of the circulation of money and of the velocity of circulation, which will be discussed in chapter 6.

distinctive feature of his model is not the relative quantitative scale attributed to agriculture, but the analytical role ascribed to it.

A second distinctive feature of Cantillon's model is the dominant role of landowners. In the (purely hypothetical) story of the isolated estate, the landowner is dominant simply because he is the absolute ruler (like the absolute monarch of a seventeenth or eighteenth century state). In the more realistic model of a market system, which Cantillon developed from the simple story of the isolated estate, the preferences of landowners govern the allocation of resources because they are the only ones with enough income to have any real scope for choice. Cantillon knew that that was not quite true, but claimed that those non-landowners with enough disposable income to spend significant amounts on luxuries followed the pattern of spending set by the landowners.

It was certainly true, at the time, that most of the richest people were landowners. During the eighteenth century, at least in Britain, ownership of the land became more, not less, concentrated, and the great land owning families consolidated their social and political dominance (cf. Stone and Stone, 1986). This process was well under way during Cantillon's lifetime, and was described, in outline, in chapter 2 of the *Essai*, in which he argued that land ownership would inevitably be concentrated in the hands of a minority. Great fortunes could be made in trade and finance – as Cantillon's own career shows – but they were the exception, not the rule (and the main opportunities for gain in trade and finance were to be found in the money markets and in international trade, which were ruled out by assumption in the first part of the *Essai*, dealing with a closed economy). Manufacturing was still mostly carried out in small establishments, which offered few opportunities for large entrepreneurial gains.

Analytically, the centrality of land and land ownership rests on the implicit assumption that land is the only truly scarce resource, because labour and capital are in elastic supply in the long run. If land is the only scarce resource, then the surplus must accrue to the owners of land. The elastic supply of labour to the system as a whole depends on Cantillon's population theory, which will be discussed in the next chapter. Cantillon's systematic neglect of capital has been noted already, and will be discussed further in chapter 4. Briefly: he did recognize that individual entrepreneurs had to have access to enough funds to finance their activities, and he explained interest rates in terms of the potential returns to investment. At the same time he implicitly assumed that capital would always be forthcoming to carry out all the activities for which there was enough demand. This may not have been an unreasonable assumption at the time, given the still very slow progress of technical change. It is, at least, arguable that capital was being accumulated fast enough to keep pace with the (limited) new investment opportunities created by technical change.

Cantillon, of course, spent most of his life in France. The last work of the great French historian Fernand Braudel (1990) is a magisterial work of synthesis, dealing with the history of population and production in France. It is striking how much Braudel's account has in common with Cantillon's. According to Braudel, French population had been roughly constant for many centuries up to Cantillon's time (with a collapse in the fourteenth century and a recovery from 1450 to 1600), and it remained constant because France simply could not support a larger population. He cited Spooner's (1972) estimate that French GNP was stationary during the first half of the eighteenth century, and described France as a 'peasant economy' (up to the twentieth century), with patterns of rural settlement and rural life that changed only very slowly over the centuries. This, and much more in Braudel's account, matches Cantillon's story strikingly well; Cantillon's approach seems to have been quite appropriate to the French economy of the time.

It is, however, much harder to defend Cantillon's model as a representation of England in the early eighteenth century. One can, of course, find elements of rural life in England that were relatively constant, but new methods of cultivation, and continued investment in agricultural improvements, led to relatively rapid changes in British agriculture. Cantillon was, of course, careful not to limit his model to any particular place or time. His examples were drawn both from England and from France.

3

Population

Two opposed views of population dominated the literature in the seventeenth and early eighteenth centuries. William Petty, who was one of the founders of modern demography, as well as an important pioneer of economics, was perhaps the most convincing supporter of the 'populationist' view. He claimed that there was plenty of underused land in both England and France (Petty, 1690: 285), and that there were also many opportunities to employ additional workers outside agriculture. He even advocated shifting most of the population of Ireland to Britain, in order to increase the population of Britain (Petty, 1690: 285ff and 1687, passim). An increase in population would, he claimed, allow an increase in both output and tax revenue.

Cantillon took the opposite view. 'Men multiply like mice in a barn if they have unlimited means of subsistence' (*Essai*: 83). Population always expands to take up the economic opportunities open to it, but if there are no new opportunities, population cannot increase. If, for example, a village continues to work the same lands in the same way, and if its circumstances remain the same, 'it will not increase in population in a thousand years' (*Essai*: 23). The same is true of a whole economy. A larger population would indeed be a good thing, but population can only increase if there is an increase in the demand for labour.[1]

The notion of an endogenous population, governed by the availability of food, was not new: there is little point in tracing

---

[1] Cantillon is sometimes counted as a populationist, like Petty, because he thought of population increase as a desirable aim of policy, but for him population increase was a *result* of other economic changes, not a *cause* of economic growth in its own right.

it back to its origins, since it must be about as old as discussion of population itself (cf. Spiegel, 1983: 277–8; Spengler, 1942). Cantillon's importance is that he made it a cornerstone of his economic analysis. Even his best known phrase, 'men multiply like mice in a barn' (*Essai*: 83), was not original; it was said in Languedoc in the mid sixteenth century that 'people are multiplying like mice in a barn' (Braudel, 1990: 171, citing Ladurie, 1966).

Cantillon's 'Malthusian' analysis (set out, of course, many decades before Malthus) was adopted by almost all economists for more than a century after his death. Unlike most of his successors, he stressed economic influences on marriage rates and birth rates, rather than on death rates. As a result, his theory was more flexible than most other versions of 'Malthusian' population theory, and did not require wages to be reduced to the bare physiological minimum of subsistence. Like many other writers, Cantillon recognized a conventional element to wages, but his theory, unlike most, could incorporate them in a natural fashion.

3.1 BIRTHS, DEATHS, AND MARRIAGES

Cantillon based his theory of population on simple premises. He argued that

> most men desire nothing better than to marry if they are set in a position to keep their families in the same style as they are content to live themselves. (*Essai:* 77)

He then adduced evidence to show that actual birth rates were far below the biological maximum. Since 'a single generation suffices to push the increase of population as far as the produce of land will supply means of subsistence' (*Essai*: 81), he concluded that population growth must be constrained by economic circumstances.

Most people want to marry and to have children, but not if this would reduce them (and their children) to poverty, or to a level of living that they would consider unacceptable. The nobility are used to living well, so younger sons, who do not stand to inherit the family estate, become priests or soldiers and remain celibate (perhaps Cantillon should have said 'do not acknowledge their children'), but they will 'seldom be found unwilling to marry if they are offered heiresses' (*Essai*: 79). In all classes, people will marry, but they would consider it 'an injustice to their children' to allow them to fall into a lower class than themselves. If incomes are high enough to support a family at an acceptable living standard, a single man could live well, since Cantillon thought that a family cost twice as much to support as a single man. Some men choose to remain single for this reason, but most do not.

There must be some constraint to population growth, he argued, since four out of six fertile women who could have children in any given year, do not. Population growth is far below what would be biologically possible, because many women do not marry (either because they choose not to or because they cannot find anyone to marry), and unmarried women take care not to give birth without a husband (*Essai*: 81; cf. Braudel, 1990: 195, on illegitimacy rates and contraceptive use in seventeenth and eighteenth century France). A few men refrain from marriage because they prefer the easy life of a single man, or for other personal reasons, but they are a minority (*Essai*: 79); the dominant factors governing the overall rate of population growth are economic.

Cantillon's argument does not imply that the mass of the people are reduced to the verge of starvation, even in bad years, since the population can be restrained at levels well above physiological subsistence, once these higher standards are built into people's expectations of an acceptable living standard. The harsher Malthusian mechanism of starvation remains to deal with the improvident, who marry without providing for the future: 'if they marry, the children who come will soon die of starvation with their parents, as we see every day in France' (*Essai*: 23).

3.2 POPULATION AND LAND

Population is limited by the amount of land available. This is true of human beings as it is of any other sort of plant or animal:

> Experience shows that trees, plants and other vegetables can be increased to any quantity which the extent of ground laid out for them can support.... In a word,... the multiplication of animals has no other bounds than the

greater or less means allotted to their subsistence. It is not to be doubted that if all land were devoted to the simple sustenance of man the race would increase up to the number that the land would support. (*Essai*: 67)

Cantillon devoted a substantial amount of the generally very terse *Essai* to discussion of the amount of land needed to support each person.[1] He argued that it took about twice as much land to support a family (large enough to replace the population, generation after generation) as it did to support a single man at a given standard of living (*Essai*: 33–5). The earnings of the wife, and her cost of living, are left out of the calculation, on the assumption that her labour covers her own living but no more (*Essai*: 37); the husband's earnings must support the children. Cantillon's calculations do not, perhaps, inspire any great confidence, but the principle is clear enough (he himself remarked that 'it suffices to be near enough to the truth' *Essai*: 35).

It is interesting to note that Marx, who seems to have known Cantillon through a passage quoted by Smith, completely misunderstood this part of Cantillon's argument, which he took to mean that each worker *produced* twice what he (and his family) consumed (Marx, 1963: 73). Tarascio (1981: 14) made the same mistake, and was led to claim that Cantillon thought agricultural workers got half of what they produced, regardless of whether the land was fertile or not. In fact, the doctrine of the three rents implies that agricultural workers get a third of the produce (so each, presumably, produces enough to support three families, and hence six single men). It is true that Cantillon implied that agricultural producers (farmers and hired hands taken together) produced about twice the agricultural produce that they consumed, since he claimed that they made up about half of the population, supporting themselves and an equal number of city dwellers. The farmers, however, get more (per head) than the workers they employ, and spend some of their income on manufactures, so there is no conflict with the doctrine of the three rents. In yet another context (*Essai*: 87, discussed in section 3.3 below),

---

[1] The amount of *land* matters, in population theory, because land is the only scarce resource. In addition, land requirements have a special significance in Cantillon's theoretical system, because his theory of value was based on land.

Cantillon claimed that 25 workers could support a population of 100, including non-producing landlords and dependents. This particular numerical example is rather difficult to square with the rest of Cantillon's calculations, and may be the source of some of the confusion.

Having established the rule of thumb that the average income must be twice what it costs to support a single adult, Cantillon presented a number of calculations (based on fuller details in the lost supplement) of the actual amount of land it took to support a single worker in various different places, at different standards of living. In China, intensive cultivation of rice together with a low standard of living (so low that many starved in bad years) allowed an extreme density of population (*Essai*: 67–9): one acre per person. At the opposite extreme, 'the savages in the interior parts of America' need 50 to 100 acres each, because they rely on hunting, and the forests support relatively little game (*Essai*: 69). Here the contrast is clearly between different ways of life, and different technologies, together with different levels of fertility of the soil.

The maximum population that a given territory can support also depends on the amount each person consumes. With European methods of cultivation and average soil, a man can live at a minimal level of subsistence on the produce of one and a half acres ('like many peasants in the south of France' *Essai*: 71).[1] The norm in southern England was much higher, five to eight acres (*Essai*: 39). Tarascio (1981) took this to mean that land in southern England is less fertile than land in the south of France, since he thought that workers only got a minimum subsistence wage (in Cantillon's system); the context seems to me to make it quite clear that Cantillon was describing a difference in standards of living, not simply of fertility, since he specified the diet and clothing corresponding to a land requirement of five to eight acres in some detail (*Essai*: 37, 71), contrasing it with that of the poor peasant of southern France. In any case, it seems unlikely that Cantillon would have thought that output per acre was lower in the

---

[1] Cantillon seems to have thought that peasants in the south of France drank only water – either things have changed, or he was ill informed. According to Goubert (1973), the south of France was richer than the north in the pre-revolutionary period, contrary to Cantillon's implication.

south of England than in France, since England was the more developed country, and agricultural productivity was almost certainly higher in England than in France.

A lower standard of living, then, allows a larger (potential) population (*Essai*: 83). Cantillon was very careful in the way he dealt with this issue: 'It is also a question outside of my subject whether it is better to have a great multitude of inhabitants, poor and badly provided, than a smaller number, much more at their ease' (*Essai*: 85).

3.3 THE OCCUPATIONAL STRUCTURE

The productivity of the land may determine the maximum population, but the actual population, and its composition, depends on the use made of the land. In Cantillon's story, the decisions made by landowners govern the overall allocation of resources, and thus determine the demand for labour, the total size of the population, and its distribution between different occupations.

> It is need and necessity which enable farmers, mechanics, officers, soldiers, sailors, domestic servants and all the other classes who work or are employed in the state to exist. All these working people serve not only the prince and the landowners but each other, so that there are many of them who do not work directly for the landowners, and so it is not seen that they subsist on the capital of these proprietors and live at their expense. (*Essai*: 47)

In other words, each occupational group makes a living because there is a demand for its services, and that demand stems ultimately from the spending decisions made by the landlords.[1]

The numbers in each occupational group adjust to the demand. Cantillon described a number of mechanisms which operate to restore equilibrium – if there were too many people competing for too few jobs, the result might be unemployment, forcing the unemployed to change their plans, or it

---

[1] The word 'capital' in the quoted extract is a translation of the French 'fonds', and does not imply a modern concept of capital; it could be translated as 'estate' or 'property'.

might instead be a general reduction in incomes as a limited amount of work is shared out among them, reducing incomes below the level regarded as adequate. Some will then migrate to other places, switch occupations, or refrain from marriage, reducing the next generation. Between them these mechanisms ensure that the supply of labour matches the demand in each trade, in each locality, and in total. Thus:

> If all the labourers in a village breed up several sons to the same work there will be too many labourers to cultivate the lands belonging to the village, and the surplus adults must go to seek a living elsewhere, which they generally do in cities. (*Essai*: 23)

The same is true for all the different trades found in market towns and cities. If there are too many tailors, for example, none can make a satisfactory living (*Essai*: 25).

It is clear that Cantillon expected most children to follow the occupations or trades of their fathers. Each trade then reproduces itself from generation to generation, in the same way as the population as a whole, and the numbers in successive generations are controlled by the same demographic mechanisms that govern the population as a whole. Thus:

> As the handicraftsmen earn more than the labourers they are better able to bring up their children to crafts, and there will never be a lack of craftsmen in a state when there is enough work for their constant employment. (*Essai*: 27)

The better-off parts of the population may produce more children than are needed to replace the previous generation, in which case younger sons must find some other occupation; the younger sons of the nobility become soldiers or priests, while members of other classes become soldiers (presumably as lower ranks), lackeys, and the like. Occupational status is partly, but not wholly, inherited.

3.4 POPULATION AND POLICY

Total population is limited by the carrying capacity of the land, but it normally falls below that limit, since the use of the land is not calculated to maximize population. Population size

POPULATION

is an unplanned side-effect of the consumption decisions of landlords. Cantillon introduced this idea in his discussion of an isolated estate (already discussed in chapter 2).

If a lord or owner who has let out his lands to farm, take the fancy to change considerably his mode of living, if for instance he decreases the number of his domestic servants and increases the number of his horses, not only will his servants be forced to leave the estate in question but also a proportionate number of artisans and of labourers who worked to maintain them. The portion of land which was used to maintain these inhabitants will be laid down to grass for the new horses, and if all landowners in a state did the like they would soon increase the number of horses and diminish the number of men. (*Essai*: 63–5)

There are several points to be made about this argument. First, it does not depend on the direct control of the landlord over the estate. Decentralization through the market has no effect on the outcome; that is the point of Cantillon's example of the isolated estate. When the owner 'has let out his lands to farm', a change in his buying habits sends market signals which lead farmers to produce less human food and more hay for the horses (in this example), as Cantillon explained in the paragraph following the one quoted above.

Second, the important point is not that the landowner dismisses servants and spends the money on something else, it is that he has switched from labour intensive to land intensive forms of consumption. Thus, if he switched from employing servants to buying a very labour intensive product such as lace, the effect on the total demand for labour would be very small. In a slightly different context, Cantillon explained that the value of lace was almost wholly made up of labour cost, and for a watch spring the labour proportion was even higher, with a ratio of labour to material cost of a million to one (*Essai*: 28–9).

Cantillon was particularly concerned with the effect of transport by horses on population, since production of fodder for horses competes directly for land with the growing of human food. 'The more horses there are in a state the less food will remain for the people' (*Essai*: 75; cf. Braudel, 1990: 248). Huge numbers of horses were, of course, used for transport in the eighteenth century. Sea transport, by contrast, was labour intensive, so spending on goods transported by water did not reduce population in the same way; the buyer had to pay enough to cover the labour costs of shipping, sailors then spent their wages on food, so land was allocated to producing food for them. Cantillon had a very firm grasp of the implications of his fundamental assumption that land was the only scarce resource.

The determinants of population play a substantial role in the *Essai* because Cantillon accepted that a large population was a good thing, or at least that it was thought of as a good thing and that people were concerned about it; 'the more labour there is in a state, the more naturally rich it is esteemed' (*Essai*: 87, chapter title). The market does its job well, in that it produces the same pattern of output that the landlords would have chosen had they controlled the use of land directly, while saving them the trouble of managing their states directly, but it leaves the total population to be determined as a side-effect of the process. If population is a matter for concern, perhaps for military reasons, there is a case for some sort of state intervention.

Concern with the economic determinants of population becomes a much more significant issue in an open economy. Indeed, Cantillon broke his general rule, that part one of the *Essai* was confined to the discussion of an open economy, in his discussion of population. The basic point is simple. Population depends on the extent to which land is used to provide food, and other necessities of life, for the people. If food is exported, then the population which consumes it is located in another country, and population is reduced in the food-exporting country. If other land intensive products are exported, land is diverted away from food production, and population falls. On the other hand, if labour intensive manufactures are exported and the proceeds used to import food, population is increased. The same is true if exports of manufactures are used to pay for imports of raw materials which would otherwise have been produced by using local land. This was one of the main reasons for Cantillon's support for 'mercantilist' policies of trade restriction, which will be discussed more fully in chapter 8.

Similar issues emerge in a rather odd chapter in the *Essai*, titled 'the more labour there is in a state the more naturally rich the state is esteemed' (*Essai*: 87–95). Suppose that 50 out of 100 people are fit to work (excluding children, the old, the landowners, and others who do not need to work), but that 25 can provide all the necessities of life ('according to the European standard') for themselves and all the others. What do the other 25 do? On the face of it, this is an odd question. The 25 surplus workers correspond to the surplus available to the landowners as rent, and will be occupied in whatever trades satisfy the demands of landowners, as Cantillon indicated only a few pages later. In this chapter, however, he approached the question from a political angle. What should they be set to do? Their labour can be used to raise the quality of goods: fine cloths, linen, and the like involve more labour than coarser equivalents, even though they are no more serviceable. A state where fine clothes are worn, 'where feeding is dainty and elegant', will be more highly esteemed.

Better, though, to produce durable goods and store them up as a 'reserve stock' (*Essai*: 89–91), and best of all if the reserve stock is of gold or silver, which 'are not only durable but so to speak permanent, which fire itself cannot destroy, which are generally accepted as the measure of value, which can always be exchanged for any of the necessities of life' (*Essai*: 89). If all else fails, the surplus part of the population can be employed to produce pure luxuries, since work, however pointless, is better than idleness.

At first sight, it might seem that Cantillon was concerned with the possibility of chronic unemployment as a result of lack of demand. The whole of the chapter is very similar to passages in Petty, who certainly did think of unemployment as a problem. In Cantillon's model, however, the population adapts to fit the demand for labour, which is determined by the available land and the spending decisions of landowners, so unemployment is not an issue, at least as long as landlords spend their incomes. Cantillon recognized this implication of his own theory, since the paragraph in which he says that work is better than idleness is immediately followed by a paragraph insisting that 'it is always the inspiration of the proprietors of the land which encourages or discourages the different occupations of the people' (*Essai*: 93).

Unemployment is not the problem; the point is that some uses of the surplus are better than others, and should be encouraged, a theme which appears several times in Cantillon's policy discussions (cf. Boss, 1990: 29–30). The system responds to the fancies of the landowners, but the ruler should encourage some tastes rather than others.

3.5 THE THEORY OF POPULATION IN CONTEXT

It may seem odd that Cantillon saw population as essentially static, when we know that the population of all the main countries in Europe has in fact grown over the centuries. Modern estimates of population growth were not, of course, available to Cantillon: demography was in its infancy when he wrote. He could, however, use his eyes, and draw on what was known at the time. In fact, modern estimates suggest that population growth for Western Europe as a whole was very slow in the century or so before Cantillon wrote. The first half of the seventeenth century was disastrous, with massive loss of life in wars, especially in the thirty years war in northern Europe. The second half saw some recovery, but that would not have posed any problem for Cantillon, since his theory would have predicted that any major population loss for exceptional reasons would soon be replaced. Many commentators at the time thought that population was actually falling, or had fallen. Cantillon's idea of the facts of the case can be judged by his (very dubious) claim that Italy had a population of 26 million in classical times, 'now reduced to 6 millions at most' (*Essai*: 83).

Braudel's discussion of the evidence for France leads him to suggest that population stagnated between about 1600 and 1750. Since population in 1600 had only just recovered to the level of about 1300, before the plagues and other disasters of the fourteenth century, he estimates that there had been little net change in the population of France over more than four centuries (Braudel, 1990: 170, 173–6). What is more, Braudel's synthesis of the evidence for France suggests that population stagnated for exactly the reasons that Cantillon emphasized. Given the technology of the time, France could not support a larger population, so whenever population grew beyond an optimum level, there were setbacks of some sort to right the balance. Peasants were prevented from marrying for fear of poverty, and forms of contraception were used, along with late marriage and celibacy, from the seventeenth or even the sixteenth century (Braudel, 1990: 174, 192, 195, 200–1). A respected observer said as late as 1787 that French agriculture had made no progress since Roman times (Gilbert, 1787, cited by Braudel, 1990: 353–4). This may not have been literally true, but it indicates that Cantillon's implicit assumption of static technology in agriculture was fairly accurate as a description of the situation in France. The same could not be said of Britain.

Cantillon's only references to the scanty demographic literature of the time are, in fact, to British writers (Petty, Halley, King, and Davenant). Britain (specifically, England) was the most successful and most rapidly growing economy of the time, but even in England population growth was slow. Modern estimates suggest that population grew rapidly in the sixteenth century, and again from the middle of the eighteenth century, starting at about the date of Cantillon's death, but they suggest that the seventeenth and early eighteenth centuries were a period of relative stagnation.[1] Petty suggested that population doubled in a period of a few hundred years,[2] which is not a particularly striking rate of growth. In any case, Cantillon was not impressed by Petty's work; he remarked of Petty's attempt to 'estimate the propagation of the race from Adam', and of Davenant's similar effort, that their calculations 'seem to be purely imaginary and drawn up at hazard' (*Essai*: 83).

Petty, with John Graunt, had produced estimates of population growth in London and in country districts. They found that the population of London was growing rapidly (this was in the late seventeenth century), but the population of the country towns they looked at seemed to have been constant for a very long time, with positive natural growth of population offset by emigration. Petty treated this as a coincidence. It is easy to see how it could be accounted for in Cantillon's scheme; population in country districts is constant because employment opportunities there are constant. At the same time, London could grow, drawing in migrants from the country, because it was becoming a great centre of international trade. London's gain was Amsterdam's loss.

I conclude that Cantillon's population theory was perfectly reasonable, given the evidence available to him. That is not to say that it was true. In the second half of the eighteenth century, after Cantillon's death, population grew rapidly in most parts of Europe. The agricultural revolution in Britain, which was already under way in Cantillon's lifetime, led to an

---

[1] Interestingly, there was a demographic crisis among the landed élite in Britain in this period (Stone and Stone, 1986).

[2] There are different estimates in different parts of his writings; it is difficult to be sure which of them Cantillon would have known.

expansion of grain exports from Britain in the mid eighteenth century, despite a considerable growth in the number of mouths to be fed. Agricultural growth depended on capital investment in hedging, drainage, and the like, and also on the adoption of new crops and new agricultural methods, precisely the factors that Cantillon left out of his account.

4

Incomes

In Cantillon's system, the primary division in the population is between landowners and the rest. Landowners either cultivate their land directly, pay the costs, and enjoy the surplus of output over cost, or they let the land to farmers, and enjoy the rents. Rent income is simply the surplus of output over the incomes of farmers and farm labourers. The prices of all non-agricultural goods adjust to cover the costs of producing them. All non-rent incomes, in this framework, are part of costs, so Cantillon said that non-landowners all lived 'at the expense' of the landlords. His discussions of incomes are mainly taken up with discussions of the incomes of non-landowners; once they are determined, landlords get what is left over.

Cantillon's theory of distribution is thus a 'surplus' theory, in the terminology adopted by many recent writers. To say this is not to say very much, merely that one category of income (in this case, rent) is treated as a residual after subtracting other incomes (treated as costs) from total output. Without an explanation of total output, of input requirements, and of the incomes paid to those who supply other inputs, it is vacuous. In particular, surplus theories cannot provide an alternative to supply and demand as an explanation of incomes, since supply and demand factors inevitably enter into the explanation of the level and composition of output and of the levels of those incomes which are not treated as part of the surplus.

O'Donnell (1990: 23–4, cf. Blaug, 1991b) has proposed a pair of definitions of 'surplus' and neoclassical theories. In his account, surplus theories take as data (1) the size and composition of the social product, (2) the technique in use, and (3) the real wage, while neoclassical theories take as data (1) the preferences of consumers, (2) the size and distribution of endowments, and (3) the technology of production. By these standards, Cantillon must be counted as a neoclassical, because he did indeed take preferences ('fancies'), endowments (of land), and technology, as given. He also meets two of the three conditions needed to count as a surplus theorist, since he took the real wage and the techniques in use as given, though he fails on item (1), since he devoted a great deal of attention to the determinants of the size and composition of total output. Perhaps this should not be counted against him, because no significant economist ever did treat total output as given, at least before Sraffa (1960), so Cantillon is not alone (cf. Blaug, 1991b).

4.1 ENTREPRENEURS AND HIRED MEN

In a market system, commodities have to be produced, transported, and stored, before they are sold to final consumers. If production is out of line with demand, prices will adjust, incentives will change, and equilibrium will eventually be restored. In the meantime, some will have lost and some will have gained. Someone has to take these risks. Cantillon drew a distinction between entrepreneurs ('undertakers' in Higgs' translation), who produce or trade on their own account, and thus carry risks, and 'hired men', who do not:

> it may be laid down that except the prince and the proprietors of land, all the inhabitants of a state are dependent; that they can be divided into two classes, undertakers and hired people; and that all the undertakers are as it were on unfixed wages and the others on wages fixed as long as they receive them though their functions and ranks may be very unequal. (*Essai*: 55)

Entrepreneurs are not necessarily rich: anyone who bears risks by trading on his or her own account counts as an entrepreneur. So, for example, water carriers in Paris (one of Cantillon's favourite examples), who used to collect water from the Seine and sell it to households away from the river, were entrepreneurs, although they ranked very low in income and social standing. Courtiers at the royal court who lived on pensions (salaries) awarded by the king (as opposed to independent landlords who visited the king's court) were hired men, however rich and powerful some of them may have been. Cantillon was probably the first to use the term 'entrepreneur' in this way, at least in a theoretical context (Hoselitz, 1951).

According to Hoselitz, the word 'entrepreneur' goes back to the middle ages, when it simply meant someone who gets things done, or who undertakes some project (such as a war). By Cantillon's time, it had acquired an economic meaning, and was used to mean a large scale contractor, particularly a contractor to the state. The equivalent word in English was 'undertaker', or 'adventurer' (as in 'merchant adventurer'). Cantillon reinterpreted the word, applied it specifically to risk taking, and generalized it to cover anyone who received a residual income, as opposed to a contractual income, regardless of the scale of their business. Say, who wrote nearly a century later, is often wrongly credited with inventing the term. His usage, however, was different – he saw the entrepreneur primarily as a planner, not as a risk taker – so he probably developed the idea independently (Hoselitz, 1951).[1]

Tribe (1978: 91–2) cites Cantillon's division between the two classes of entrepreneurs and hired men, to support a claim that Cantillon (along with everyone else of his time) was not an 'economist'. He seems to think that Cantillon's classification can be dismissed as eccentric and irrelevant simply because generals, courtiers, and domestic servants all fall into the class of hired men, while both farmers and beggars are counted as entrepreneurs. Part of his difficulty seems to be that he reads the division between the two as a division between productive and unproductive sections of the population, though which Cantillon is supposed to have regarded as productive and which as unproductive is not obvious – agricultural workers and domestic servants both count as 'hired men'.

To avoid such confusions, it may be worth repeating that Cantillon's division is between those who receive contractual incomes, and those who trade on their own account, and hence take risks. The distinction is relevant to any account of the workings of the economy, because the two take different

---

[1] This distinction should not be overstressed. Cantillon's entrepreneur takes risks because he or she is operating as an independent trader, and therefore must be taking decisions and making plans.

kinds of decisions and play different roles in the working of markets. It is not a division by income or status, nor is it a division between productive and unproductive. It does not imply that the two classes are opposed to each other, or anything of the sort. As for Tribe's claim that Cantillon was not an economist, it seems to rest on a peculiar definition of the term, and little else.

4.2 WAGES

Cantillon treated all non-rent incomes as essentially the same, whether they were wages in the modern sense (the wages of 'hired men'), or entrepreneurial incomes (which modern theorists would treat as partly wages of management, partly return on capital, partly risk premium, and so on). The difference between the two is that entrepreneurs receive 'unfixed wages'. It is, of course, true that a large part of the population in the early eighteenth century were self-employed peasants, artisans, traders, and the like (entrepreneurs, in Cantillon's terms), though many were employed as wage earners. There was no clear separation between rich employers and poor workers. It is therefore not surprising that Cantillon did not make a sharp distinction between wages and profits, in the way later writers did. He discussed non-rent incomes from different points of view in different contexts, so it is difficult to find a definitive statement of his wage theory. It may be significant that he did not even have a consistent terminology to deal with wages – he wrote of the amount different people are paid, the amount labour is worth, and so on.

The overall level of wages is not determined, except by social custom or habit. In his discussion of an estate run by its owner, the basic statement of his theory of distribution, Cantillon first assumed that the living standards of workers were set by the owner. Slaves[1] must be given enough to live on, and to support their children. Overseers 'must be allowed advantages proportional to the confidence and authority' given them (*Essai*: 33). (Slave) craftsmen must be better

---

[1] Cantillon presumably discussed slavery mainly in order to make his point in a context in which the owner was the only active decision maker, but his interests in America may well have influenced him in this choice of example.

provided for than labouring slaves, because the loss of a trained artisan would be worse than the loss of an untrained slave. It seems that a scale of 'wages' emerges even among slaves, for wholly functional reasons.

If the owner employs free peasants, 'he will probably maintain them on a better foot than slaves according to the custom of the place he lives in' (*Essai*: 35). This is one of Cantillon's few explicit statements about the general level of wages. Wages are ('probably') set by 'the custom of the place', but subject to the landowners choice (as with almost everything, in Cantillon's model). In the case of an isolated estate, the owner clearly could have discretion, as monopoly employer. In a market system, employers do not have the same kind of direct control over wages. In Cantillon's account of an isolated estate (discussed in chapter 2 above), he got round this problem by arbitrarily assuming that wages in the market system were the same as those which the landowner would set, were he dictator.

Cantillon's population theory explains how demand and supply of labour are maintained at a customary or habitual level, but gives no clue as to how that level came to be established. It is clear, from his examples, that Cantillon knew that living standards were very different in different places, as in the comparison between England (Middlesex) and the south of France (section 3.1 above). Presumably, the level of output per head must set an upper bound to wages, though Cantillon did not say so explicitly – in one of his examples, that of native American hunters, there are no landlords, so the whole of output must go to the hunters themselves (*Essai*: 69).

Cantillon's account of wage differentials in a market system is more straightforward, at least for hired men, or for entrepreneurial incomes which do not include any return on capital. Costs of training are one relevant factor, used to explain why the handicraftsman earns more than the husbandman (*Essai*: 19). Rural children can do useful work from an early age, and can learn as they go. To learn a trade involves a long apprenticeship. Parents are therefore reluctant to support their children during an apprenticeship unless there is a corresponding return during the remainder of a working life, in the form of higher wages. Craftsmen's wages are therefore raised, 'in proportion to the time lost in learning the trade and the cost and risk incurred in becoming proficient' (*Essai*: 19). There has to be due compensation for risks to life or health, for skill, and for responsibility. Silver miners, for example, must be paid well 'because they rarely live more than five or six years at this work, which causes a high mortality' (*Essai*: 111). In Cantillon's words, 'the difference of price paid for daily work is based upon natural and obvious reasons' (*Essai*: 21–3).[1]

4.3 PROFITS AND INTEREST

In part one of the *Essai*, Cantillon's discussions of incomes make no explicit allowance for returns on capital, though there are signs that he felt uncomfortable about the issue. For example, he estimated that farmers got a third of the harvest as their profit, though he did not link that profit clearly to the need for capital investment.[2] At the same time, he wanted to argue that the value of different kinds of labour could be estimated in terms of the amount of land needed to produce subsistence, at the appropriate level, for each type of work (for his land theory of value, to be discussed in chapter 5). Entrepreneurial incomes might vary from individual to individual and from day to day, but the average would reflect subsistence needs. Unfortunately, he found a difficulty:

> Farmers and master craftsmen, if they superintended the labour of 10 labourers or journeymen would equally be capable of superintending the labour of 20, according to the size of their farms or the number of their customers, and this renders uncertain the value of their labour or superintendence. (*Essai*: 41)

A larger enterprise makes correspondingly larger profits, so treating those profits as the wage of superintendence leads to problems. Similarly, he recognized that successful entrepreneurs might become wealthy, threatening his claim that only landlords are 'independent' (*Essai*: 55).

---

[1] Petty repeatedly stressed the difference in earnings between husbandmen and handicraftsmen, without providing any explanation of it, which may have stimulated Cantillon to give the subject a chapter to itself.

[2] Hollander is more charitable than I am in his interpretation of Cantillon's notion of profit (Hollander, 1987: 28).

A related problem emerged in Cantillon's discussion of his claim that only landlords are truly independent, where he seemed to concede that the intensity of cultivation was a variable:

> The land belongs to the proprietors but would be useless to them if it were not cultivated. The more labour is expended on it, other things being equal, the more it produces. (*Essai*: 47)

If output, and the rent of land, are left indeterminate, because the intensity of cultivation remains unexplained, Cantillon's theory loses much of its force.

Cantillon's successors, notably the Physiocrats, emphasized the scope for increased agricultural output, and explained the intensity of land use in terms of the available capital. Cantillon himself hinted at something similar, in a digression on the share of rent (in his analysis of the velocity of circulation of money in part two of the *Essai*).

> When a farmer has some capital to carry on the management of his farm the proprietor who lets him the farm for a third of the produce will be sure of payment and will be better off by such a bargain than if he let his farm at a higher rate to a beggarly farmer at the risk of losing all his rent. The larger the farm, the better off the farmer will be. This is seen in England where the farmers are generally more prosperous than in other countries where the farms are small. (*Essai*: 123)

On the argument presented in this extract (reminiscent of the – later – Physiocrats), a landlord should prefer a prosperous tenant because it reduces risk, even if it means a lower rent. Again, one feels that Cantillon was close to recognizing the role of capital, without actually spelling it out or allowing it any active role in his theory.

In much of the *Essai*, then, Cantillon treated profit as a form of wage, though he was clearly rather unhappy with this procedure. Later in the *Essai*, in the discussion of interest, a rather different story emerges, as Prendergast (1991) has pointed out.

The main purpose of the chapters on interest in the *Essai* was to reject monetary theories of interest, and thus (at least implicitly) Law's claim that increasing the money stock by issuing notes would lower interest rates.[1] Cantillon also, in passing, made fun of 'casuists' who passed moral judgement on interest but 'seem hardly suitable people to judge the nature of interest'.

> Nothing is more amusing than the multitude of laws and canons made in every age on the subject of the interest of money, always by wiseacres who were hardly acquainted with trade, and always without effect. (*Essai*: 209)

Legal restrictions on interest rates were ineffective unless they simply ratified the rates the market would have arrived at anyway.

Cantillon started his analysis of interest with a robust assertion that interest rates, like any other price, are determined by demand and supply.

> Just as the prices of things are fixed in the altercations of the market by the quantities of things offered for sale in proportion to the quantity of money offered for them, or, what comes to the same thing, by the proportionate number of sellers and buyers, so in the same way the interest of money in a state is settled by the proportionate number of lenders and borrowers. (*Essai*: 199)

Lenders demand interest because of the risks involved in lending.

> A man who lends his money on good security or on mortgage runs at least the risk of the ill will of the borrower, or of expenses, lawsuits and losses. But when he lends without security he runs the risk of losing everything. (*Essai*: 199–201)[2]

Borrowing may simply fund extravagance, but the main demand for loans comes from entrepreneurs. The example of farming makes the point.

---

[1] Cf. Low (1954) on the theories of interest current at the time.
[2] Cantillon had personal experience of lawsuits, and of ill will, arising from financial transactions.

If the farmer have enough capital to carry on his enterprise, if he have the needful tools and instruments, horses for ploughing, cattle to make the land pay, etc. he will take for himself after paying all expenses a third of the produce of his farm. But if a competent labourer who lives from day to day on his wages and has no capital, can find someone willing to lend him [funds], he will be able to give the lender all the third rent, or third part of the produce of a farm of which he will become the farmer . . . However he will think his position improved since he will find his upkeep in the second rent and will become master instead of man. (*Essai*: 201)

I have altered the translation of this extract; the French has 'fonds' where I have 'funds', but Higgs translates it as 'land', which makes nonsense of the passage; after all, the farmer is going to rent the land from a landowner; what he lacks is the capital (cf. Hennings, 1987: 328). The three 'rents' may also need some explanation. As Cantillon explained at several points, it was widely believed that rent (at least in England) accounted for a third of the output of a farm,[1] the costs of production for another third, while the remaining third was the farmer's income or profit. The French text has 'rente', which is not as specific as the English 'rent', and can mean simply a return or yield.

Details of translation apart, the meaning is clear. A farmer who owns his own capital can expect a comfortable return on it. A labourer without capital cannot be a farmer unless he borrows and pays (some or all) the profit as interest. Cantillon argued that a borrower would be prepared to pay all the profit (over and above a labourer's wage) in interest, for the sake of the independent life of the entrepreneur. The same goes for all other lines of investment; for hat making, and so on (*Essai*: 203–5). Interest rates, therefore, reflect the potential returns on capital investment. This is quite different from the vague hints found in earlier parts of the *Essai*.

There are two main problems with Cantillon's treatment of

---

[1] It may be worth noting that Goubert (1973), summarizing modern estimates of the exactions to which peasant farmers were subject in pre-revolutionary France (rent, tithes, taxes, and seigneurial dues), concludes that they varied between a fifth and a half of the produce, and adds 'call it a third'.

capital and profit. First, an explanation of the level of profits in different lines of business is needed to complete the model. Wages have to cover a (conventionally determined) level of subsistence, graduated according to the status and responsibility attached to different occupations, with appropriate allowances for risks, training costs (costs of apprenticeship), and so on. If, as it now seems, there is an element of return on capital in incomes and costs, this has to be accounted for, which it is not, in much of the *Essai*. Second, if capital is needed, it is necessary to consider whether capital constrains output. If so, Cantillon's basic model, in which land is the only constraint, needs to be modified in a very fundamental way.

It is hard to find a definite model of the determinants of profits in the section of the *Essai* on interest, itself the only place where the question is discussed at all seriously. Cantillon calculated profit rates as the ratio of the entrepreneur's total income to the capital needed to set up in business. For a water carrier in Paris, the capital needed was no more than a couple of buckets to take water from the river to be sold to those who did not want to go and fetch it themselves. The total return on the water carrier's investment might be as high as 5,000 or 10,000 per cent per year (*Essai*: 205), but this includes the water carrier's subsistence. Since subsistence is so large a part of the total, and the 'clear profit' (net of subsistence) is so small, Cantillon thought it impossible, in practice, to calculate the per centage rate of profit; it might be as much as 500 per cent. For a hatter, the calculation was easier, because the element of clear profit was much more substantial; Cantillon suggested that the total profit rate might be 50 per cent, with the clear profit (and the interest rate), 20 to 30 per cent.

In all the examples he gave, Cantillon assumed that the profit rate in any particular line of business was equal to the interest rate charged on borrowing by the entrepreneurs concerned. There was, he said, a scale of interest rates, depending on credit-worthiness. Water carriers could not normally borrow at all. Fishwives at Billingsgate in London paid 260 per cent, market women in Paris, 'whose business is smaller', paid 430 per cent, and so on. Cantillon concluded that:

> there are in a state many classes and channels of interest or profit, that in the lowest class interest is always highest in

proportion to the greater risk, and that it diminishes from class to class up to the highest which is that of merchants who are rich and reputed solvent. The interest demanded in this class is called the current rate of interest. (*Essai*: 211)

So far, this is straightforward, and consistent with modern economics: there is a 'current' rate of interest for the best risks, while other borrowers have to pay a risk premium, which may be very large if the risks are large. The profit rate, in equilibrium, is equal to the interest rate, including the appropriate risk discount. This implies an equalization of profit rates for equal risks, though the emphasis in Cantillon's discussion is on the variability of returns caused by differences in risk, rather than on equalization.[1]

The main weakness of the analysis is that the risks described by Cantillon are risks to the lender – risks due to asymmetric information or to lack of collateral are certainly relevant to the determination of interest rates, but not necessarily to profit rates, unless it is assumed that all entrepreneurs operate with borrowed funds. In addition, there is no obvious explanation of the current interest rate, the rate for the best risks, which modern theorists would treat as the true return on capital.

One possible reading would be to make the current rate a risk premium too, on the grounds that even the highest class of borrowers are not risk free. This would be consistent with Cantillon's initial comments on interest, in which he claimed that the 'origin of interest' was the desire to borrow by lenders, set against the 'fear and avarice' of the lender (*Essai*: 201), and insisted that even with the best security there are risks. To explain the demand for loans is easy: it comes from entrepreneurs:

> If there were in a state no entrepreneurs who could make a profit on the money or goods which they borrow, the use of interest would probably be less frequent than it is now. (*Essai*: 211)

If this reading were accepted, the basic framework of part

---

[1] Prendergast (1991) has persuaded me to change my view since Brewer (1988a, b), where I argued that Cantillon did not recognize profit rate equalization.

one of the *Essai* could be preserved. Capital is not scarce, so the true interest rate on risk free lending, and the corresponding pure rate of return on capital, are zero. Zero interest rates are not observed, because there are no risk free assets. Costs include risk premiums, whether they take the form of higher wages for jobs involving risks to life and limb, or risk premiums on investments which involve a risk of capital loss. Rent remains the only true surplus.

Cantillon was, however, far from clear. It is rather difficult to square the reading suggested here with his discussion of differences in interest rates between different places and times. The interest rate in China is high even in the highest class (30 per cent), because of the multitude of small entrepreneurs, who have, seemingly, a high demand for loans. Equally, the interest rate varies over time, as the demand and the supply of loans change. Anything that creates investment opportunities, such as a war, raises interest rates by raising the demand for loans (and in the case of war, by raising the government's demand for loans as well). A balance of payments surplus, on the other hand, lowers the interest rate because the inflow of money comes into the hands of merchants and entrepreneurs, who add to their own resources and borrow less. It would be possible to explain these variations in terms of short run fluctuations around a long run equilibrium, in which capital is not scarce, but Cantillon did not do so.

It seems, then, that Cantillon did (sometimes) recognize a role for capital investment, at least at the level of the individual enterprise, and that he recognized profit (or interest) as an independent source of income, which might be regarded as part of the surplus, along with rent, rather than as the cost of an input in elastic supply, like wages. He was not clear about it, and did not fully integrate it into his main theoretical framework. In the main part of the *Essai*, non-landowners receive conventionally determined wages, and the surplus of output over costs (including the 'wages' of entrepreneurs as well as hired men) accrues to landlords as rent.

5

The Land Theory of Value

Cantillon summarized his theory of value in the very first sentence of part two of the *Essai*.

> In part I an attempt was made to prove that the real value of everything used by man is proportionable to the quantity of land used for its production and for the upkeep of those who have fashioned it. (*Essai*: 115)

The land theory of value, set out in this extract, is unique – no other significant economist has claimed that value is determined by the amount of land used in production, though several have held a labour theory of value. (cf. Brems, 1978; Herlitz, 1961; Samuelson, 1959: 19).

Cantillon distinguished between market prices and what he called 'intrinsic values'. Market prices are, of course, the actual prices paid in the market on any particular occasion. Intrinsic values are the centre of gravity around which market prices fluctuate, and are relatively unchanging.

> There is never a variation in intrinsic values, but the impossibility of proportioning the production of merchandise and produce in a state to their consumption causes a daily variation, and a perpetual ebb and flow in market prices. (*Essai*: 31)

Intrinsic values depend on costs, which are made up of land and labour costs, so they depend on the amounts of land and labour needed to produce each good. For given wage levels, however, labour costs can be reduced to the land needed to support the labour force, so intrinsic values can be expressed in terms of land alone.

5.1 MARKET PRICES

Market prices are determined by supply and demand:

> the prices of things are fixed in the altercations of the market by the quantities of things offered for sale in proportion to the quantity of money offered for them, or, what comes to the same thing, by the proportionate number of buyers and sellers. (*Essai*: 199)

There are similar statements in several places in the *Essai*; for example: 'Prices are fixed by the proportion between the produce exposed for sale and the money offered for it' (*Essai*: 13).

Here and elsewhere it is clear that the analysis of market price is an analysis of what Marshall called the 'market period', that is a period in which the quantity produced can be taken as given, the quantity 'exposed for sale'. The analysis seems, at first sight, rather unsophisticated (though not much more so than in most economic writings up to the late nineteenth century). That the (average) price is equal to the ratio of the quantity sold to the total money exchanged for it is no more than a tautology (unless the quantity of money offered in exchange for the goods concerned is assumed to be fixed, introducing an implicit assumption that the elasticity of demand is unity). The introduction of the number of buyers and sellers, as opposed to the quantities demanded and supplied, simply muddies the waters further.

Fortunately, Cantillon gave one example in a little more detail – a market for green peas in Paris. There are a number of buyers, each of whom wants a fixed amount, subject to a maximum price. As a result, the demand curve slopes downward (in steps), and the price has to be set at the level which equates demand with the fixed supply. If the quantity offered for sale were larger, the price would have to be set at a lower level to find enough buyers for the greater supply (*Essai*: 119–21). Prices are set by bargaining. Sellers raise their price if they see more buyers, while buyers cut the price they offer if they think that demand will be low. Some are better at bargaining than others, and 'this method of fixing market prices has no exact or geometrical foundation' (*Essai*: 119). Sellers who are reluctant to cut prices may in the end gain from it, but equally, they may be left with unsold stocks and regret it. Distant markets affect each other, presumably because of arbitrage (*Essai*: 121). In sum, Cantillon's analysis of market price is well worked out, for its date, but it contains little that is surprising.

5.2 INTRINSIC VALUE

Most of Cantillon's argument is conducted in terms of 'intrinsic value', or long run equilibrium price, not market price. The distinction between market prices and intrinsic values is exactly the same as the distinction between market prices and natural prices in the writings of classical economists like Smith and Ricardo, or between market prices and prices of production in Marx.

Intrinsic values are determined by costs of production, which can be reduced to the costs of the land and labour used in production.

> The price or intrinsic value of a thing is the measure of the quantity of land and of labour entering into its production, having regard to the fertility or produce of the land and to the quality of the labour. (*Essai*: 29)

The price of any commodity must be enough to pay all the people required to produce it, and to pay rent at the going rate on the land used. Cantillon took the example of a pound of flax made up into fine Brussels lace, which required 14 person-years of labour; he claimed to have shown (in the now lost supplement) that the price covered the wages of these people, plus the (trivial) costs of producing the flax. Some goods are even more labour intensive than this; water sold in the streets of Paris costs nothing to obtain from the river, so the price is wholly accounted for by the labour required to carry it from the river. On the other hand, some goods require no labour at all (or so Cantillon implied); standing hay or timber are examples. Note that capital costs, or returns on capital, do not play any part in Cantillon's account of the determination of intrinsic values. In so far as he recognized the existence of capital costs, and the corresponding incomes, at all, they are hidden in the labour component of costs, where they are treated as part of the cost of entrepreneurial labour.

Market prices may differ from intrinsic values.

> If the farmers in a state sow more corn than usual, much more than is needed for the year's consumption, the real and intrinsic value of the corn will correspond to the land and labour which enter into its production, but as there is too great an abundance of it and there are more sellers than buyers the market price of the corn will necessarily fall below the intrinsic price or value. If on the contrary the farmers sow less corn than is needed for consumption there will be more buyers than sellers and the market price of corn will rise above its intrinsic value. (*Essai*: 29–31)

Any divergence of market price from natural price implies a divergence between quantities produced and sold, and their equilibrium values, and a corresponding divergence between actual incomes and their normal levels, setting up incentives to restore equilibrium. The process by which incomes are brought to equilibrium, and the numbers of people employed in different trades brought into equilibrium with the demand for their services (discussed in chapters 2 and 3 above), is, of course, also a process by which market prices are brought into line with intrinsic values. So, if farmers sow too much corn, its price falls, and they must adjust their plans (*Essai*: 61–3).

Changes in demand (normally caused by changes in landlord's tastes, according to Cantillon) induce corresponding changes in production through the price mechanism. Cantillon's example was a shift in a landlord's tastes away from the employment of servants, towards the possession of horses.

> When a landowner has dismissed a great number of domestic servants, and increased the number of his horses, there will be too much corn for the needs of the inhabitants, and so the corn will be cheap and the hay dear. In consequence the farmers will increase their grass land and diminish their corn to proportion it to the demand. In this way the fancies or fashions of landowners determine the use of land and bring about the variations of demand which cause the variations of market prices. (*Essai*: 65)

5.3 THE 'PAR' BETWEEN LAND AND LABOUR

Different goods are produced by land and labour in very different proportions, so their relative equilibrium prices depend on the relation between the unit costs of labour and land. Cantillon wanted to find a 'par or relation between the value of land and labour' (*Essai*: 31, chapter title):

> land is the matter and labour the form of all produce and merchandise, and as those who labour must subsist on the produce of the land, it seems that some relation might be found between the value of labour and that of the produce of the land. (*Essai*: 31)

Cantillon's chapter on the 'par' is mainly devoted to a discussion of the cost of maintaining a worker, measured by the land needed to provide the worker's subsistence.[1] He considered a single self-sufficient estate, worked either by slaves or by free men. If the landowner controls the use of the estate directly, he must provide for all those he employs, at a standard of living appropriate to their status and skills (allowing each man twice what a single man would need, in order to cover the costs of raising children). Some of the land of the estate can be used directly to produce the things the landlord wants, but part is needed to support the labour force.

> If the owner of a large estate (which I want to consider here as if there were no other in the world) has it cultivated himself he will follow his fancy in the use to which he puts it. (1) He will necessarily use part of it for corn to feed the labourers, mechanics and overseers who work for him, another part to feed the cattle, sheep and other animals necessary for their clothing and food or other commodities according to the way in which he wishes to maintain them. (2) He will turn part of the land into parks, gardens, fruit trees or vines as he feels inclined and into meadows for the horses he will use for his pleasure, etc. (*Essai*: 59)

---

[1] I have drawn on the chapter on the 'par' at some length already (in chapters 3 and 4), to illustrate Cantillon's treatment of wage levels and wage differentials.

This extract is not from the chapter on the 'par', but it makes the point that the cost of anything the landowner wants to consume consists of the land that is needed directly to produce it (meadows for horses, if he wants to ride, and so on), and also of the land needed to support the workers involved. The same is true in a market system; the landowner does not directly allocate the land, but the workers still need to eat, the price paid by the landowner must cover that cost, and land must be used to produce the appropriate wage goods.

The labour component of intrinsic value can therefore be reduced to the land needed for subsistence, so the value of anything can be expressed in terms of land alone.

> By these examples . . . it is seen that the value of the day's work has a relation to the produce of the soil, and that the intrinsic value of any thing may be measured by the quantity of land used in its production and the quantity of labour which enters into it, in other words by the quantity of land of which the produce is allotted to those who have worked upon it; and as all the land belongs to the prince and the landowners all things which have this value have it only at their expense. (*Essai*: 41)

The land theory of value is a logical conclusion of Cantillon's assumption that land is the only scarce resource.

The basic principle is clear, but the exact procedure is hard to disentangle from Cantillon's verbal argument. In the appendix to this chapter I present a formal model designed to show the logic of Cantillon's arguments – I have relegated it to an appendix, because it is a 'rational reconstruction' rather than something taken directly from Cantillon's text. The problem in interpreting the *Essai* is precisely that Cantillon did not present a formal mathematical model of this sort. A simple example will show what the problems are.[1]

Suppose it takes one acre-year of land and two man-years of labour to make one barrel of wine, that ten acre-years of land and one man-year of labour can produce one ton of corn, and that the (socially sanctioned) subsistence wage per person is half a ton of corn per year. How should the intrinsic value of a barrel of wine be calculated? The most natural way of

---

[1] The example is stated more formally in the appendix.

THE LAND THEORY OF VALUE

reading Cantillon's arguments is as follows. The cost of the wine is one acre-year of land and two man-years of labour. Each person needs half a ton of corn, and a ton of corn is grown on ten acres, so each person needs the produce of five acres. The labour component of the value of the wine is twice five acres, hence ten acres, plus one acre directly required, making a total of eleven acres.

This calculation of the land needed is wrong. If ten acre-years are allocated to growing corn, one man-year of labour is also needed in the corn sector, and half of the corn goes to the person who grew it. Ten acres of corn land yields a gross output of one ton per year, but the output net of the consumption of those who produce the corn is only half a ton, which is only enough to support one worker in the luxury sector, here the wine sector. To support two wine sector workers takes twenty acres, so the labour component of the value of the wine is twenty acres, plus one acre of land required to grow the grapes on, making a total of twenty one acres, which is the land value of the wine.

How can a correct calculation be set out in Cantillon's terms? The direct land requirement is not a problem. The problem arises from the need to distinguish between the net and gross product of the wage-goods sector in calculating the land equivalent of the labour costs. One possibility is to calculate the total labour required in both sectors. Taking this approach, it takes four man-years of labour to produce the wine, two working on the wine, and two growing corn to support all four, while the 'par', the land needed to support each man, is five acres, since each actually consumes the product of five acres of land. This gives the correct answer, and it is consistent with the most natural interpretation of Cantillon's 'par', but it complicates the calculation of the labour required. In particular, it is now impossible to calculate the labour required without first knowing what the workers consume. This is not compatible with Cantillon's procedure, since he first described intrinsic values in terms of the (separate) land and labour requirements of production, which he identified with rent and wage costs, and only then went on to discuss the workers' consumption needs in order to convert the labour element in costs into its land equivalent.

An alternative way of setting out the calculation would be to calculate the labour component in the natural way, counting direct labour only, and then to compute the land required to support it using the net, not the gross, product of each acre. In the example, the labour needed to produce a barrel of wine is two man-years, and it takes ten acres to support each man-year of labour in the wine sector, since ten acres has a net product (and thus a rent) of half a ton of corn.

This seems a more plausible reading than the alternative, but it is still quite difficult to square it with Cantillon's explanation. For example, his discussion of population (*Essai*: 65–73) includes a discussion of the amount of land needed to support a person in different places. Here it is clearly the gross product of the land[1] that should be considered to determine the total population that can live on a given amount of land. The case of the native Americans, one of those described, is very clear, since there cannot have been any surplus at all in this case – the net product per acre was zero. It is just possible that Cantillon's discussion of the par, which employs very similar numbers, apparently derived in the same way, involves quite different definitions from those used in the discussion of population, but it does not seem likely.

It is hard to avoid the conclusion that Cantillon overlooked the distinction between net and gross output in the wage-goods sector, and thus that his presentation of the land theory of value is faulty. If the supplement to the *Essai* (which apparently contained the details of calculations which are reported in the main text) had survived, it would probably be possible to settle the issue. In any case, the basic idea is clear enough; the error, if there is one, is in the details of the calculation.

5.4 HETEROGENEOUS LAND

Land is heterogeneous, as Cantillon realized (*Essai*: 27), but heterogeneity only figures in his main analysis of value in the phrase 'having regard to the fertility or produce of the land' (*Essai*: 29), appended to a mention of the quantity of land used to produce a good. In effect, Cantillon assumed that land could be reduced to a common denominator and treated as if it were homogeneous. This rather cavalier approach contrasts with his treatment of labour, where he was careful to explain the reasons for wage differentials. Heterogeneous land is, of

---

[1] Net of seed corn, which Cantillon allowed for (*Essai*: 71), but which I neglect throughout for simplicity.

course, a much more serious problem for his analysis than heterogeneous labour, since each kind of labour has a given real wage, which can be reduced to its equivalent in land. To solve the problem of heterogeneous land in the same way, different kinds of land must have fixed values relative to each other. That is what Cantillon assumed.

If one piece of land were, say, twice as productive as another, then it could simply be treated as equivalent to twice as much 'land', in the abstract. However, the ratio between the productivities of the two pieces of land would have to be the same in all uses, since otherwise their relative rents, and hence their relative contributions to the value of the outputs produced on them, would depend on relative prices. This problem would arise, for example, in Cantillon's treatment of location (discussed in section 2.4). The relative prices of different agricultural products vary with distance from the capital – products which are in demand in the capital, and have high transport costs, are produced close to the capital, and so on. Clearly, the value of any land which is specially suited to growing these products will vary according to its location relative to the capital.

One of the few places where Cantillon gave any indication of how to tackle the problem was in his discussion of mining. A mine clearly cannot be compared with an acre of pasture in terms of physical productivity, because it produces something quite different.

> The real or intrinsic value of metals is ... proportionable to the land and labour that enters into their production. The outlay on the land for this production is considerable only in so far as the owner of the mine can make a profit. (*Essai*: 97)

This seems to mean that the mine only counts as land if it commands a rent, which might imply that land was to be aggregated by its rent. From the point of view of the arithmetic of prices, of course, this must be true (prices must cover rent on the different types of land employed, plus other costs) but it risks reducing the theory to a tautology; price governs rent (for a mine, at least), and rent governs price. The chapter on metals and mines contains a hint of a theory of differential rent (*Essai*: 97), but also a hint that price is governed by the cheapest source (*Essai*: 101).

Cantillon's idea was to explain money prices by real, permanent factors (land and labour), and to express these in terms of land alone. Heterogeneity of land evidently poses a serious problem for a land theory of value. He seems not to have had any satisfactory solution to the problem.

APPENDIX: A FORMAL MODEL OF LAND VALUES

The logic behind the land theory of value can be demonstrated using a formal model. Cantillon did not set his model out formally, so the model must be regarded as a rational reconstruction, or perhaps as a representation of what Cantillon would (or should) have said, if he had access to modern analytical techniques.[1]

Cantillon's system can be represented formally in terms of an input–output model, treating each type of labour as a separate 'product' alongside other products.[2] Labour is produced by inputs of consumer goods, and goods are produced by other goods, including labour, and by inputs of land. Let there be a single homogeneous type of land, and n goods (labour included). Then

(1) $y = x - Ax$,

where y is the vector of net outputs, x the vector of gross outputs, and A the input–output matrix, with typical element a_{ij} representing the amount of good i required per unit of good j produced. Given a desired net output vector, the corresponding gross outputs are given by

(2) $x = (I - A)^{-1} y$,

and the land required by $mx = m(I - A)^{-1} y$, where m is the vector of (direct) land requirements per unit of (gross) output of each good, and I is the identity matrix. The land constraint, the only constraint in Cantillon's system, can be written as

(3) $m(I - A)^{-1} y \leq M$,

---

[1] It is based on Brewer (1988a). A rather similar model is in Brems (1986: 40–9).

[2] It is an input–output model, not a circulating capital model of the von Neuman or Sraffa type, because Cantillon did not allow for any time lags in production, or for any return on capital.

where M is the total land available. This constraint will be satisfied as an equality, if such uses of land as parks, hunting grounds, and so on are included in the list of 'goods' produced.

Let v be the vector of integrated land requirements, so any element of v represents the land directly and indirectly employed to produce a net output of one unit of the corresponding good. Then

(4) $\qquad v = m(I - A)^{-1}$

and the land constraint can be rewritten

(5) $\qquad v.y \leq M.$

The ratio between any two elements of v shows the opportunity cost of one good in terms of the other, so the elements of v are the natural shadow prices to use in making choices between different net output vectors. I shall call them 'land values'; it remains to be seen how they are related to Cantillon's intrinsic values.

The argument so far depends only on the technology and on the living standards of workers. It could be used as a description of Cantillon's isolated estate run by its owner, or of a market system. In the case of an isolated estate run entirely by its owner (a miniature centrally planned dictatorship), the vector of net outputs is simply a list of all the things the landlord consumes.

Cantillon claimed that a market system would give the same result, with prices set to allow the labour force to enjoy the same living standards in both cases. Prices must be set so that revenue covers costs in the production of each good, including workers' consumption and rent payments. The prices which satisfy this condition are given by

(6) $\qquad p = pA + rm,$

where p is the vector of prices (in terms of an arbitrary numeraire; Cantillon suggested silver), and r is the (scalar) rent per unit of land, in terms of the same numeraire. These prices are proportional to land values (as defined above), since (6) can be rewritten as

(7) $\qquad p = rm(I - A)^{-1} = rv.$

The constant of proportionality is the rent per acre, r, which is governed by the (arbitrary) choice of numeraire.

Using a land theory of value, it is natural to use the rent per unit of land as numeraire, so r could be set equal to unity, making equilibrium prices equal to land values. Combining (7) with (5), and assuming that all land is used, so that (5) is satisfied as an equality, yields:

(8) $\qquad rM = rv.y = p.y,$

so total rent, rM, is equal to the value of net output, py.

The simple example given in section 5.3 can be restated in similar terms to those used above. Consider the production of a single final good, wine, and suppose there is only one type of labour and one wage good, corn. Production of a unit of wine requires inputs of l_w labour and m_w land, production of a unit of corn requires l_c labour and m_c land, and the wage in corn is b. The value (integrated land requirement) of a unit of corn, as defined above, is $m_c/(1 - bl_c)$, so the value of one unit of labour is $bm_c/(1 - bl_c)$. The value of a unit of wine must then be:

$$wine\ value = m_w + l_w bm_c/(1 - bl_c).$$

This is the total land required to produce a net output of one unit of wine, including the land required to support all the workers involved. As shown above, money prices must equal values multiplied by r, the money rent of a unit of land.

The question now is how to arrange the analysis of this example in the format proposed by Cantillon. His presentation takes the form

$$wine\ value = wine\ land + (wine\ labour \times par)$$

where *par* is the conversion factor between labour and land. The first term, *wine land*, is the land required excluding that used to support labour, since land used to support labour is dealt with by the second term. In the example, *wine land* is given by m_w.

What of *wine labour*? Two measures could be proposed. First, *wine labour* could be identified with the direct labour required to produce a unit of wine, excluding the labour employed in the corn sector. Call this *wine labour$_1$*; in the example it is l_w. This definition is natural, it is consistent with the treatment of *wine land*, and it seems on the face of it to be consistent with Cantillon's examples.

Second, to be consistent with the discussion of the isolated estate, where the emphasis is on the total labour required, *wine labour* could be defined as the labour required, *directly and indirectly*, to produce a unit of wine, including labour needed to produce corn for the wine sector workers. Call this *wine labour$_2$*; in the example it is:

$$l_w + bl_w l_c/(1 - bl_c) = l_w/(1 - bl_c).$$

Two definitions of *par* are also possible. Cantillon introduced it in terms of 'the quantity of land of which the produce is allocated' to the labour concerned (*Essai*: 41). This definition is most naturally read as the land needed to produce a *gross* output sufficient to support one unit of labour. Call this *par$_1$*; in the example it is bm_c, since the corn wage is b and the land required to produce it is bm_c. Cantillon's extensive examples (e.g. *Essai*: 37–41) seem to be constructed on this basis.

However, note that Cantillon identified the par with the value of labour. In discussing the par, he stated explicitly:

> The money or coin which finds the proportion of values in exchange is the most certain measure for judging of the *par* between land and labour. (*Essai:* 41)

The value (or price) of labour must equal the value (or price) of the required subsistence, which must itself include the labour cost of producing subsistence. To be consistent with the definition of the par as the value of labour, it must be measured by the land required directly and indirectly to sustain one (non-agricultural) worker, that is, as the land needed to produce a *net* output of subsistence for one. Call this *par$_2$*; in the example it is $bm_c/(1 - bl_c)$.

To recapitulate, Cantillon's writings could be used to defend either of two definitions of *wine labour* (in the example), and two definitions of *par*, giving four possible formulations of the term (*wine labour* × *par*) in the derivation of intrinsic value. One patently involves double counting and need not be considered (*wine labour$_2$* × *par$_2$*), but the remaining three must be considered as defensible readings of Cantillon's text. Consider them in turn:

(V1)   *wine value* = *wine land* + (*wine labour$_1$* × *par$_1$*)
         = $m_w + (l_w \times bm_c)$.

This formulation uses the most natural and plausible readings of *wine labour* and *par*, taking each separately, but together they yield an indefensible result for the value of wine, because the consumption of corn sector workers is omitted. The result is incompatible with the basic requirements of the model; for example, the labour cost allowance in the value of wine is insufficient to allow the workers to buy the corn they need, even calculating the value of corn in the same way.

(V2) $\quad$ *wine value* $=$ *wine land* $+$ (*wine labour*$_2$ $\times$ *par*$_1$)
$\qquad\qquad\quad = m_w + (l_w/(1 - bl_c) \times bm_c)$,

giving the 'correct' answer. Unfortunately, this measure of *wine labour* seems to be inconsistent with some of Cantillon's examples.

(V3) $\quad$ *wine value* $=$ *wine land* $+$ (*wine labour*$_2$ $\times$ *par*$_1$)
$\qquad\qquad\quad = m_w + (l_w \times bm_c/(1 - bl_c))$,

again giving the 'correct' answer. This formulation embodies the idea that the par should be measured by the value of labour, but is harder to reconcile with Cantillon's examples of how the par should be calculated. This third reading may be the best chance there is of rescuing him from a charge of inconsistency, but the defence will not be easy.

On the evidence to be found in the surviving part of the *Essai* (without the supplement) it seems impossible to be certain of Cantillon's intentions, and at least possible that he was inconsistent. It is clear, at the least, that Cantillon set out to construct a pure land theory of value, and that he provided the basis on which to construct one. Whether he completed the job remains open to doubt.

6

Money, Prices, and the Trade Balance

Cantillon's monetary theory is, perhaps, the best known part of his work. There is even a 'Cantillon effect': the effect of an increase in the money supply (at least in the short run) depends on the route by which the additional money gets into the system (Blaug, 1985: 21). Cantillon understood both the quantity theory of money (which Locke and others had already stated, in a rather crude form) and the specie-flow mechanism (which earlier writers had hinted at), and he set out to investigate the mechanisms involved. Locke 'has clearly seen that the abundance of money makes everything dear, but he has not considered how it does so' (*Essai*: 161).[1]

Cantillon insisted that the value of money was based on the value of gold and silver:

> Money or the common measure of value must correspond in fact and reality in terms of land and labour to the articles exchanged for it. Otherwise it would have only an imaginary value. (*Essai*: 111)

> [Gold and silver] are not only durable and easily transported but correspond to the employment of a large area of land for their production, which gives them the real value desirable in exchange. (*Essai*: 117)

The links between Cantillon's theory of intrinsic value and his theory of money are less direct than these extracts make

---

[1] See Low (1952) and Vickers (1959) on the state of informed opinion on monetary theory in the mid eighteenth century.

them seem, since he presented his monetary theory entirely in terms of market prices, not the underlying intrinsic values. Indeed, the chapter on market prices in the *Essai* is placed near the beginning of part two, the part devoted to money and its effects, not where one might expect to find it, alongside the discussion of intrinsic value.

It is possible to suggest a number of reasons for this. First, Cantillon's main aim was to show the mechanisms by which monetary changes affected prices, so the focus was on disequilibrium processes. Second, although money has to have an intrinsic value, reflecting the cost of producing the monetary metals, these metals were not in fact produced in any quantities in the main countries of Western Europe, so Cantillon's monetary theory was concerned with the effects of changes in the money supply caused by surpluses and deficits in the balance of trade. What is more, he thought that the relative levels of prices in different countries would not remain constant, but would constantly change, as one country after another rose to a dominant position. Again, it was the process of change, the rise and fall of different centres, that mattered.

After the chapter on market prices, the first of part two of the *Essai*, Cantillon dealt with the circulation of money, the velocity of circulation (a phrase he invented), and the effects of changes in the money supply, with particular emphasis on the effects of a surplus or deficit in the balance of trade. I shall follow this order, and I shall relegate consideration of the intrinsic values of monetary metals to an appendix to this chapter, since intrinsic values play very little active role in this part of Cantillon's argument.

6.1 THE CIRCULATION OF MONEY

Cantillon's analysis of the circulation of money, of the velocity of circulation, and hence of the demand for money, is based on an account of the flows of spending between city and country, and between three components of the economy: (1) the rural sector (farmers and others), (2) the urban sector (including merchants and non-agricultural producers), and (3) landlords (who do not produce or sell anything, but receive rents from farmers and spend them in the urban sector). He presented, in effect, an early version of the circular flow of income and expenditure.

He used a numerical example, which he evidently thought to be a reasonable approximation to the facts of the time. The example is sketched in part one of the *Essai* (45), and then developed at greater length in part two (121ff). Farmers are assumed to earn 'three rents', meaning that the output of the farm (presumably net of seed corn, but gross of wage costs) is divided into three equal parts: one third goes to the landowner as rent, a second goes to pay the wages and other costs, and the remaining third is the farmer's profit.

> The assumption I shall make . . . is that farmers earn three rents and spend the third rent on living more comfortably instead of saving it. It is in fact the case with the greatest number of farmers in all countries.
>
> All the produce of the country comes directly or indirectly from the hands of the farmers as well as all the materials from which commodities are made. . . . The three rents of the farmer must therefore be considered as the principal sources or so to speak the mainspring of circulation in the state. (*Essai*: 123)

Farmers pay rents in cash to the landlords, who are assumed to spend them in the city, where their spending supports manufacturing, services, and so on. In addition, a further one-sixth of gross farm output is spent on 'Iron, tin, copper, salt, sugar, cloth and generally all the merchandise of the city consumed in the country' (*Essai*: 123). Cash payments to the urban sector by farmers (representing the rural sector) therefore amount to half of total farm output (a third for rent and a sixth for purchased commodities).

Transactions within the rural sector are assumed to be carried out by barter, without using money. Rural output measured by the methods used in modern national accounts would be larger than farm output, because the output of rural craft activities would be added. Cantillon ignored all dealings between farmers and rural artisans, in his discussion of the circulation of money, because they were assumed to be outside the monetarized sector.

If cash payments to the city correspond in value to half of farm output, half of the physical output must be sold to the city to raise the money to make these payments. Foreign transactions are assumed to go through the city, so they can be ignored at this stage. Correspondingly, half the population is said to live in cities; half the food stays in the country, half feeds the urban population. As noted already (in chapter 3), modern estimates put the urban population at the time far below 50 per cent, so one is led to ask: can Cantillon's estimates be taken seriously at all?

Cantillon himself seems to have been somewhat sceptical about the estimate that half the population lives in cities (the French, incidentally, is *villes*, which might be read as 'towns' rather than 'cities'):

> It is generally calculated that one half of the inhabitants of a kingdom subsist and make their abode in cities . . . . This idea is only to convey a general idea of the proportion; but in fact, if half of the inhabitants live in cities they consume more than half of the land's produce, as they live better than those who live in the country. (*Essai*: 45)

The principles, not the numbers, matter.

There are, in any case, a number of corrections to make to the simple story, which produce a more sensible estimate of the urban fraction of the population. In the extract above, Cantillon suggested the first. If city dwellers consume half the produce of the rural sector, the urban population will still be less than half of the total, if city dwellers eat better than the inhabitants of the country. Second, it is necessary to correct for the part of farm produce that is used as raw materials, and hence does not support a human population, plus the part used to feed horses.[1] Third, the assumption that rents are entirely spent in the city is unrealistic. Elsewhere, Cantillon noted that landlords who live in the country support an enlarged rural population (*Essai*: 9). Even landowners who lived most of the year in the capital typically maintained country houses – the eighteenth century was an era of great country houses. Finally, some of the things which the rural sector is described as buying from the city (metals and sugar, for example) were not produced in the urban sector, but simply traded there on the way from a rural origin to a rural destination. Cantillon was, of course, right to include them in urban–rural trade when dealing with the circulation of

---

[1] Transport costs absorbed a large part of the value of the rural produce shipped to the city, on Cantillon's own account, leaving little for the producers (section 2.4 above).

money. In sum, Cantillon's estimate, that half of farm output was sold to non-farm buyers, is compatible with a rural share of the total population well above 50 per cent.

Whatever the size of the urban population, it is fed and provided with materials by the rural sector. Farm produce is shipped to the cities by merchants, and distributed there through the wholesale and retail trades, before it is finally consumed. The corresponding flow of payments from the country to the city passes partly through the hands of the landlords, and partly through the hands of the traders who sell urban products to the country. Their spending passes through various channels, since urban tradesmen deal with each other as well as with landlords and farmers, but eventually it is used to pay for agricultural products, so the money flows back from the city to the country to restart the cycle again (*Essai*: 125–7).

As Cantillon presented it, this is an account of the interdependence of city and country. Quesnay took it as the basis for his *Tableau Economique*, the most famous element of Physiocratic economics. Unlike Cantillon, however, Quesnay drew the conclusion that only agriculture was productive. Quesnay's economics, and its relation to Cantillon's, will be discussed in chapter 10, but it is worth asking here whether Cantillon's model could legitimately be used in this way.

Modern national income accounting methods would, of course, show a considerable amount of production in the urban sector, including not only the goods sold to the country and to the landlords, but also all the consumption goods produced in the city for consumption there. If, however, intermediate goods are eliminated as double counting (as they are in modern national income accounts) and if labour, and hence consumption out of wages and profits, is treated as an intermediate good (contrary to modern practice), the city would appear as adding nothing to the value of national output at all. Cantillon did not make such a claim, but it clearly follows from the logic of his case, since urban output derives its intrinsic value, in Cantillon's framework, from the land used to support the labour force. Quesnay did indeed draw this conclusion. The classical economists, on the other hand, treated profit and wages separately, so they were able to treat profits as part of net income whichever sector they came from. Neither the Physiocrats nor the classical economists treated wages as part of net output.

6.2 THE VELOCITY OF CIRCULATION

Cantillon gave the velocity of circulation (*vitesse de circulation*) its name (e.g. *Essai*: 130, 134).[1] He treated velocity as substantially determined by institutional factors, and discussed the institutional determinants of velocity at some length. At the same time, his discussion of the impact of monetary changes involves short run changes in the velocity of circulation. He criticized Locke's rather mechanical quantity theory, because Locke had not adequately explained the mechanisms by which monetary changes affected the economy, and had not allowed for the time lags involved. In this section I shall concentrate on the institutional, long run, aspect of Cantillon's analysis, leaving discussion of the response to monetary shocks to the next section.

In Cantillon's account, flows of money between country and city, and in particular rent payments, play the main role, because they involve substantial payments made at intervals. The farmer sells produce in bulk, to a merchant, and pays the rent with a large part of the proceeds. Other exchanges tend to proceed much more rapidly.

> The principal rent of the landowner must be considered to be the most necessary and considerable branch of the money in regard to circulation. . . . The circulation consists always of this, that the large sums which the farmer receives on the sale of his produce are split up in detail and then brought together again to make large payments. . . . All the circulation takes place between the inhabitants of the state, and they are all fed and maintained in every way from the produce of the soil and raw materials of the country. (*Essai*: 137)

Using the numerical example discussed in the last section, which Cantillon devised for the purpose, half of agricultural output is traded with the cities, using cash. The other half is consumed in the country, with little need for cash, since exchanges are made by barter at valuation (*Essai*: 125). The money paid in rent is spent in detail, in the city, by the landlords, so the money farmers receive from the cities, in return for half of their total output, flows back to the cities as rent or

---

[1] Higgs translated it as 'rapidity of circulation'.

as payments by farmers for urban products. It circulates in the cities, and is eventually collected together in the hands of the merchants who bring farm produce from the country, and used to pay the farmers.

Cash transactions between city and country therefore amount to half the produce of the land, so cash of equal value must change hands. Cantillon assumed that a little more would be needed 'in order that the country circulation should be easily conducted' (*Essai*: 127), so he worked on the basis that the ready cash involved should equal two thirds of the value of the produce, or twice the rent.

If rent were paid annually, and if all transactions between city and country took place once a year, the money stock needed, simply to pay rents with, would be twice the annual rent (two thirds of annual output). If, however, rent is collected, and other transactions carried out, every six months, the money stock required would only be equal to twice a half-years' rent, half as much as with an annual cycle, and so on.

Many transactions are carried out much more rapidly, since individuals often spend money they receive almost immediately. In particular, transactions within the urban sector take place rapidly, so the lengthy interval between rent payments allows plenty of time for the money to be spent by the landlord, passed from hand to hand within the city, and sent back to the country as payment for agricultural products. The money may be back in the farmers' hands in (say) a month, but it will then be held immobile for (say) two months until the next quarter's rent is due. In this case, the speed of the urban circulation makes no difference to the required money stock (*Essai*: 135–7). As farmers have to make large rent payments at intervals, and as other large transactions are carried out infrequently (tax payments, for example, are retained by the collectors and paid over at intervals), 'there must be enough ready cash in circulation to make these large payments without difficulty' (*Essai*: 129).

The velocity of circulation can be accelerated in various ways (*Essai:* 139–45). If the landlord spends his rent immediately (or pays off debts with it), so that it goes into circulation immediately, and if the farmer waits to sell the produce of his farm until the rent is due, money will only be tied up for a very short time, and the circulation of money will be accelerated. If the landlord deposits the money with a 'goldsmith or banker' who lends it out again, the effect on the circulation of money will be the same as if the money had been spent immediately. If mutual debts between merchants or artisans are cancelled off without any need for money to change hands, this again will reduce the amount of money needed, and increase the velocity of circulation.[1]

The use of banknotes also reduces the demand for money, by replacing it for some transactions (Cantillon did not consider notes to be money, but simply a substitute for it). On the other hand, the price of all non-agricultural goods can be reduced to wage costs, and wages must always be paid in coin, and spent in coin on everyday living expenses, so the scope for notes to replace coin is limited (*Essai:* 145–7).[2] The velocity of circulation is reduced when money is hoarded, or saved up for indivisible purchases, and so on.

Characteristically, Cantillon was more interested in showing that the velocity of circulation could be explained, than in establishing any particular figure for it:

> It will be seen from this that the proportion of the amount of money needed for circulation in a state is not incomprehensible, and that this amount may be greater or less in a state according to the mode of living and the rapidity of payments. (*Essai:* 129–31)

He thought of velocity as substantially constant, which implies that prices vary with the quantity of money. The quantity theory of money underlies the whole of his analysis, no matter how much he stressed the qualifications to it.

> Whether money be scarce or plenty in a state this proportion [money stock to total rent] will not change much because where money is abundant land is let at higher rents, and where money is scarce at lower rents. . . . But it usually happens in states where money is scarcer that there is more barter than in those where money is plentiful, and circulation is more prompt and less sluggish than in those where money is not so scarce. (*Essai:* 131)

---

[1] It is not clear that this line of argument is consistent with Cantillon's claim, discussed above, that large and infrequent payments govern the stock of money needed, though it might be possible to make them compatible if indivisible payments are not synchronized.
[2] Notes were only issued in large denominations at that time.

6.3 MONEY AND THE PRICE LEVEL

> Everybody agrees that the abundance of money ... raises the price of everything. ... Mr Locke lays it down as a fundamental maxim that the quantity of produce or merchandise in proportion to the quantity of money serves as the regulator of market price. ... He has clearly seen that the abundance of money makes everything dear, but he has not considered how it does so. The great difficulty of this question consists in knowing in what way and in what proportion the increase of money raises prices. (*Essai*: 161)

Prices, Cantillon argued, are determined by demand and supply in the market for each good. An increase in the money supply can only lead to increased prices by increasing the demand for each good; in Cantillon's words, it leads to an 'increase of consumption which gradually brings about increased prices' (*Essai*: 163). Note the word 'gradually' – there are lags in the response of prices.

Suppose that there is an increase in the money supply caused by the opening of a gold or silver mine.[1] The owners of the mine, and those who work in it, will spend their increased incomes, driving prices up. Producers and sellers of food and the like gain, and increase their spending (*Essai*: 163–5). All goods (apart from gold and silver) are assumed, at this stage in the argument, to be in fixed supply, so the new demand must bid supplies away from others. The losers, at this stage, are landowners with rent incomes fixed in nominal terms, and wage earners on fixed wages. Some are forced to emigrate, said Cantillon, reducing population. This part of the argument is not wholly clear: why should the loss of non-miners not be counterbalanced by the numbers employed in the mines, or employed in providing for the miners?

Given time, rents and wages adjust to the new price level, raising costs and reducing competitiveness. Imports from low cost suppliers abroad displace domestic production; 'this will gradually ruin the mechanics and manufacturers of the state who will not be able to maintain themselves by working at

---

[1] The nearest thing to printing money, given Cantillon's implicit assumption that money consists of gold or silver; he dealt with banking operations separately.

such low prices owing to the dearness of living'. Eventually an equilibrium is reached in which the population is lower, the money produced by the mine flows out to pay for imports, and 'poverty and misery follow' (*Essai*: 165–7). The money stock is no higher than in other countries. This sad tale was clearly inspired by the experience of Spain, following the discovery of gold in the Spanish possessions in the Americas.[1]

It is not at all clear why the results of gold mining should be so dire. Cantillon thought that an increase in the price level resulting from a balance of trade surplus in manufactures was not at all harmful, at least in the medium run (see the next section), and production of gold or silver is surely just a particular example of industrial success. The extra money enters circulation directly, rather than doing so in return for export sales of manufactures, but it is hard to see why that should make so much difference. In the case of Spain, the (admittedly dismal) record could be explained by pointing to the enormous costs of the attempt by successive Spanish kings to create a European empire – Spain actually went bankrupt, despite the gold inflows from the Americas. More generally, it could be argued that gold mining was very profitable, so wage costs were a small part of the revenues, while the manufacturing industries which were displaced by imports were labour intensive, so the result was unemployment and population decline. In this case, it is not the increase in the money supply which did the damage, but a shift in the aggregate land–labour ratio as a result of a change in the composition of output.

6.4 BALANCE OF PAYMENTS ADJUSTMENT

Monetary theorists often try to present their theories as if they were timeless (Cantillon was no exception), but the subject is inevitably shaped by the institutional arrangements of the time. Modern monetary theory assumes fiat money (that is, money which has no value in itself, such as banknotes) or forms of money which have no physical existence at all except

---

[1] It has, incidentally, a lot in common with some explanations of the decline of British manufacturing industry in the 1980s after the discovery of oil, the twentieth century equivalent of gold, in the North Sea.

in electronic storage systems (such as bank deposits transferable by cheque). In the early eighteenth century money was gold or silver, and governments could not print gold as they can notes. The only way a country with no gold or silver mines of its own could increase its stock of monetary metals was by importing them, as the counterpart of a surplus in the balance of trade in all other goods. Monetary theory and the theory of balance of payments adjustment were inseparable.[1]

Cantillon's discussion of the effects of changes in the money supply is mainly about the effects of a balance of trade surplus.[2] The basic assumption is that the surplus is the result of competitive success in the export manufacturing sector. The money stock is increased, as money flows in because exports exceed imports, and the extra money comes into the hands of merchants and manufacturers. Employment expands as jobs are created in the export industries, so wages are bid up. The general price level only increases slowly, because the main gainers are the sort of people who will save in order to buy property, so a substantial part of the inflow of money will be hoarded, to begin with, and demand will not increase until it is spent. This only delays the inevitable – sooner or later the money will be spent in one way or another, and the general price level will be bid up.

An equilibrium can be reached in which the successful country has a high price level, a large money stock, and balanced, or near balanced, trade.

> In this situation the state may subsist in abundance of money, consume all its own produce and also much foreign produce and over and above all this maintain a small balance of trade against the foreigner or at least keep the balance level for many years. (*Essai*: 169)

In this extract, 'produce', of course, means agricultural produce; by manufacturing for export the country can afford net imports of foreign food and raw materials.

Can this be right? It appears to contradict conventional

---

[1] Cantillon did write about the effects of issuing banknotes, but not in his main discussion of money (see chapter 7 below).

[2] Cantillon generally wrote 'a balance of trade', or 'a balance against the foreigner', to refer to a surplus in the trade balance. In context, his intention is always clear.

notions of international equilibrium, in which price levels are usually assumed to be equalized between countries, and to reject the specie-flow mechanism, in which money stocks are automatically redistributed between countries. As Cantillon himself emphasized in his discussion of the effects of gold mines:

> All the gold and silver which [Spain and Portugal] extract from the mines does not supply them in circulation with more precious metal than others. *(Essai*: 167)

There is in fact no contradiction, since the trade surplus which started the story is assumed to be the result of an exceptionally competitive export manufacturing sector. If manufacturing was competitive enough to generate a surplus at the initial price level, it must be able to sustain a smaller surplus or balanced trade at a higher domestic price level. In the new equilibrium, domestic wages and rents are higher (in nominal terms) than those in less successful countries.

Cantillon suggested, in one place at least, that short run demand elasticities were very low. Suppose, he said, that the export of money from Portugal is forbidden. English traders will be unable to repatriate the revenue from selling cloth, because Portugal has a trade deficit, so they will find no-one to exchange the Portuguese currency they have earned into English currency. In this case, they will simply refuse to trade, so the price of English textiles in Portugal will become extraordinarily high, and smugglers will evade the prohibition. More money, he said, would leave the country than if its export had not been forbidden (*Essai*: 267), which implies that the demand elasticity is (numerically) less than one. Cantillon, obviously, did not know about the Marshall–Lerner condition, but it is possible that he intended to imply that an increase in export prices will increase, rather than decrease, the trade surplus, at least in the short run. If so, it seems that there may not be a stable equilibrium in relative price levels in the short run at all. This would fit Cantillon's general story quite well. Success, he implied, breeds success, at least for a while. A successful country, with an abundance of money, eventually declines, because new competitors emerge, and because success breeds luxury. Short run instability, at least within a certain range, plus long run corrective forces, could account for such a pattern.

Relative prices change in the process. Again, this seems to contradict standard presentations of the quantity theory of money, but again there is no contradiction, given Cantillon's assumptions. The economy is, of course, open, so changes in the relative prices of tradable and non-tradable goods are to be expected. As domestic costs and prices rise relative to those abroad, the price of non-tradables rises relative to tradables, the price of imported goods with high transport costs rises relative to goods with lower transport costs, and so on. The allocation of resources adjusts to the new prices.

> Increase of money only increases the price of products and merchandise by the difference of the cost of transport, when this transport is allowed. But in many cases the transport would cost more than the thing is worth, and so timber is useless in many places. This cost of carriage is the reason why milk, fresh butter, salads, game, etc. are almost given away in the provinces distant from the capital. (*Essai*: 179)

Cantillon's example was England, where meat imports were forbidden, while corn imports were permitted. As England increased its share of the world market for manufactures, and for other labour intensive activities like shipping and trade, the demand for food grew, the price of meat increased relative to that of corn, land was reallocated from corn growing to stock raising, and rents on meadows rose relative to those on corn fields (*Essai*: 173–5, 179).

Cantillon had a second argument about the relative prices of meat and bread. He argued that, as incomes rose, demand for meat would increase as more people could afford it (a third instead of a quarter of the population, in his example), forcing prices up. On the other hand, an increase in population (as a result of employment in export trades) would increase the demand for bread, but the increased demand would be a smaller proportion of the total output in the case of bread, and would therefore have a smaller effect on price (*Essai*: 173).

It is difficult to see why this should be true, except as a result of the rather arbitrary numbers Cantillon chose to illustrate his case. Perhaps the point is that export revenues accrue to those who are most likely to consume meat, and thus have a large relative effect on the demand for meat. In any case, it is clear that Cantillon was not considering the standard case preferred by modern theorists, in which the money supply changes with everything else staying constant, but a case in which the change in the money supply is the result of a prior change in export competitiveness, so incomes and relative prices change.

He also introduced a notion of hysteresis (as it would now be called) to deny Locke's strict quantity theory. An increase in the money supply, this time caused by the 'residence of ambassadors and foreign travellers' (a successful tourist industry?) will enter circulation through payments to servants, mechanics, and the like, who provide the 'equipages, amusements, etc. of these foreigners' (*Essai*: 177). Many who had not used money before (including the newly successful, and even their children) will become accustomed to using it, and habits will change.

> From all this I conclude that by doubling the quantity of money in a state the prices of products and merchandise are not always doubled. A river which runs and winds about in its bed will not flow with double the speed when the amount of its water is doubled. (*Essai*: 177)

A state can 'subsist in abundance of money' for many years, but not for ever.

> When a state has arrived at the highest point of wealth (I assume always that the comparative wealth of states consists principally in the respective quantities of money which they possess) it will inevitably fall into poverty by the ordinary course of things. The too great abundance of money, which so long as it lasts forms the power of states, throws them back imperceptibly but naturally into poverty. (*Essai*: 185)

There are two main mechanisms at work: the emergence of new competition from other countries, and increased spending on 'luxury' in the high price country, leading to increased imports.

In a successful country, the money stock, the general price level, and export prices all rise, and 'some foreign countries endeavour to set up for themselves the same kinds of manufactures, and so cease to buy those of the state in question' (*Essai*: 183). To begin with, the existing producers continue to dominate, at least in their own home market and in third markets, because of their great reputation, and because they enjoy economies of scale in transport, 'the facility of navigation affording the means of sending them at little cost into distant countries' (*Essai*: 183). Established producers can keep the upper hand for 'many years'.

Cantillon repeatedly stressed the difficulties of setting up manufactures in a new location. So, for example, Poland could replace imports of manufactures with locally produced goods, since 'bad as they might be at the outset', the local producers would 'soon' improve (*Essai*: 75–7). He recommended setting up manufactures in areas of the country remote from the capital, because prices are low there, but argued that 'much encouragement and capital' would be needed, because 'perfection is not at once attained' (*Essai*: 155). This is the main reason why the specie-flow mechanism takes so long to work: high prices eventually call forth low cost competitors, but the cost gap has to become large before the competitors can even get started, and then it takes quite a long time for them to establish themselves fully enough to make headway in third markets.

Cantillon's argument is clearly an early version of the 'infant industry' case for government intervention. He did not use that phrase, nor did he go into detail, but it is easy to see that the difficulties of setting up new industries were particularly strong in the pre-industrial period, when technology was embodied in the craft skills of the work force, and was learned through a long apprenticeship. It was not impossible to set up new competing centres of production, of course (that such centres would arise was precisely Cantillon's point), but learning new skills, perfecting them, and building up a good reputation were bound to take many years.

A major method by which technology was transferred, at the time, was by migration of skilled craftsmen. There would, presumably, be little incentive for those who were doing well in the established centres of an industry to move elsewhere, though they might be tempted if offered high rewards to teach others; it is not, of course, possible to establish a cheap manufacture by offering high rewards to all the work force. Once the tide turns, and the previously dominant centre starts to decline, its work force will face redundancy and will have to emigrate; 'many of its workmen and mechanics who see labour fallen off leave the state to find more work in the countries with the new manufacture' (*Essai*: 183). The tide can, presumably, turn very fast once this stage is reached. Political events might have the same effect. The expulsion of Huguenots from France in the late seventeenth century was a major blow to French industry, and corresponding gain for their competitors, especially England, where Huguenots founded several important industries (cf. *Essai*: 187).

To recapitulate, a balance of trade surplus can persist for some time, and a high price level can be maintained for much longer, perhaps for several decades.[1] Eventually, the downturn will come, and a period of depression will ensue, as other countries occupy the leading position. In time, the wheel turns again, and the depression is, or at least can be, brought to an end, allowing another upswing to begin. The specie-flow mechanism generates very long cycles, not static equilibrium.

A modern reader of Cantillon will often mentally substitute 'balance of payments' for 'balance of trade'. The phrase, 'balance of payments', had not then been invented, but Cantillon was well aware of the effects of trade in invisibles and of capital flows. Thus, he wrote about ambassadors and foreign travellers as a reason for an inflow of money (*Essai*: 177), and about shipping (*Essai*: 239–41).

He also discussed borrowing from abroad, public or private (*Essai*: 191–3). Such borrowing brings in money, and also diminishes the rate of interest.[2]

> By means of this money the entrepreneurs in the state find it possible to borrow more cheaply to set people on work and to establish manufacturies in the hope of profit. (*Essai*: 191)

This is, incidentally, about the only place where Cantillon suggested that capital investment might matter to employment and to output levels. An inflow of capital leads to an increase in employment and spending, driving prices up. This is very like the effect of a balance of trade surplus brought

---

[1] France, for example, did well from 1646 to 1687, a period of four decades (*Essai*: 187).

[2] The interest rate falls not because of the increase in the money stock, but because of the direct effect on the supply and demand for loans when demand is diverted abroad or supply augmented by foreign lenders (see section 6.5).

about by other causes, and is pleasant enough in the short run ('sums lent to the state . . . bring with them many present advantages'; *Essai*: 191), but Cantillon mistrusted borrowing from abroad, because it involved an outflow of interest payments, and because it made the borrowing state vulnerable to capital outflows at a time of crisis.

6.5 MONEY AND INTEREST RATES

Cantillon insisted that market prices were determined by demand and supply, so monetary changes could only affect prices through their effects on demand. This emphasis comes out very clearly in his account of the effect of monetary changes on interest rates.

Cantillon's explanation of interest rates has been discussed already (in section 4.3). I return to it here because interest rates were then, as now, often thought of as monetary phenomena. 'It is a common idea', Cantillon remarked, 'that the increased quantity of currency in a state brings down the price of interest there' (*Essai*: 213), on the grounds that where there is more money there is more to be borrowed. He rejected this idea, citing the conditions of 1720 in England as a counter example. In that year, the year of frantic speculation in the shares of the South Sea Company, 'nearly all the money in England was brought to London', and there was a large and increasing volume of banknotes in circulation, but interest rates rose from 5 per cent to 20 per cent. The explanation, of course, is simple: there was a very large demand for loans to buy shares with, and the increase in the money supply was a response to the demand. That was precisely Cantillon's point. The rate of interest depends on the demand and supply of loans, which may or may not be correlated with the money supply.

The normal cause of an increase in the money supply, in Cantillon's account, was a positive trade balance driven by a successful export sector. The increased money supply enters the system in the hands of entrepreneurs, the main borrowers of money, as increased profits, allowing them to reduce their borrowing and therefore lowering interest rates (*Essai*: 217–19). In this case an increased money supply is associated with a lower interest rate, but the relation is not one of cause and effect. Both are the effect of increased export competitiveness and hence increased profits in the export sector. If, however, the state is wealthy and contains great landowners, the increase in prices and thus (eventually) in rents which results from the increased money supply, tempts them to increase their spending, creating opportunities for investment, and thus keeping the demand for loans and interest rates up.

High public spending on war, on the other hand, raises interest rates, both by creating additional demand for goods, and thus additional investment opportunities, and also by raising risks, which raises interest rates by making lenders reluctant to lend. Borrowing from abroad lowers interest rates, as explained in the last section, because it adds to the supply of loans. Cantillon worked through a number of similar examples, concluding that the interest rate depends on the demand and supply for loans, and hence on the opportunities for profitable investment, independent of the money supply.

> Plenty or scarcity of money in a state always raises or lowers the price of everything in bargaining without any necessary connection with the rate of interest, which may very well be high in states where there is plenty of money, low in those where money is scarcer. (*Essai*: 215)

In this, as in much else, Cantillon was the proximate ancestor of classical economics (and the distant ancestor of modern monetarist, or new-classical, economics – see Bordo, 1983). The classics, however, did not learn from his analysis of monetary disequilibrium, which had to be rediscovered after a century and a half by Cairnes (1873) and again by Keynes (1930) – 'in virtually identical form' (Bordo, 1983: 253).

6.6 AUGMENTATION AND DIMINUTION

Only historians are now likely to take an interest in 'augmentations' and 'diminutions' of the currency, but they were a matter of great practical concern in the seventeenth and eighteenth centuries. Law used them deliberately to try to manipulate the portfolio choices of individuals (for example, to try to induce people to hold notes issued by his bank). Cantillon therefore had to say something about them.

The circulating currency consisted of gold and silver coins (and copper coins, used for small transactions, which can be ignored here). In origin, of course, coins simply served as a way of dividing gold and silver up into convenient quantities and of guaranteeing the quantity and purity of metal in each coin, to save the trouble of testing and weighing metal each time it was offered in exchange. In Cantillon's time, coins were still valued for their metal content. One problem arose from the simultaneous use of the two metals, gold and silver, which meant that their relative value had to be determined; that issue will be discussed later in the appendix to this chapter.

A second problem arose from the use of a money of account distinct from the coinage. In Britain, for example, the money of account was the pound sterling, but there was no pound coin. There were silver shillings and gold guineas (as well as copper pennies). The value of the shilling and of the guinea had to be defined in terms of pounds (or vice versa). Various obligations and debts, including public debt, were denominated in the unit of account. A somewhat similar situation exists now within the European Community, which uses a unit of account, the ecu, defined in terms of the various currencies of the member states.[1]

The relation between the unit of account (the pound sterling in Britain, for example) and the circulating currency was defined by law, so it could be changed by decree. 'Augmentation' of the currency involved declaring that each coin should count for more units of account. In other words, it was a devaluation of the unit of account relative to metallic coins. 'Diminution' was the reverse; reducing the value of coins in terms of money of account, and thus increasing the value of the unit of account in terms of gold and silver.

Cantillon's position was very simple. Money was based on gold and silver because these metals were really scarce, and had a real value, determined by the costs of producing them.

---

[1] The European Community's ecu may become a real currency. Coins have been issued, though they are not yet in general use anywhere. There was a real French coin, in Cantillon's time, called the ecu, while the guinea came into use as a unit of account for some purposes in Britain at a time when it had ceased to exist as a coin – well within living memory some rather pretentious establishments used to announce their prices in guineas.

The price level in terms of metallic coins was determined by the quantity of coins in circulation. He restated this theory very clearly as a preliminary to dealing with augmentation and diminution:

> According to the principles we have established the quantity of money circulating in exchange fixes and determines the price of everything in a state taking into account the rapidity or sluggishness of circulation. (*Essai*: 287)

It follows that augmentation or diminution should have no effect on prices measured in terms of the circulating coins. It should simply alter the real value of the unit of account. The problem was that augmentations and diminutions in France had in fact led to price changes (in terms of metallic coins), as Cantillon's readers would have known well. He had to explain this fact, in terms of his general theory.

The point is that various assets, notably instruments of the public debt, were denominated in units of account, so augmentations or diminutions led to capital gains or losses for holders of these assets, while expectations of an augmentation or diminution would induce changes in portfolios, with real effects.

In 1714, the king of France decreed that the ecu would be lowered in nominal value from 5 to 4 livres. There was, of course, a scramble to get out of cash and to acquire assets denominated in livres. Debts were repaid, and borrowing (in livres) became very easy. Merchants tried to build up stocks, including stocks of imported goods, rather than holding money. (This part of Cantillon's story might be thought to depend on ignorance on the part of merchants and other actors: if there was not going to be a real fall in the value of coins, there was no need to switch from cash to goods.)

Money circulated more rapidly, and prices rose, making it look as though the purely nominal diminution of the currency (which still contained just as much gold) really made it worth less. The king, we are told, borrowed at low interest rates, willingly losing from the diminution because he planned an augmentation to offset it. The king then hoarded money, and money had also left the country to buy stocks of imports, so the price level (calculated in terms of gold and silver coins) fell again, after having risen. Even after an augmentation which restored the ecu to its previous value in terms of the livre, prices were lower than before, because money had left the country and not returned.

The point of all this, of course, is to show that prices are determined by supply and demand, and changes in the price level have to be explained by changes in the conditions of supply and demand.

> After explaining the effects of raising and lowering the coinage, as practised in France, I maintain that they neither destroy nor weaken my principles, for if I am told that what cost 20 livres or 5 ounces of silver before the lowering referred to does not even cost 4 ounces or 20 livres of the new money after the augmentation, I will assent to this without departing from my principles, because there is less money in circulation than there was before the diminutions. (*Essai*: 295–7)

APPENDIX: THE VALUE OF MONETARY METALS

Money, for Cantillon, meant metallic money: gold, silver, and copper. Since copper was only used for small change, and since the value of copper coins diverged widely from its value as a metal, because of the relatively high cost of coining a low value metal (*Essai*: 269–71), it can be ignored. Gold and silver are uniquely suitable for use as money: they have a high intrinsic value per unit of volume, so high values can be transported without too much difficulty; they are divisible, durable, and 'beautiful and brilliant in the articles made of them' (*Essai*: 111). Their intrinsic value is essential.

> [If] a prince or republic gave currency to something which had not such a real and intrinsic value, not only would the other states refuse to accept it on that footing but the inhabitants would reject it when they perceived its lack of real value. (*Essai*: 111–13)

Locke was right to claim that the value of gold and silver depends on the consent of mankind, in that there is no absolute need to use them, but there are good reasons why they are always chosen as money. Their value is not imaginary, but depends on the real costs of producing them (*Essai*: 113).

The value of metals (not merely the monetary metals) depends on the land and labour required to produce them, just like any other goods. Cantillon had some difficulty fitting them into his framework, because the 'land' directly required to produce metals, that is the mines, is clearly a very special sort of land, and is not directly comparable to normal agricultural land (the land needed to support the workers, on the other hand, raises no new difficulties). His solution (already discussed in section 5.4) was to ignore the mine as a type of land, unless it was very productive:

> The outlay on the land for this production is considerable only so far as the owner of the mine can obtain a profit from the work of the miners when the veins are unusually rich. The land needed for the subsistence of the miners and workers, that is the mining labour, is often the principal expense and the ruin of the proprietor. (*Essai*: 97)

There is more than a hint of circularity in this extract: if the 'land' concerned, the mine, yields a lot of rent, it counts as a lot of land, making the land theory of value a tautology, since any part of the value of the product not accounted for by labour costs can be automatically counted as 'land'.

In practice, Cantillon fell back on a demand and supply explanation of the price of metals, and the claim that they possess intrinsic value amounts simply to an assertion that they are costly to produce. If demand fell, the price would fall, and production would cease (*Essai*: 97–9). When there was only one silver mine (this is part of a conjectural account of how silver first came into use), the owner had a monopoly, and 'was in a manner master to demand in exchange an arbitrary quantity of other produce and merchandise' (*Essai*: 101). When several mines were opened, 'the metal was esteemed at its cost value' (*Essai*: 103; an unusually unclear remark by Cantillon's standards).

In all of Cantillon's discussion of monetary theory, the focus is on market prices, not intrinsic values, and the value of (gold or silver) money is determined in the market:

> the quantity of money, as of all other commodities, determines its value in the bargaining of the market against other things. (*Essai*: 175)

MONEY, PRICES, AND THE TRADE BALANCE

The relative values of gold and silver were a matter of concern in a system in which both metals circulated. Cantillon repeated that their values depend on the land and labour needed to produce them, but his discussion of the ratio between the (market) values of silver and gold was conducted entirely in terms of their relative abundance (*Essai*: 273–7). This ratio had varied at different places and dates depending on the amount produced by the mines. The ratio must be the same everywhere, subject to adjustments for transport costs, because any profit opportunities would soon be removed by arbitrage (*Essai*: 279). The ratio depends on the relative quantities available and on the relative demands (*Essai*: 277–9).

The relative values of gold and silver coins must follow the relative price of the metals in the market, since if one metal were undervalued as a coin, the coins would be melted down for their metal content. Isaac Newton, as master of the mint in England, faced a problem of this sort, which Cantillon took as an example. Silver shillings and gold guineas were fixed in value in terms of the pound sterling, the money of account, and were hence fixed in relation to each other. The ratio of the value of gold coins to silver coins was fixed, in this way, at sixteen to one, by weight, while the ratio of their market prices had drifted down to fourteen and a half to one. Silver coins were thus undervalued (or gold overvalued) relative to the market value of their metallic content, so silver crowns, shillings, and sixpences were exported and melted down (*Essai*: 281). Newton recommended cutting the value of the gold guinea from 21s 6d (£1.075) to 21s (£1.05), a recommendation that was adopted by Parliament. Cantillon disagreed, on the grounds that Britain's debt to foreign lenders was denominated in pounds sterling, so reducing the value of gold in terms of the pound meant repaying more gold. Better, he said, to increase the value of the silver shilling, thus keeping the debt the same in gold and reducing it in terms of silver. Newton replied that the law made silver the 'true and only monetary standard' (*Essai*: 283).

7

Banking and Exchange Rates

The third part of the *Essai* is more obviously policy oriented and more obviously linked to the issues of the day than most of the book, though the approach remains resolutely theoretical. Apart from the first chapter (on foreign trade), it deals with the workings of the banking sector; Cantillon treated exchange rates as a part of the business of transferring money from one place to another, within or between countries, and hence part of the work of a banker.

There can be few better guides to the financial issues of the early eighteenth century than Cantillon, since he was both the greatest economic theorist of the time and a practical banker, who had been close to the great events of the preceding two decades. Even where his analysis was not original, the exposition is excellent. His treatment of exchange rates, for example, is similar to that found in Law's *Money and Trade Considered* of 1705, even though Cantillon disagreed with Law on almost everything else – it simply reflects the common experience of all those close to the financial markets of the time. I shall summarize it here (in section 7.2) for the sake of completeness. Cantillon's treatment of general banks, on the other hand, while also based on the conventional wisdom of the time, is significant as an implicit critique of Law's projects.

7.1 TRANSFERS OF MONEY

Modern economists tend to ignore location, unless they are really forced to consider it. They treat money in a very abstract way anyway, so it is natural for them to think of an exchange rate as the price of one abstract kind of currency, say a dollar, in terms of another, say a Deutschmark or a yen, in a market which has no particular location. Since trading is done by telephone, or some similar form of electronic communication, while the money concerned is often no more than an entry in an electronic record anyway, this may be a reasonable way of thinking about it (though anyone who has tried to get hold of some actual cash, in a hurry, in a strange country, knows that it is not really quite that simple). In Cantillon's time, money consisted of gold or silver coins. The coins of one country often circulated in another, since they were all made of the same physical stuff, gold or silver. Transport, however, was both costly and risky. There was nothing abstract about the problem of transferring money.

The primary function of the exchanges, as Cantillon saw it, was to transfer money from one geographical location to another, preferably without actually shipping the physical coins. Even within Paris, there was a cost to transporting money 'from one house to another', of 50 sols per 1000 livres, or 0.025 per cent. Between Paris and Rouen (less than an hour's drive today), the cost was 0.25 per cent. If there are payments to be made from one place to another, and payments to be made in the opposite direction, they can be offset against each other without anybody having to carry the actual coins in either direction.

Cantillon used an example in which tax payments had to be transferred from Châlons sur Marne to Paris, while payments for purchases of champagne had to be transferred by the Paris agents of the Châlons wine merchants to Châlons itself. The tax office in Paris could give bills of exchange to the wine merchants' agents, in return for cash payments in Paris, and the bills could then be presented to the tax receiver in Châlons sur Marne, who would pay over the money there. Note that bills of exchange are presented not as credit instruments (which became, later, their main function), but as simple devices for transferring money. Cantillon in fact spoke of 'cheques or bills of exchange' (*Essai*: 247), at least in Higgs' translation ('rescriptions ou lettres de change' in the French).

If there were enough trade between two centres, bankers would set up in business – acting as agents, arranging offsets, and issuing bills. Finding a partner in the way described above would clearly be difficult for a non-specialist. It is easy to see how merchants engaged in trade with a particular region could become agents, and thus bankers – there was no clear distinction between merchants and bankers at the time.

7.2 EXCHANGE RATES AND THE TRADE BALANCE

Bills of exchange can eliminate the costs of shipping money, provided the sums to be transferred in each direction balance each other. If they do not, some actual cash will have to be transported in one direction or the other. If the value of the bills presented for payment in one place exceeds the money received there from the issue of bills payable in the other, money has to be moved, and the cost must be paid by those who want to transfer the money. As long as trade between the two places is balanced, bills can be issued at 'par', that is, 1 livre in Paris exchanges for 1 livre in Châlons.[1] If, however, Châlons has a trade surplus with Paris, those who want to send money to Châlons will have to pay the cost of shipping the cash, so the exchange rate diverges from par by enough to cover this cost. In Cantillon's example, the divergence from par is 2.5 per cent, so 102.5 livres at Paris will buy a bill for 100 livres payable at Châlons.[2] The principle is clear; the exchange rate differs from par when there is an imbalance in trade, and it has to be sufficient to cover the cost of physically transporting enough money to transfer the balance.

The transfer of money between places which are in different countries raises no new issues. Transport costs may be higher, but that is a matter of physical distance, and has nothing to do with national boundaries. Between Paris and Châlons the exchange may be as much as 3 per cent either side of par, when one city has a deficit with the other, while between London and Amsterdam the divergence from par was rarely more than 2 per cent in peacetime (*Essai*: 253). In places which use the same money ('like Paris and Châlons sur Marne, London and Bristol'), 'par' simply means exchange at one for one, £1 in London for £1 in Bristol, and so on. Where the money has different names, as between London and Amsterdam, par means 100 ounces of gold or silver for 100

---

[1] This use of the word 'par' is, of course, quite different from its use in Cantillon's land theory of value, the 'par' between land and labour.

[2] Cantillon's arithmetic is a bit difficult to follow, since he says that transport itself costs 1 per cent, and he allows 1.5 per cent as the bankers' commission – it is not clear whether this is charged on all exchanges, regardless of the balance, or whether it only appears when money has to be shipped.

ounces of the same metal in a different coinage. Note that Cantillon ignored mint costs here; if the owner of the metal had to pay the costs of melting down one kind of coin and minting it into a different coinage, mint costs would have to be added to transport costs.

This basic analysis was easily developed to deal with more complicated cases. In a system of multilateral exchange involving many places, bills of exchange can be offset against each other, so the exchange rates reflect the overall balance of each country or city (*Essai*: 257). Further, if the balance between, say, London and Amsterdam shows a deficit for London in a particular month which is expected to be reversed in the next month, bankers who anticipate a reversal of the exchanges will postpone payments from London to Amsterdam, in order to avoid the unfavourable exchange rate, and this will prevent unnecessary shipments of money to and fro.

> This is what bankers call speculation, which often causes variations in the exchanges for a short period independently of the balance of trade; but in the long run we must get back to this balance which fixes the constant and uniform rule of exchange. (*Essai*: 259)

Cantillon presented his main analysis in terms of the trade balance, because he clearly thought that trade was the main source of international payments, but he knew that other payments, such as 'the sums of money which one state sends into another for its secret services and political aims, for subsidies to allies', and so on, had to be taken into account (*Essai*: 263).

The essential point is that the exchange rate mirrors the balance of payments, so that if a country's currency is above par, it is a signal that it has a surplus, while a currency below par signals a deficit. The exchange rate does not, however, indicate the size of the surplus or deficit, because the rate only has to move far enough away from par to cover the costs of transporting the money (per unit of currency), which depend on physical distance and the like, not on the amount of specie being transported. In a multilateral trading system, each country has a different exchange rate with each different trading partner, so the best indicator of the overall balance of payments is the price of gold or silver. If gold rises above the price at which the mint will buy it (i.e. turn it into coin), the balance cannot be favourable, because a favourable balance would mean gold imports, which would force the price down to the mint price.

Exchange rates do not play any active role in Cantillon's story. He presumably went through the analysis of the determinants of exchange rates in order to demystify the subject. Some writers of the time attached great importance to exchange rates, and wanted to manipulate them in various ways. Cantillon wanted to shift attention back to the fundamental determinants of a country's performance.

7.3 FRACTIONAL RESERVE BANKING

As well as taking responsibility for transfers of money from one place to another, banks can take deposits, issue notes, and make loans. These, of course, are now regarded as the main functions of (retail) banks. Goldsmiths had long since had a sideline in storing money for safekeeping, and had started to carry out some other banking functions, but the development of deposit taking banks as distinct institutions was far from complete in Cantillon's time. At one point he referred to 'a goldsmith or a banker', in this context (*Essai*: 303).

As Cantillon described it, clients would deposit money (coins or bullion) in a bank, or with a goldsmith, and take notes in return. The banker could then lend some of the money, relying on getting it back before his clients returned to demand repayment. It was essential to hold enough cash on hand, because confidence in the bank would be wrecked by any failure to supply cash on demand. How much the bank could safely lend would depend on the habits of its clients. 'Economical gentlemen', who build up savings to buy land, would often leave the money in the bank for a long time, or give notice of their intention to withdraw well in advance. The banker could then lend as much as nine tenths of the money deposited. On the other hand, if the customers were entrepreneurs and merchants, depositing and withdrawing large amounts from day to day, the banker might only be able to lend a third of the deposits, keeping two thirds in cash, to meet possible withdrawals (*Essai*: 299–303). Banknotes could circulate from hand to hand. Cantillon evidently did not expect them to circulate very far – he remarked at one point that the notes may circulate through 'several' hands before being presented for payment. One reason is that notes were, at that time, only issued in rather large denominations, and were only used in large payments.

The effect of the introduction of (private) banks of this sort was to accelerate the circulation of money, by freeing money which would otherwise be held in private hoards, and by replacing money with notes for some (but only some) kinds of transactions. So, in an example, 100,000 ounces of silver are deposited, and the banker is able to lend out 90,000, returning them to circulation. Note that Cantillon did not count notes or bank deposits as money, but as substitutes for money, so he saw them not as adding to the money supply but as speeding up the circulation of metallic money.

7.4 NATIONAL BANKS

> A general national bank has this advantage over the bank of a single goldsmith that there is always more confidence in it. (*Essai*: 305)

The limitations of a 'national' bank, however, emerge rather clearly in the next sentence, when Cantillon remarked that people will bring the largest deposits (but presumably not smaller deposits, which are left to local bankers) to it 'even from the most remote quarters of the city'. In other words, Cantillon did not conceive of a national bank whose operations stretched beyond the capital. This explains his otherwise obscure comment:

> I think public banks of very great utility in small states and those where silver is rather scarce, but of little service for the solid advantage of a great state. (*Essai*: 313)

In a 'great state', only the capital would be served by the bank. Branch banking was unknown then, and would probably not have been feasible, because of the poor state of communications.

Even national banks cannot enlarge the money supply by very much, since if they issue too many notes they will find themselves unable to redeem them. For example, Venice was a city state, and thus well placed to benefit from a national bank. Indeed, all transactions above a certain size had, by law, to be carried out using bank money, but even so:

> If the explanations given to me in round figures in 1719 on the receipts of the Bank of Venice are correct it may be said of national banks generally that their utility never corresponds to the tenth part of the current money circulating in a state. This is approximately what I ascertained there. (*Essai*: 309)

In any substantial state, the maximum scale of operation of a national bank (relative to the total money stock) must be much less. If a national bank tries to expand credit too far, as the bank of Venice did in an emergency when the state was 'pressed for money', withdrawals soon exhaust reserves. All of this was presumably directed against Law, who wanted to issue paper money to expand the money supply and stimulate the economy.

A bank can, then, accelerate the circulation of money, effectively raising the money supply, but only within limits. It may not be advisable anyway:

> when money circulates [in a state] in greater abundance than among its neighbours a national bank does more harm than good. An abundance of fictitious and imaginary money causes the same disadvantages as an increase in real money in circulation, by raising the price of land and labour, or by making works and manufactures more expensive at the risk of subsequent loss. But this furtive abundance vanishes at the first gust of discredit and precipitates disorder. (*Essai*: 311)

This gnomic comment is as close as Cantillon came to a direct criticism of Law and his schemes.

8

Trade and Trade Policy

Cantillon is generally recognized as one of the most important predecessors of Adam Smith and of classical economics. His account of the workings of the economy provided a strong, if implicit, case for the efficiency of markets. In particular, his argument that the owner of a large estate need not manage it himself, but can rent the farms to individual farmers and rely on the market mechanism to supply him with everything that he could have got by ordering its production himself, makes a strong case for the market. His distinction between market price and (cost-based) intrinsic value is very much in the classical tradition, as is his theory of wages and of population. Above all, he was one of the first to show a clear understanding of the specie-flow mechanism, which is sometimes thought to be the decisive refutation of mercantilist theories.[1]

At the same time, Cantillon's views on policy were clearly 'mercantilist', in the rather loose sense in which the word is usually used. Mercantilism is not easily defined. It consisted mainly of pamphlets on immediate policy issues, and lacked any common theoretical framework. In writings on economic and political history, the term is usually used to refer to a set of policies associated with nation-building and with economic and military competition between emergent nation states. In discussions of the history of economics, it refers to a rather inchoate body of literature advocating nationalist economic policies and centring on the control of trade. Nevertheless, Blaug (1985: 10) argues that 'as a description of a central tendency in economic thought from the close of the 16th to the middle of the 18th century, the label retains general

---

[1] See section 10.3 for a fuller discussion of the relation between Cantillon and classical economics.

validity'. It refers to 'the doctrine that a favorable balance of trade is desirable', and that a favourable balance in manufactures is particularly desirable. All that matters here is that Cantillon held views on policy of the sort that Smith associated with the 'mercantile system'.[1]

In particular, Cantillon supported policies designed to promote exports of manufactures, and regarded a positive trade balance, and the accumulation of gold and silver, as legitimate aims.

> It is by examining the results of each branch of commerce singly that foreign trade can be usefully regulated. . . . It will always be found by examining particular cases that the exportation of all manufactured articles is advantageous to the state, because in this case the foreigner always pays and supports workmen useful to the state, that the best returns or payments imported are specie, and in default of specie the produce of foreign land into which there enters the least labour (*Essai*: 233).

One could hardly ask for a clearer statement of the views that are conventionally described as mercantilist, or of the views that Smith spent about a quarter of the *Wealth of Nations* castigating.

This combination of classical and mercantilist elements in Cantillon's writings may seem surprising. After all, Adam Smith, and other classical writers, dismissed mercantilism as a tissue of error and special pleading. I will argue that there is no inconsistency; Cantillon's 'mercantilist' views on policy were based directly on his analysis of the economy, together with a number of assumptions, on matters of fact and on the aims of policy, which differ from those of the classics, but which were not at all unreasonable in the context of the times.

8.1 THE CASE FOR THE MARKET

Mercantilist writers are often accused of a childish confusion of money with wealth. That was a major element in Adam Smith's case against them, and his critique of mercantilism is

---

[1] On mercantilism in general see Allen (1987), Coleman (1969), Heckscher (1931), Perotta (1991), and Viner (1937, 1968).

often repeated by unsophisticated modern writers. According to this reading, mercantilists wanted a balance of trade surplus to bring more money, that is more gold and silver, into the country, because they thought that a country with more money, like an individual with more money, is richer. Some mercantilists may have thought in this way (though it is not easy to find any serious writer against whom the charge could be proved). Cantillon was certainly not guilty of it. In the very first paragraph of the *Essai*, he defined wealth in almost exactly the same terms that Smith used in the first sentence of the introduction to the *Wealth of Nations*. Smith spoke of 'the necessaries and conveniencies of life' (1776: 10), and Cantillon said that 'wealth in itself is nothing but the maintenance, conveniencies and superfluities of life' (*Essai*: 3).

There is a strong case for *laissez-faire* implicit in Cantillon's analysis of a closed economy. His account of an isolated estate (discussed in section 2.3) makes the case particularly clearly. He did not, it is true, actually use the phrase, 'the invisible hand', which was invented by Smith, but he could have done, and it would not have seemed out of place. His claim that

> the fancies, the fashions and the modes of living of the prince, and especially of the landowners, determine the use to which land is put in a state, and cause the variations in the market price of all things (*Essai*: 59, chapter title)

seems strange to modern readers, but it is no more than a special case of the doctrine of consumer sovereignty. The landowners have disposable income to spend, on a sufficient scale to be able to make some real choices. Most of the population do not: 'labourers and mechanics who live from day to day change their mode of living only from necessity' (*Essai*: 63), while the few farmers and businessmen who have something to spare, copy the landowners.

How can this analysis of the smooth working of the market and of the way it satisfies consumers' wants be squared with the extract quoted at the start of this chapter, or with these words from the beginning of the chapter on foreign trade?

> When a state exchanges a small product of land for a larger in foreign trade, it seems to have the advantage; and if current money is more abundant there than abroad it will always exchange a smaller product of land for a greater.

> When the state exchanges its labour for the produce of foreign land it seems to have the advantage, since its inhabitants are fed at the foreigner's expense. (*Essai*: 225)

There are two main reasons why the state should interfere with the market. First, because the number of people in the state is important (for military reasons), and individual landowners need not take account of the effects of their consumption choices on the size of the population. Second, because successful trade policy can raise the money stock and the price level in a state relative to its neighbours and rivals, improving the terms of trade and (again) increasing its military power. I will deal with them in turn.

8.2 TRADE POLICY AND POPULATION

Concern over population was a major reason for Cantillon's mercantilist policy recommendations. His analysis of the determinants of population has been dealt with in chapter 3, so only a brief summary of the basic theory is needed as a basis for examination of the policy issues.

In a closed economy, output and employment are constrained by the availability of land, which is, in the long run, the only scarce resource. Given the supply of land, employment depends on the land–labour ratio in production, while population adjusts to bring the labour supply into line with employment. For a given scale of real wages, the division of the (land) value of any good between the land used to support the labour force and that used to produce materials is a direct measure of the labour–land ratio, and hence of the employment generated by demand for that good. In the example of the isolated estate, Cantillon worked through the results of cutting down on domestic servants to increase the number of horses (*Essai*: 65); land has to be reallocated from producing food for servants to producing fodder for horses, and employment falls. For a given level of real wages, then, employment depends on the composition of output. Higher real wages mean that a given territory supports fewer people.

> If the proprietors of land had at heart the increase of population . . . they would doubtless increase the population up to the point which the land could support,

according to the produce which they allotted for each person whether an acre and a half or four to five acres a head. But if . . . by the prices they offer in the market for produce and merchandise they determine the farmers to employ the land for other purposes than the maintenance of man (for we have seen that the prices they offer in the market and their consumption determine the use made of the land just as if they cultivated it themselves) the people will necessarily diminish in number. (*Essai*: 73)

In an open economy, employment depends on the composition of trade, as well as the composition of demand. The main point is very simple. In a closed economy, workers in the manufacturing sector live on the produce of domestic agriculture, and the size of the manufacturing sector is limited by the surplus produced by the agricultural sector. In an open economy, by contrast, workers employed in manufacturing can consume imported food, or use imported materials, paid for by exports of manufactures. Employment and population can expand beyond the limits set by local agriculture. Equally, local demand for manufactures can be met by imports, paid for by exports of agricultural products, but in this case, employment and population will be below their closed economy levels. Total employment in the world system will remain the same (to a first approximation), but it will be concentrated in countries which export manufactures, at the expense of those which export primary products. The notion of the 'export of work' was fairly common among mercantilist writers at the time;[1] the point here is to show how it fits in with Cantillon's system as a whole. Cantillon's theory provided a more rigorous justification of it than any of his predecessors had been able to provide.[2]

Cantillon returned to this line of argument repeatedly (*Essai*: 25, 45, 75–7, 225–35, 239); for example:

---

[1] See Johnson (1937, chapter XV).
[2] Perotta (1991: 320) identifies the 'exchange of labour with land' as part of Cantillon's case, but also claims that Cantillon favoured the exchange of luxuries for necessities. In Cantillon's example of the exchange of (labour intensive) lace for (land intensive) wine (*Essai*: 77), he claims that Cantillon thought of wine (in this case, champagne) as a necessary wage good. I can find no textual justification for this odd claim.

England buys from abroad considerable amounts of timber, hemp and other materials or products of the soil and consumes much wine for which she pays in minerals, manufactures, etc. That saves the English a great quantity of the products of their soil. Without these advantages the people of England ... could not be so numerous as they are. (*Essai*: 85)

Given Cantillon's assumptions and his method of analysis, his conclusion is clearly correct. It differs from that of his classical successors because they assumed that the availability of capital was the main constraint on output. Ricardo, and other classical writers, recognized diminishing returns to land, of course, but the size of the capital stock determined how much of the land was used, and how intensively it was cultivated, whereas Cantillon did not treat capital as a scarce resource at all. Adam Smith, for example, argued that investment in agriculture is preferable to 'manufactures for distant sale' (Smith, 1776: 378), so long as land is relatively abundant – in Smith's model, manufacturing and agriculture are alternative uses of scarce capital (cf. Smith, 1776: 453), so the best policy is to invest first in the activities which give the highest return on capital, which is exactly what capital owners will do without any need for government intervention.

In Cantillon's account, by contrast, manufacturing for export is a net addition to domestic production, though not to rent incomes. Cantillon's claim that food imports can allow an enlarged population has much in common with the Ricardian case for free trade in corn. The difference is that the price mechanism will do the job automatically, in Ricardo's version, because the country with abundant capital will cultivate the land more intensively (in the absence of trade), and will have a higher relative price of corn. In Cantillon's model, success in external markets for manufactures depends mainly on skills and reputation.

Why should a large population be regarded as a good thing? Clearly not for the sort of reasons dealt with in the mainstream of modern welfare economics, in which a desirable allocation of resources is one which best satisfies consumers' preferences. Final demand comes from landlords, who presumably buy imports because they prefer them. According to Cantillon, the creation of a new manufacturing industry, to produce for export or to displace imports, would help to increase population, but it would normally involve putting up with low quality, at least for a considerable time (*Essai*: 77, 155), which could hardly be in the consumers' interest. He did not rely on the workers' interest in jobs either. Other things being equal, high wages mean a smaller population, because the land supports fewer people if consumption per head is higher (*Essai*: 81–3). Cantillon refused to take sides on that issue:

> It is also a question outside of my subject whether it is better to have a great multitude of inhabitants, poor and badly provided, than a smaller number, much more at their ease. (*Essai*: 85)

In general, Cantillon accepted that states had certain aims, one of which was to increase population, and he simply offered expert advice on how they should be attained. 'The more labour there is in a state the more naturally rich the state is esteemed', according to a chapter heading (*Essai*: 87). He qualified this argument, in his discussion of foreign trade, by conceding that 'great states have no need to increase the number of their inhabitants' (*Essai*: 233). On the other hand, small states, with little 'raw produce' of their own, needed to import it, and thus needed manufactured exports. Examples like the Netherlands, a small state which had attained a position in Europe quite out of proportion to its limited territory, must have been in his mind. In so far as he did offer any explanation of his concern with population, it seems to be military. Exports of agricultural products are not only 'abstracted from the food of the people', but 'what is worse, mostly sent to the foreigner and often serving to support the enemies of the state' (*Essai*: 77).

Cantillon stressed one particular application of this argument; a state should encourage the use of its own ships in trade. Shipping is labour intensive, so population is increased by the use of local, rather than foreign ships, and a strong merchant fleet is very directly linked to naval power (*Essai*: 243). He therefore praised the Navigation Acts in England (*Essai*: 241). His arguments contrast with those of Smith, who argued that shipping was best left to foreigners until a late stage of development, on the grounds that it is a capital intensive activity (Smith, 1776: 379–80, 454–5), though Smith also, rather inconsistently, praised the Navigation Acts for military reasons (Smith, 1776: 463–4).

A particularly full version of Cantillon's arguments linking population, manufacturing, and economic policy is to be found in his discussion of Poland (*Essai*: 75–7). Poland, along with other states near the Baltic, was a main source of food and raw materials for Western Europe at the time. If Polish landowners spend half of their rent (assumed to be a third of the produce of the land) on manufactures from Holland, and if farmers imitate them, and spend half of their profits on imports, a third of the output of Polish agriculture will be exported to pay for imports, and will support the population of Holland.

> If the proprietors of land and the nobility in Poland would consume only the manufactures of their own state, bad as they might be at the outset, they would soon become better, and would keep a great number of their own people to work there, instead of giving this advantage to the foreigners: and if all states had the like care not to be the dupes of other states in matters of commerce, each state would be considerable only in proportion to its produce and the industry of its people. (*Essai*: 77)

One thing that is missing from Cantillon's discussion of trade is any real recognition of the existence of gains from trade. He did not explicitly deny them, but the remark about states becoming the 'dupes' of others, in the quoted extract, is difficult to square with any idea that a state might gain from specializing in some things and exporting others. His comments on Poland suggest that manufactured goods could be produced anywhere, given initial encouragement, and given time to build up experience, though he did add a word of caution in his discussion of new manufactures in remote provinces:

> When these manufactures are set up perfection is not at once attained. If some other province have them better or cheaper or owing to the vicinity of the capital or the convenience of a sea or river communication have their transport considerably facilitated, the manufactures in question will have no success. (*Essai*: 155)

In the case of a sovereign state like Poland, one has to assume either that any substantial state is sure to be able to pick a location which will be good enough to be competitive, at least in local markets, or that the state can always protect local producers.

In sum, this part of Cantillon's analysis of trade policy combines (1) a model of the determinants of population, which is entirely coherent given the key assumption that land is scarce but capital is not, (2) an argument for state support of infant industries, and (3) a belief that a larger population is desirable on military grounds. All of these might be criticized, but they do not deserve the sort of scornful dismissal that mercantilist ideas have often suffered.

8.3 POLICY AND THE TRADE BALANCE

The second and more prominent part of Cantillon's case for intervention in foreign trade rests on his case for a positive trade balance.

> I will conclude then by observing that the trade most essential to a state for the increase or decrease of its power is foreign trade, . . . and above all that care must always be taken to maintain the balance against the foreigner. (*Essai*: 243)

> Enough to say that it should always be endeavoured to import as much silver as possible. (*Essai*: 235)

One could hardly hope to find a more unequivocal statement of mercantilist policy.

Cantillon's analysis of the effects of an increase in the money stock have been discussed in chapter 6. Briefly, he was well aware that a positive balance of trade involved an inflow of the monetary metal, silver, and that this would increase the money supply, increase the price level, reduce competitiveness, and eventually reverse itself. Indeed he provided as clear a statement of the specie-flow mechanism as any writer of the time, or for a century after (Blaug, 1985: 21). However, he argued that the eventual decline of a successful trading nation, though (almost) inevitable, would take a long time, and that the advantages of a positive trade balance, although temporary, were well worth having (cf. Low, 1952).

Cantillon did not advocate a trade surplus for its own sake, and he insisted that the only surplus likely to persist was a surplus based on competitive success in manufacturing. The point seems to be that the factors which generate the surplus in the first place allow the country concerned to sustain a strong position, despite increasing costs and prices. The argument has already been outlined in chapter 6 above; the next three paragraphs are a brief summary, to provide a basis for discussion of Cantillon's policy views.

In the first instance, Cantillon argued, an inflow of money caused by a balance of trade surplus accrues as income to merchants and the like, who are particularly likely to save the money and hoard it until they have accumulated enough to buy property (*Essai*: 167), so the increase in prices is delayed. During the period of rising prices and high demand, the use of money in exchange tends to expand, at the expense of barter, increasing the transactions demand for money, and limiting the extent of price rises (*Essai*: 179). Cantillon concluded that prices need not increase in proportion to the increase in the money stock. (Other writers of the time, such as Potter, Law, and later Hume, held the same view; see Viner, 1937: 36–40.)

Prices must increase, and competitiveness must be affected (*Essai*: 169), but Cantillon thought that

> the state may subsist in abundance of money, consume all its own produce and also much foreign produce and over and above all this maintain a small balance of trade against the foreigner or at least keep the balance level for many years. (*Essai*: 169)

He gave several grounds for this optimistic view. First, although rivals will spring up, they will not succeed immediately, since they 'will not at first be so perfect or so highly valued' (*Essai*: 169). Markets are difficult to enter, because skills take time to acquire, and reputation counts for a lot – a large part of trade, then as now, consisted of highly differentiated manufactured goods, and manufacturing skills at the time were largely transmitted by apprenticeship and were therefore difficult to establish in new areas. A large money stock based on foreign borrowing or artificial credit creation, on the other hand, was unlikely to last (*Essai*: 191–3).

Second, the high price country enjoys favourable terms of trade, selling dear and buying cheap (*Essai*: 189). Even if the quantity of exports and imports moves against it, the balance may remain favourable because of these price changes.

Taken together, Cantillon's arguments amount to an assertion that a higher price level may actually have favourable effects on the balance of payments to begin with, and that this effect lasts for a long time. Cantillon's mercantilism, then, is both defensible and fairly familiar to modern readers, taking account of the conditions of the time. He did not think that it was possible to maintain a (large) surplus on the balance of trade for long, but he did think that a country could sustain a relatively high price level for a considerable period, provided it was based on real competitive strength in manufacturing.

Suppose Cantillon's positive economics were correct, and a high price level could be sustained. Why should this be a good thing? Cantillon offered two main reasons. First, a high price level for exports means favourable terms of trade, which raises real consumption and allows the inhabitants to 'live there on the raw produce of the state with more comfort and ease' (*Essai*: 233). This is a relative of the case for an optimal tariff, albeit in a very crude form. Second, cash comes in useful in war.

> [T]he revenues of the state where money abounds, are raised more easily and in comparatively much larger amount. This gives the state, in case of war or dispute, the means to gain all sorts of advantages over its adversaries with whom money is scarce . . . [the Prince] will be better able to attach to himself generals and officers by gifts of money. . . . With money munitions of war and food are bought even from the enemies of the state. Money can be given without witnesses for secret service. After all it seems to me that the comparative power and wealth of states consist, other things being equal, in the greater or less abundance of money circulating in them. (*Essai*: 189–91)

As well as giving a revealing view of the conduct of international relations in the early eighteenth century, this extract presents an entirely rational argument for trying to maintain a high price level and a large money stock.

Cantillon did not, however, expect that high prices would prove sustainable in the long run.

When a state has arrived at the highest point of wealth (I assume always that the comparative wealth of states consists principally in the respective quantities of money which they possess) it will inevitably fall into poverty by the ordinary course of things. (*Essai*: 185)

The goods and manufactures will in the long run cost so much that the foreigner will gradually cease to buy them . . . and this will by imperceptible degrees ruin the work and manufactures of the state. The same cause . . . will draw [landlords] into the habit of importing many articles. . . . States who rise by trade do not fail to sink afterwards. (*Essai*: 235)

It is possible to delay decline, by withdrawing money from circulation to slow down the price increase, and by avoiding excessive state spending (*Essai*: 185), but not to postpone it indefinitely. In any case Cantillon was too much of a political realist to expect much of governments.

[Princes use] the abundance of their state revenues, to extend their power and to insult other countries on the most frivolous pretexts. And all things considered they do not perhaps so badly in working to perpetuate the glory of their reigns . . . for since . . . the state must collapse of itself they do but accelerate its fall a little. (*Essai*: 185–7)

But, he added thoughtfully, 'they ought to endeavour to make their power last all the time of their own administration' (*Essai*: 187).

A state that has declined in this way can be revived again, at least provided it is 'a considerable state':

To revive a state it is needful to . . . bring about the influx of an annual, a constant and a real balance of trade, to make flourishing by navigation the articles and manufactures which can always be sent abroad cheaper when the state is in a low condition and has a shortage of money. . . . An able minister is always able to make it recommence this round. Not many years are needed to see it tried and succeed, at least at the beginning. (*Essai*: 193–5)

One might ask why Cantillon advocated policies whose

effects were bound to be transitory. One answer is that the time taken to complete the cycle is considerable (though Cantillon described it as 'not a great many years'). By his reckoning, the upswing in France lasted from 1646 to 1684, and the downswing from 1684 to the date at which he was writing, around 1730:

> one may say that the power of France has been on the increase only from 1646 (when manufactures of cloths were set up there, which were until then imported) to 1684 when a number of Protestant undertakers and artisans were driven out of it, and that the kingdom has done nothing but recede since this last date. (*Essai*: 187)

Given a plausible time horizon, a forty year upswing looks pretty attractive.

In any case, Cantillon seems not to have thought it possible to enjoy permanent growth, or to remain in equilibrium at any but the lowest level. The options are to start on the merry-go-round, or to remain stuck in poverty. An increase in 'power and wealth' initially feeds on itself, as the quality of locally manufactured goods improves, through learning by doing, and their reputation increases. This must happen faster than the consequent price increases, or the process could not get off the ground, but eventually the balance is reversed. By juggling the time lags involved, it would clearly be possible to construct a formal model with the property that no stable static equilibrium exists, but Cantillon's analysis is too informal for his implicit model to be reconstructed with enough confidence to make formalization worthwhile.

An essential component of the story, for Cantillon as for other mercantilist writers, is that the world market is limited, so one country can only expand its exports and population at the expense of others.

> But as to Italy, Spain, France and England . . . they are always capable of being raised by good administration to a high degree of power by trade alone, provided it be undertaken separately, for if all these states were equally well administered they would be great only in proportion to their respective capital and to the greater or less industry of their people. (*Essai*: 195)

In this extract, as elsewhere in the *Essai*, 'capital' is Higgs' translation of 'fonds', which has a much broader meaning than the English word 'capital', at least as the latter is used by modern economists. 'Fonds' includes land, so there is no implication that general accumulation of capital would allow all countries to expand together.

In Cantillon's analysis (in contrast to that of most other mercantilist writers), the assumption that markets are limited is inherent in the basic theoretical framework. Land is the only ultimate scarce resource, and rent is the only net income. Output and demand, on a global scale, are fixed, because land is fixed. International competition, therefore, can only be competition over shares in a given market.

8.4 CANTILLON AND MERCANTILISM

If this interpretation of Cantillon's theory is correct, it did indeed contain mercantilist elements. The main aims of policy are to increase the power and wealth of the state; these aims generally coincide, so there is no need to choose between them (cf. Viner, 1948); they are achieved by maintaining a trade surplus (as far as possible), by accumulating precious metals in the country, and by exporting manufactures rather than agricultural products. The standard view of mercantilism, descended from Adam Smith, treats it as either the rationalization of special interests or as the result of simple error. There is no doubt that many mercantilist writers deserve to be dismissed in this way, but Cantillon does not.[1]

Cantillon did not naively identify money with wealth. Some of his comments, taken out of context, could, it is true, be read this way, but in the context of the analysis as a whole it is clear that 'abundance of money' is both cause and effect of wealth, which is defined independently. He was not guilty of overlooking the specie-flow mechanism either, as I have argued at length above. It is true that he did not hold a quantity theory of money, in any simple form, though it is not clear that this should be counted as a fault. He argued, very reasonably, that in an open economy an increase in the money

---

[1] As Herlitz put it (1961: 134): 'In the hands of Cantillon and Steuart the earlier "doctrine of the balance of trade" . . . is cast in a more rational mould'.

stock led not only to an increase in the general price level, but also to consequent changes in real incomes and relative prices, so it could not be assumed that all prices would change in the same proportion. He also argued that the process through which prices increased could induce permanent changes in habits.

An increase in the money stock will therefore not in general lead to an increase in all prices in the same proportion as the increase in the money stock (the simplest version of the quantity theory). Sophisticated proponents of the quantity theory would only expect the simple result under rather special circumstances anyway. Cantillon was dealing with the effects of real changes in competitiveness or policy, which would be expected to have real effects, so there need be no conflict between his views and those of quantity theorists. He argued that no long run equilibrium existed, as far as the trade balance and the price level were concerned, so that policy had to be directed to initiating and accelerating the upswing and retarding the downswing.

It might be thought that the aims of a positive trade balance and a large population conflict, on the grounds that maximizing population requires food imports, not imports of specie. Cantillon did not consider this possibility. If he had, he could have argued that it was irrelevant, since a positive trade balance is a temporary phenomenon, followed by a higher price level and a rough balance in international payments. The aim is to sustain a high price level and favourable terms of trade, which does not conflict with (and may help in) maintaining a large population.

Cantillon has a very special position in the history of economics, as the first to provide a coherent theory of prices, outputs, and incomes. Unlike preceding mercantilist writers, his policy recommendations about international trade were firmly based on an analysis of the economy as an interrelated system. With land as the only scarce resource, world income is essentially fixed, and the main aim of policy is to gain a larger share of the total.

Part II

Cantillon's Place in the History of Economics

9

Cantillon and his Predecessors

Any assessment of Cantillon's contribution to the development of economics must depend on a comparison of his work with that of his predecessors and his successors. In this chapter, I will examine his most important predecessors, to see how much he took from them, and how much of his theory was entirely original. I will argue that none of them conceived of the economy as an interconnected system, in the sort of way Cantillon did, and that none of them had a theory of allocation, distribution, and pricing remotely comparable with Cantillon's.

In their very different ways, William Petty, John Locke, and John Law must all have had some influence on Cantillon.[1] Of the three, Petty is generally regarded as Cantillon's most direct and most important precursor. I shall argue that the connection between the two was a great deal less direct than many, following Schumpeter, have thought, but there is no doubt that the relation between them deserves careful scrutiny. Locke is important, in this context, primarily as a

---

[1] It is an interesting comment on the late seventeenth and early eighteenth centuries, that Petty, Locke, and Law, like Cantillon himself, were able to rise from relatively obscure beginnings to positions of considerable wealth and standing. Petty started as a cabin boy on a ship, and ended up wealthy, well known in intellectual and political circles, and personally known to two successive kings of England. Locke started from almost equally unpromising circumstances, and became prominent in politics, and then, late in life, lionized as a great philosopher. Law had a small inheritance, but he squandered most of it, spent many years on the run (facing a charge of murder), and then, against all the odds, became for a while the most powerful man in France.

possible influence on Cantillon's monetary theory. He was among the first to present a quantity theory of money, and his writings were a major focus of debates on monetary issues in the early eighteenth century. His influence on Cantillon may, indeed, have extended beyond monetary issues, narrowly defined, and may have been more important than Petty's. Law, on the other hand, was mainly a negative influence. Cantillon did not mention him by name, but parts of the *Essai* may well have been intended to refute Law's system and his theory.

There were, of course, many others who contributed to the active pamphlet literature of the time, especially in England. Cantillon's intellectual background, at least in economic matters, seems to have been mainly English: with the exception of one reference to an anonymous French author, all of the (very few) economic writings which Cantillon referred to in the *Essai* were written in English. He must have been aware of the work of such writers as Mun (1664), Child (undated), North (1691), Barbon (1690, 1696), Mandeville (1714), and King (1936), though he only referred to a few of them in passing and there is no way of knowing exactly what he had read. They formed the intellectual climate of the time, but I can find no evidence of any direct borrowings by Cantillon from any of them, or of any other connections substantial enough to justify examining their work in detail.[1]

Finally, there is one French writer, Pierre de Boisguilbert (1645–1714), who deserves mention as a possible precursor, though Cantillon did not refer to him, and there is no direct evidence that he influenced Cantillon's work. Boisguilbert thought that France was in a state of severe economic decline at the time he was writing (around 1700), and that this decline dated from the introduction of Colbert's mercantilist policies. Cantillon's account of French economic history was almost the reverse; he thought that France had prospered under Colbert from 1646, and that it had declined from 1684, when the Huguenots were expelled (*Essai*: 187). According to Boisguilbert, the problem was a decline in agriculture; according to Cantillon it was a decline in manufacturing. Cantillon, of course, assumed that agriculture always remained essentially unchanged. Although they used different assumptions, and drew very different conclusions, there were some similarities

---

[1] Hutchison (1988) is an excellent survey of the development of economic ideas in this period, as is Letwin (1963).

in the way their theories were constructed. In particular, Boisguilbert's concept of the circulation of money, and of equilibrium between the different sectors of the economy, may well have had some influence on Cantillon.[1]

9.1 PETTY

William Petty (1623–77) was the son of a relatively poor clothier of Romsey in Hampshire. He started work as a cabin boy on a ship, but by the age of 26 he was Professor of Anatomy at Oxford. He resigned his position almost immediately to go to Ireland with the Parliamentary army, where he bid for the contract to survey much of Ireland, and made a substantial profit from the venture. He bought large estates in Ireland, though he had to spend much of the rest of his life in legal battles to hold on to his gains. Cantillon's family, of course, lost their estates in Ireland at this time. After the restoration, Petty seems not to have suffered from his Parliamentary associations, since he was personally known to both Charles II and James II and was a founder member of the Royal Society.[2]

Schumpeter, in his magisterial *History of Economic Analysis*, claimed that there was a close connection between Petty and Cantillon:

> What Petty failed to accomplish – but for what he had offered almost all the essential ideas – lies accomplished before us in Cantillon's *Essai*. True, it was not accomplished in the style of a pupil . . . , but in the style of an intellectual peer who strides along confidently according to his own lights. . . . [But] dependence or possible dependence – there can be no certainty about it – extends beyond such important individual points as the theory of velocity of circulation or the theory of population to the fundamental

---

[1] Boisguilbert (1966) is a collection of his main economic works. See also Groenewegen (1987a), Spengler (1984), Hamilton (1969), Hebert (1987), and Hutchison (1988: 107–15).

[2] Petty's economic writings are collected in Hull (1899); on his life see Hull's short biography in the collected writings, and Aspromourgos (1988); on his life and work, see Aspromourgos (1986) and Roncaglia (1985, 1987).

features of the theoretical set-up. (Schumpeter, 1954: 218)

There is very little direct evidence of any influence of Petty on Cantillon. Cantillon's *Essai* is effectively all there is to go on, and Petty is mentioned by name only three times in the whole book. Twice, Cantillon dismissed Petty's work on particular topics in a fairly brutal fashion; Petty's research on the 'par' between labour and land was 'fanciful and remote from natural laws' (*Essai*: 43) and his calculations of population growth were 'purely imaginary and drawn up at hazard' (*Essai*: 83). The third reference is non-committal, and deals with a factual question, the amount of money in circulation (*Essai*: 131). That Cantillon did not publicly recognize any debt to Petty, of course, proves nothing, but it does mean that any judgement of Petty's influence has to be based on circumstantial evidence.

I will argue that the connections between them are considerably weaker than is often thought. It is true that there are points in common, most obviously the idea of a 'par' between labour and land, a concept found in the writings of these two writers and, for practical purposes, nowhere else. The 'par', of course, plays a fundamental role in Cantillon's land theory of value, and was described by Petty as 'the most important Consideration in Political Oeconomics' (Petty, 1672: 181). I will, however, show that their conceptions of the par are very different. On a more general level, their models are diametrically opposed to each other on a number of central issues. In particular, Petty treated population as exogenous, and claimed that land was not scarce, so output was governed by the utilization of a given labour force. Cantillon argued the opposite, that population was endogenous, while land was scarce, so the allocation of land between different uses was the key determinant of the level and composition of output, of the size of the population, and so on.

Petty's 'political arithmetic' was an application to social and economic issues of the Baconian method of the Royal Society (of which he was a prominent member), marked by the use of 'number, weight and measure' in place of rhetorical generalizations. With trivial exceptions, all of his works deal with a specific problem or with a specific economy at a specific time. He tried to estimate total population, total incomes, and so on; indeed a number of his works follow a common format, starting with a list of what he took to be the essential (numerical) facts about the economy. Schumpeter has claimed that Petty was 'first and last a theorist' (1954: 211), but his analysis was built on an accounting framework, and the theory he developed was largely aimed at providing and justifying numerical estimates to fit into this framework. What would now be recognized as economic theory, the analysis of a system of interrelated markets, played a relatively small part. Almost all modern discussions of his work concentrate on a very few pages, on rent, on the 'par', and on the value of money. These sections, on which Petty's reputation largely rests, are clearly signalled as digressions from the main theme.

Cantillon, by contrast, was a theorist of a more modern kind. He 'thought of the economy as Newton thought of the cosmos – as an interconnected whole made up of rationally functioning parts' (Ekelund and Hebert, 1983: 65). It is true that he referred repeatedly to numerical estimates of various sorts in the lost 'supplement', but these references, in the context of the main text, simply provide numerical or empirical illustrations of the general principles involved. Cantillon put the numbers into a supplement, while Petty dealt with theory in digressions. The structure of the *Essai*, or at least of the early parts of it, is determined by the presentation of a general theoretical model – Cantillon was careful to avoid limiting himself to any specific country or period of history, except by way of illustration:

> I confine myself always to the simple views of commerce lest I should complicate my subject, which is too much encumbered by the multiplicity of facts which relate to it. (*Essai*: 265)

Petty revelled in the multiplicity of facts.

It may be that other things Cantillon wrote, now lost, were more empirical in flavour. One of Cantillon's friends, quoted by Mirabeau, said that:

> In [his] voyages he made certain of everything, got out of his carriage to question a labourer in the field, judged the quality of the soil, tasted it, drew up his notes, and an accountant whom he always took with him put them in order when he stopped for the night. (Spengler, 1954: 285)

Cantillon may indeed have been very thorough in his empirical researches, but the *Essai*, his only surviving work, was a work of theory.

It would be a mistake to exaggerate the contrast between Petty's style of thought and Cantillon's, but there can be no doubt that there is a difference (cf. Spiegel, 1983: 178). Petty founded quantitative applied economics. Cantillon founded economic theory.

Population theory is one of the areas where Schumpeter (1954: 218) claimed that Cantillon followed Petty. In fact, their views on population were diametrically opposed, and Cantillon said so. Cantillon, of course, treated population as endogenous. Petty treated it as exogenous, at least in his analysis of the economy.[1] Petty's friend, John Graunt, virtually founded modern demography with his *Natural and Political Observations upon the Bills of Mortality* (1676). What part Petty played in this work is controversial, but is irrelevant here. The point is that Petty chose to take the observed rate of (natural) population growth as a given fact, and thus to treat population as exogenous, except for the effects of migration. How far he went in this is seen by his attempts to account for the growth of population since Noah's ark in these terms, using the datings for biblical events accepted at the time. It was this effort that provoked Cantillon's scorn (*Essai*: 83). Petty thought that Britain's population was doubling every 320 years (there are slightly different estimates in different writings), and seems to have been willing to project population, on this basis, for hundreds of years into the future. More sophisticated (and more cautious) calculations of this sort are used for population projections today.

Labour supply follows directly from population, for both authors. Petty did insist that high wages would lead to lower

---

[1] Petty did discuss reasons for population change – social and epidemiological factors, for example – but he did not link them to the demand for labour in the way that Cantillon (and some of Petty's contemporaries) did. Schumpeter's claim that Cantillon developed Petty's views (1954: 219) might perhaps be based on the fact that both thought of a larger population as a good thing. Cantillon, however, thought that population could only be increased by importing agricultural produce, or by reallocating land, from other uses, to feeding and providing for the population (see chapters 3 and 8).

labour supply, because workers stop when they have earned enough, but he had little or nothing to say about wage variations (or, indeed, about the determinants of wages), so for practical purposes he treated labour supply as exogenous. In Cantillon's account, labour supply adjusts to match the demand for labour, through migration in the short run, and through the population mechanism in the long run.

Petty insisted, repeatedly, that land was not scarce (though it would eventually become scarce as population growth continued). Perhaps the most dramatic example of this was his plan to move a million people from Ireland to England, on the grounds that adding a seventh to the population of England would add at least a seventh to output and rents. In some places he suggested that there were increasing returns in agriculture: 'a very little addition of husbandry . . . will produce a fifth more of food' (Petty, 1690: 289–90). Cantillon argued the reverse; population is governed by the carrying capacity of the land. For example, he argued that England imported a variety of products of the soil (timber, hemp, and the like), and also saved land by using coal in place of wood for fuel. 'Without these advantages the People of England, on the footing of the expense of living there, could not be so numerous as they are' (*Essai*: 85). The facts of the case had not changed enough to account for the difference in their conclusions.

Neither author saw capital (stock) as an important determinant of total output, though both had some idea of its importance. Petty seems to have thought that there was plenty of idle capital (or potential capital) lying around: there was enough, he claimed, in England to 'drive the trade of the whole Commercial World' (Petty, 1690: 311). Cantillon was aware that individuals needed access to capital to enter a trade, and would pay interest for it, but never treated it as a constraint on total output, perhaps because his essentially static view of the economy allowed plenty of time for enough capital to be accumulated to take up all the available investment opportunities.

The determinants of the scale of economic activity, of total output, are thus quite different in Petty and Cantillon. Petty saw output limited by population, and growing with it, with no limit set by land or capital. Cantillon's view was directly opposed to Petty's. Output is limited (in a closed economy) by the available land, with population adjusting automatically.

Petty had little to say about the general level of wages, beyond urging that they be kept low to avoid slacking, while Cantillon treated them as determined by convention. Both were aware of wage differentials, which Petty seems to have taken for granted. Cantillon's account of wage differentials was somewhat more sophisticated. Neither had much to say about profit, though both showed some awareness of it as a source of income.

Petty's remarks about rent (they can hardly be called a theory) have been the focus of rather more discussion than they really merit. In a digression in his first work on economics, he imagined a single individual growing corn, and subtracting the seed, plus everything he needed to live on, from the harvest. The remainder is the 'natural and true Rent' (Petty, 1662: 43). This is a tautology, of course, if the actual deductions are counted. If the deductions are those that are needed, it is a simple surplus theory, essentially the same as Cantillon's. Only a few pages earlier, however, he claimed that taxes on rents will be passed on to the tenant by increases in rent, and then passed on to the consumer in the price of products (Petty, 1662: 39–40). It is hard to see any theory, let alone the simple surplus story, which could justify this claim.

Elsewhere, he presented a quite different account: rent is what the land can produce if it is used for pasture, with no labour input, while the wage is the extra output that can be produced if it is worked by a unit of labour (Petty, 1672: 181). Here he was clearly groping towards some sort of marginal product theory of wages and rents, though he did not get very far with it. It is worth noting that this theory was presented in a piece about Ireland, where pasturage was the dominant use of land, so one could argue that rent would reflect the return from pasturage, leaving renters to keep whatever they could produce in addition. It seems that Petty had no well thought out theory, but that some sort of surplus theory fits more of his work than any other.

The main difference between the distribution theories of the two authors is that Cantillon's rent theory follows from his basic model, while Petty's does not. If land is scarce while labour (of various kinds) is in elastic supply at a given wage (as Cantillon held), then the surplus goes to the owner of the scarce factor, the landlord. According to Petty, land was not scarce, and the returns from it would be greatly increased by recruiting more labour (see the citations given above). He never explained why landowners would not compete for tenants, thus driving rents down. It seems that he did not realize that there was a problem.

Both Petty and Cantillon discussed interest rates, though Petty only did so in passing. Petty started from the value of land. Given a secure title, land would produce a return in perpetuity, but it clearly could not sell for an infinite price. A buyer was not likely to consider the returns to very distant descendants, so Petty suggested as a rule of thumb that the number of years purchase (the reciprocal of the annual interest rate) should be the equivalent of three lives (the expected date of the last death from three generations all alive at once) (Petty, 1662: 45–6). This would be greater than the observed figure of about twenty years (though not by very much, given the high mortality of the seventeenth century). He then said that interest on loans must at least match the return on land (Petty, 1662: 48). In general, he seems to have been more concerned with justifying the existence of interest than in explaining the rate of interest; Schumpeter suggested a scholastic influence (1954: 215).

Cantillon's interest theory has been discussed in chapter 4; he insisted that the interest rate was determined by demand and supply, and that the demand for loans was governed by the profits entrepreneurs could make on borrowed money. Since he had no very well developed theory to explain profit rates, Cantillon's theory was not by any means complete, but it was undoubtedly a huge improvement on Petty's. More to the point here, it was different from, and independent of, Petty's story.

Petty did not have any well developed theory of prices or values, though he did have some sensible things to say, for example about the higher price of provisions near London; if local production was not enough to meet demand, prices had to be high enough to cover transport costs from more distant sources (1662: 51–2). This argument has points in common with Cantillon's discussion of price levels in different regions (see section 2.4).

In two places, however, Petty hinted at something like a labour theory of value. Both of these hints, it should be noted, occur in the context of the value of money, not the relative values of commodities in general, and both occur in digressions. They have to be taken seriously, but they also need to be treated with caution. First, having derived rent as a surplus of output of corn over costs measured in corn (see above), Petty said that the money value of rent is determined by considering the silver produced by a single individual, net of all costs, including subsistence, and equating it with the rent (surplus) in corn produced by a single farm worker. This is clearly not a labour theory of value, in the usual sense, since it is the surplus, not the total output, of the two men that is equated. Corn is a very unfortunate choice of product as an example, since the amount, and the surplus, produced by one man varies with the quality of the soil, as Petty well knew. Petty's argument fails, because it would produce the same money value for the rent of different pieces of land, regardless of quality.

A few pages later, however, Petty *did* state a labour theory of value, though again for corn: 'If a man can bring to *London* an ounce of Silver out of the Earth in *Peru*, in the same time that he can produce a bushel of Corn, then one is the natural price of the other' (Petty, 1662: 50). It seems likely that Petty thought he was repeating his earlier argument, not realizing that they are different. It also seems likely that Petty threw in these comments simply to tie down the value of silver, and hence of money, to something real, and did not intend a labour theory of prices in general. In any case, as Bowley (1973: 86) notes, 'Cantillon . . . ignored Petty's silver miners'.

At the same time, Petty argued that 'all things ought to be valued by two natural Denominations, which is Land and Labour', and thus that

> we should be glad to finde out a natural Par between Land and Labour, so as we might express the value by either of them alone as well as or better than by both, and reduce one into the other as easily and certainly as we reduce pence into pounds. (Petty, 1662: 44–5)

It is difficult to know what to make of this. It is tempting to think of the value of a good as made up of land and labour costs, reduced to a single denomination by use of the par, or conversion factor. This is how Cantillon developed the idea, but it is hard to find anything so definite in Petty. Note first that the idea of the par is clearly inconsistent with a labour theory of value, though it occurs in the very passage, already discussed, that has been read as supporting a labour theory of value. Second, Petty continued from the last extract quoted to say 'Wherefore we would be glad to finde the natural values of the Fee simple of Land', that is the freehold (capital) value of land, which is clearly irrelevant to the problem, since the capital value of a piece of land cannot be compared with the labour required per unit of output. A second reference to the 'par' (the one cited by Cantillon) occurs in the *Political Anatomy of Ireland* (Petty, 1672: 181), and is directly followed by the second, marginal product, rent theory discussed above. It is thus inconsistent with the first. One can only agree with Cantillon's assessment of Petty's work on the par as 'fanciful and remote from natural laws' (*Essai:* 43).

Petty sometimes distinguished between 'natural' and 'artificial' prices. In a very few places, the distinction seems to be the same as Cantillon's distinction between intrinsic and market prices; natural prices are the effect of permanent, as opposed to temporary, causes (e.g. *Writings*: 90, where there is quite a mixed bag of 'contingent' causes). Elsewhere, the distinction seems to be between the effects of nature, in some sense, and human society: high prices near London are described as artificial, though they are clearly permanent (Petty, 1662: 51–2). Elsewhere, Petty described money prices as artificial, because money is of no natural use.

Cantillon's far more coherent analysis has been discussed in chapter 5. The par, for Cantillon, was a conversion factor which allowed him to convert labour requirements into their equivalents in land, to determine the land value of a product. Cantillon presumably took the notion of a par, or at least the term, from Petty but, beyond that, his use of the notion was entirely original (cf. Bowley, 1973: 89–90).

Petty's contribution to monetary theory was fairly limited. He insisted that the value of money derived from its metallic content, a value determined, as we have seen, by the costs of mining and transporting the metal. Cantillon agreed: this was a fairly common view at the time. Petty argued that a society needed a certain amount of money to transact its business, and discussed how this necessary amount was determined, thus presenting one of the first accounts of the institutional determinants of the velocity of circulation. Petty's purpose, characteristically, was to allow a calculation of the amount needed, compare it with the actual amount in circulation, and take the necessary corrective action, a perfect example of his policy oriented, numerical, approach. Schumpeter thought highly of this contribution (1954: 316–17). Petty was, however, distinctly vague about the effects of having too much or too little money in circulation. If there was too little money, 'we must erect a bank', if too much, melt it down, export it, or let it out at interest (Petty, 1695: 446). Shortage of cash leads to 'distress of the People and the obstruction of Trade' (Petty, 1672: 187). 'Money is but the Fat of the Body-politick, whereof too much doth as often hinder its Agility, as too little makes it sick' (Petty, 1691: 113). Cantillon may have drawn on Petty's discussion of the determinants of the velocity of circulation, but otherwise he looked to Locke, not Petty, when it came to monetary theory.[1]

Both authors wanted to encourage manufactured exports and import substitution, and to encourage shipping. They thought it was necessary, at the least, to aim at balanced trade, and better to achieve a trade surplus and hence a net import of monetary metals. There is nothing very notable about this: it would be hard to find anyone at the time who disagreed. What is interesting is the reasons they advanced for these broadly 'mercantilist' views.

Petty thought that population was exogenous, so labour supply was essentially fixed. He recognized, however, that some unemployment existed, and he was anxious to provide work for the unemployed, in order to increase total incomes and remove the threat of disorder. Import substitution offered a prospect of job creation (Petty, 1690: 309), as did public works (provided they did not involve the use of imported commodities). This is clear enough, but it points to a serious gap in his theory. If neither labour, nor land, nor capital was scarce, what governs the level of employment of resources and the total level of output? I can find no answer in his writings, and no sign that he recognized that there was a problem. His recognition of unemployment undermines, for example, his notorious proposal to depopulate Ireland and bring a million people from Ireland to England. What guarantee could there be that there would be jobs for them?

Once unemployment was absorbed, successful mercantilist policies, if carried further, would involve shifting labour from agriculture to manufacturing, shipping, and trade, since Petty (unlike Cantillon) thought of population as essentially fixed. Petty seems to have approved of this prospect, because pay was much higher in manufacturing than in agriculture, and

---

[1] Locke will be discussed in the next section.

returns from trade were higher still, so total income would be increased (Petty, 1690: 256). The fact that he had no explanation of the reasons for this gap in wage rates weakens his case, though he did argue that increased demand for labour in manufacturing would pull agricultural wages up towards manufacturing levels, at the expense of rent (Petty, 1690: 267–8). Trade and shipping also help to promulgate knowledge of foreign techniques (Petty, 1690: 258).

Why aim to import monetary metals? Petty's main reason seems to have been that they are the most durable form of wealth (Petty, 1690: 260). Any government budget surplus should also be retained in these permanent forms of wealth (Petty, 1690: 269). Cantillon supported this view, though only in passing – it was not a main component of his theory. Petty seems to have thought that the state should hoard money until there was enough for any military emergency, and the people should then sit back and rest, or devote themselves to thought (Petty, 1691: 119).

Cantillon's mercantilism, and the reasons for it, have been discussed in chapter 8. Land, not labour, is the scarce factor. A state which exports labour intensive manufactures, and imports land intensive food and raw materials, can support a larger population. A balance of trade surplus increases the money stock, and eventually increases prices, but a surplus based on real competitive advantages can persist for some time (years, even decades, it seems), and a high price level, and thus favourable terms of trade, can persist for even longer, with trade balanced. Eventually, competitors will catch up, trade will move into deficit, and both the money stock and prices will fall. The result is a long cycle, which can be influenced by policies designed to accelerate the upswing and retard the downswing. Cantillon's analysis was very much more fully worked out than Petty's. More to the point here, their arguments have very little in common, so Cantillon cannot have taken his ideas from Petty.

A direct comparison of Cantillon's *Essai* with Petty's economic writings does reveal a few places where the parallel between the two appears to be more than coincidental. With the exception of the 'par', the most obvious is Cantillon's chapter entitled 'the more labour there is in a state the more naturally rich the state is esteemed' (*Essai*: 87–95), which has already been discussed in section 3.3. It starts with a numerical example strikingly reminiscent of Petty. The labour of 25 people is enough to support 100, according to a calculation in the (now lost) supplement; of 100 people, 50 are available for work, so what are the rest to do? Petty has very similar calculations in a number of his works (e.g. *Writings*: 30, 89, 118–19, 307–8). Cantillon drew the conclusion that the labour of those who are not needed to produce subsistence would be best employed producing durable goods, or things which can be traded for durable goods, best of all gold and silver, to add to the reserve stocks of the state (*Essai*: 89). Petty made a very similar case, in several places (e.g. *Writings*: 119, 259–60). Cantillon did not refer to Petty in this chapter, but it is hard to avoid the conclusion that it was directly inspired by Petty.

On closer examination, however, these apparently similar calculations are based on very different models, and reach different conclusions. Petty thought there was chronic unemployment of resources, and wanted to find some way of putting people to work, or of ensuring that their work was more productive. In Cantillon's analysis, there is no doubt that those who are not needed to produce subsistence will be put to work; the fact that they are available to work is a reflection of the surplus in agriculture, which accrues to the landlords as rent. The question for Cantillon was not whether they will work, but what they will work at. That will be determined by the way landlords spend the rent. The prince can set them an example, and hence determine the use of the uncommitted part of the labour force (*Essai*: 93).

That Petty's economics was more limited than Cantillon's is not in doubt. After all, Cantillon wrote some half a century later, and his *Essai* sets standards of conciseness and clarity that few writers, of any date, can match. The question is: how far did Cantillon build on foundations laid, however clumsily, by Petty? Did Petty offer 'almost all the essential ideas' used by Cantillon, as Schumpeter claimed (1954: 218)? I think not.

The essential difference is that Petty thought of population and labour supply as essentially exogenous, and the size of the labour force as the limiting factor governing the scale of output. Land was not scarce, Britain was not 'fully peopled', and there were increasing returns to increasing labour inputs. Cantillon's view was the opposite. Population was endogenous, and land was fully used, given the techniques, preferences, and customary living standards of the countries of Europe. This difference colours every aspect of their work. For example, though Cantillon's rent theory is similar to one version of Petty's, Cantillon's version is a logical consequence of his model, while in Petty's framework there is no good reason for rent to be positive at all, if land is not scarce. It is not even clear that Cantillon would have known Petty's surplus theory of rent anyway, since the work he actually cited contains a 'marginal product' version of Petty's theory.

With labour as the scarce factor, Petty should have had a labour theory of value, and in a couple of places he did, though he contradicted it elsewhere and it is not compatible with his rent theory. With land as the scarce factor, Cantillon needed a land theory of value, and that is exactly what he constructed. The 'par', the most striking parallel between their work, thus functions quite differently in the two systems. It is hard to see quite what role it was intended to play in Petty's model, and he never developed the idea far enough for one to find out. In Cantillon's system it performs a necessary function in setting up the land theory of value. On trade policy, again, the difference in views about the limiting factor means that superficially similar policy proposals (which were, in any case, commonplace at the time) are in fact based on quite different considerations. Only Petty's discussion of the velocity of circulation remains as justification for Schumpeter's claim that Petty led the way. Cantillon, however, took monetary theory much further, drawing on Locke rather than Petty, and adding much of his own.

9.2 LOCKE

John Locke (1632–1704) was the son of a rather poorly paid functionary, the clerk to the Justices of the Peace in Somerset. His prosperous and influential uncle arranged for him to go to Westminster School, and then to Oxford. Like Petty, who was nine years older, he qualified as a doctor, and pursued medical research for a time. When he was 35, he found a patron in the Earl of Shaftesbury, became involved in politics at a very high level as a member of Shaftesbury's entourage, and was driven into exile with him for a time. His writings about economics stem from this involvement with the practical issues of economic policy.

The philosophical works which made him famous came late in his life: the *Essay Concerning Human Understanding*, his masterpiece, appeared in 1689, when he was 56. Many of his political and philosophical works had to be published anonymously, since they were considered seditious, but the importance of the *Essay Concerning Human Understanding* was soon recognized. Lady Mary Calverley, for example, described him as 'the greatest man in the world' (Dunn, 1984: 1). By far the most substantial of his economic writings was *Some Considerations of the Consequences of the Lowering of Interest and Raising the Value of Money* (or *Some Considerations*, for short), published in 1691, that is a few years after Petty's death, and about forty years before Cantillon wrote the *Essai*.[1]

Locke's main focus was on monetary questions. He claimed that money has only an 'imaginary' value (1691: 31), a claim rejected by Cantillon, among others (*Essai*: 113). Locke seems to have meant, first, that silver is used as money by general consent to its use, not because it has to be, and, second, that it is valuable only because it is so used, and because it is scarce. Cantillon accepted the first part of this, but not the second. He held that silver has an intrinsic value governed by its cost of production, like anything else. Locke too had argued that the value of silver, and hence the value of money, was determined by the same factors as the value of anything else, but he treated all prices as governed by scarcity. As far as the value of money is concerned, the disagreement between Locke and Cantillon was more apparent than real. Both knew that the stock of silver changes only very slowly. Locke chose to treat changes in the world stock as exogenous, and Cantillon did the same when he came to deal with monetary issues in their own right; the claim that silver had a value like anything else is to be found in the chapter dealing with the value of metals, but nowhere else.

Locke argued that the price or value of anything was determined by the quantity of it relative to the 'vent'. For example:

> He that will justly estimate the value of any thing, must consider its quantity in proportion to its vent, for this alone regulates the Price. (Locke, 1691: 61)

Locke did not define 'vent' explicitly. The vent of some commodity clearly means the demand for it, or the size of the market (vent, literally, means 'outlet').

---

[1] On Locke's economics, see Vaughn (1980, 1987), Leigh (1974), and Vickers (1959: 43–73).

> The price of any Commodity rises or falls, by the proportion of the number of Buyers and Sellers. (Locke, 1691: 45)

> The Vent of any Thing depends on its Necessity or Usefulness, as Convenience, or Opinion guided by Phancy or fashion shall determine. (Locke, 1691: 46)

Sometimes, 'vent' seems to mean total expenditure on the good concerned. For example:

> The Vent of any Commodity comes to be increased or decreased as a greater part of the Running Cash of the Nation is designed to be laid out by several People at the same time rather in that, than another, as we see in the change of Fashions. (Locke, 1691: 46)

This could be taken to mean that the elasticity of demand is unity; expenditure, or 'the part of the running cash of the nation', is invariant to changes in the quantity available, and hence the price. Locke in fact discussed reactions to price changes, showing some awareness of the factors which affect the elasticity of demand. Necessities must be had at any price, so scarcity can raise the price to extraordinary levels. If wheat were scarce enough, its price might rise ten times. For things that are merely convenient, on the other hand, the effect of scarcity on price depends on the availability of substitutes (Locke, 1691: 46–7). Even so, the assumption of a unit elasticity of demand seems to lurk behind a lot of Locke's arguments, notably his quantity theory of money.

Note, incidentally, an implicit confusion between stocks and flows in the last extract quoted. A 'part of the running cash of the nation' is presumably a stock, a component of the stock of money in the country, but it is equated to the expenditure on a particular commodity, a flow. Despite Locke's quite careful discussion of the velocity of circulation (Locke, 1691: 33–9), his writings rarely distinguish clearly between the money stock and money expenditure. He also seems to have confused money and wealth; for example, he claimed that 'A Kingdom grows Rich, or Poor just as a Farmer doth, and no otherwise', by spending more or less than it earns abroad, and thus by subtracting from or adding to the stock of money (Locke, 1691: 26).

Locke derived his theory of the value of money directly from his theory of prices.

> Money therefore in buying and selling being perfectly in the same Condition with other Commodities, and subject to all the same Laws of Value. (Locke, 1691: 55)

> But because the desire of Money is constantly, almost everywhere the same, its vent varies very little, but as its greater scarcity enhances its Price. . . . The lessening its quantity therefore, always increases its Price, and makes an equal portion of it exchange for a greater of any other Thing. (Locke, 1691: 62)

It is a rather odd argument. Locke did not treat the value of money as a simple inverse of its purchasing power over commodities. He had a notion of the absolute value of each commodity, including money, even though he understood well that only relative prices are actually observable.[1] When the price of one good changes relative to another, consideration of the quantity and vent of each will reveal which of them has changed in value.

> It being only the change in the quantity of Wheat to its Vent, supposing we have still the same Summ of Money in the Kingdom; or else the change of the quantity of our Money in the Kingdom, supposing the quantity of Wheat, in respect to its Vent be the same too, that makes the change in the Price of Wheat. (Locke, 1691: 62–3)

The conclusion that a change in the quantity of money will cause an equal and opposite proportional change in its value rests on the rather obscure claim that its 'vent' is always constant. The 'vent' of money cannot, clearly, be identified with money spending on it, like the 'vent' of anything else, but some analogue of a unit elasticity of demand seems to be implied.

Little wonder that Cantillon treated this argument with great caution, and insisted that the effect of a change in the quantity of money must be traced through its effects on the

---

[1] Some of his successors, most notably Ricardo and Marx, had the same idea.

demand for goods, and hence the price of goods. He concluded that the change in the value of money need not take place immediately, and that relative prices were likely to be affected, at least in an open economy.

Locke's main aim, in *Some Considerations of the Consequences of the Lowering of Interest*, was defined by its title – to analyse the effects of changes in interest rates. He therefore devoted particular attention to the connection between interest rates and money. He had two different accounts of the determinants of interest rates. In the first pages of *Some Considerations*, he treated interest[1] as the price of money, and argued that the price was high when money was scarce.

> That which constantly raises the Natural Interest of Money, is, when Money is little in proportion to the Trade of a Country. (Locke, 1691: 10–11)

If the money stock were half what is needed, its price (that is, the interest rate) would be raised

> as it is of any other Commodity in a Market, where the Merchandize will not serve half the Customers, and there are two Buyers for every Seller. (Locke, 1691: 11)

This argument is, at least on the face of it, incompatible with his account of the value (that is, the purchasing power) of money.[2] Cantillon argued very firmly that a change in the money supply would normally alter the price level, not the interest rate.

Locke had an alternative story about interest rates, much more like Cantillon's.

> Money is a barren thing, and produces nothing, but by Compact transfers that Profit that was the reward of one Man's Labour into another Man's Pocket. That which occasions this, is the unequal Distribution of Money. (Locke, 1691: 55)

Here the 'unequal distribution of money' clearly means the

---

[1] He also used the term 'use', as in 'usury', for interest.
[2] It might be compatible with his account of prices and money in an open economy – see below.

unequal distribution of wealth. Those with money to lend can lend it to those who can make a profit from using it in trade.[1]

> For as the unequal Distribution of Land, (you having more than you can or will manure, and another less) brings you a Tenant for your Land; and the same unequal distribution of Money, (I having more than I can or will employ, and another less) brings me a tenant for my Money: my Money is apt in Trade, by the Industry of the Borrower, to produce more than Six per Cent to the Borrower. (Locke, 1691: 56)[2]

This argument is very similar to Cantillon's: the interest rate depends on (or at least has some connection with) the profit rate that the borrower can earn by using the borrowed money. Locke used this line of argument mainly to explain the existence of interest, as Cantillon did, but Cantillon went on to argue that interest would account for all of the increase in net income that the borrower could earn on the borrowed money, while Locke, as in the above passage, thought the borrower could retain some of the surplus. The difference may be only that Locke was referring to the legally regulated interest rate rather than to the rate that would clear the market. Cantillon argued that interest rates were set by demand and supply, so he was evidently thinking of the market clearing rate.

Like Petty, Locke considered the relation between the price of land (capitalized rent) and the interest rate. Petty thought the number of years purchase of land (that is, the inverse of the rate of return on the capital value of land) determined, or at least set a lower limit to, the interest rate on money loans. Locke was aware that the two ought to be equal, if buying land or lending money were perfectly substitutable as uses of wealth, but he thought that the two markets were rather separate (Locke, 1691: 57–9). His main concern was to argue that lowering the legal rate of interest would not raise the price of land, mainly because controls on the interest rate were rather ineffective, and also because lowering the interest rate would tend to depress the economy (for reasons to be discussed below), and thus to depress, not raise, land prices. There may

---

[1] Locke always said 'trade', rather than production, though it may be that production was included in the term.
[2] Six per cent was the maximum legal interest rate.

be an element of special pleading in these arguments, since Locke was strongly opposed to lowering the interest rate on other grounds.

The main policy issue, of course, was whether there was enough money in circulation to 'drive' the nation's trade, and whether lowering interest would help. One might expect that Locke would not be concerned with the absolute quantity of money, because his quantity theory suggests that any deficiency in the quantity of money would be offset by a higher value. For a closed economy, that was indeed the conclusion he reached.

> That supposing any Island separate from the Commerce of the rest of Mankind, if Gold and Silver . . . be their Money, if they have but a certain quantity of it, and can get no more, that will be a steady standing Measure of the Value of all other Things. . . . [Such a money] would serve to drive any proportion of Trade, whether more or less, there being Counters enough to reckon by, and the value of the Pledges being still sufficient, as constantly increasing with the Plenty of the Commodity. (Locke, 1691: 75–6)[1]

In an open economy, however, the quantity of money, relative to other states, matters.

> That in a country that hath open Commerce with the rest of the World, and uses Money made of the same Materials with their Neighbours, any quantity of that Money will not serve to drive any quantity of Trade; but there must be a certain proportion between their Money and Trade. (Locke, 1691: 77)

> Riches do not consist in having more Gold and Silver, but in having more in proportion, than the rest of the World, or than our Neighbours, whereby we are enabled to procure to ourselves a greater Plenty of the Conveniencies of Life than comes within the reach of Neighbouring Kingdoms and States. (Locke, 1691: 15)

---

[1] Money serves, according to Locke, as 'counters', that is, in modern terms, as a unit of account, and as a 'pledge', that is as a reliable store of value, however temporary.

If one country has less money, relative to its trade (that is, relative to economic activity as a whole, given the determinants of the velocity of circulation), than others, then either its trade is restricted, and resources are left unemployed, or its price level will be below that of its neighbours. Locke seems to have found it difficult to decide which of these two alternatives would occur in practice (Locke, 1691: 78–9).

> The Value of Money in general is the quantity of all the Money in the World, in proportion to all the Trade: but the value of Money in any one Country, is the present quantity of the Current Money in that Country, in proportion to the present Trade. (Locke, 1691: 77)

This formulation leaves the scale of the 'present trade' open; it may be below the optimum level, or it may not. Most of Locke's explicit arguments seem to assume that prices will be lower in a country with a relatively small stock of money.[1]

The case against a low price level is that the terms of trade are worse. It makes native commodities sell cheap, while imports are dear (Locke, 1691: 78). Cantillon said the same. In addition:

> It endangers the drawing away of our People, both Handicrafts, Mariners, and Soldiers, who are apt to go where their Pay is best, which will always be where there is greatest plenty of Money; and in time of War must needs bring great distress. (Locke, 1691: 79)

This is not, on the face of it, a very good argument; pay may be lower where prices are low, but the cost of living would also be low. If, however, mariners, soldiers, and the like want to save, or to earn where pay is high and send the money back to a family, there may be some justification for it. Locke's rather crude argument is an obvious ancestor of Cantillon's more sophisticated arguments about the military benefits of a high relative price level.

Locke's main argument against cutting the interest rate was that it would reduce the effective supply of money, both by

---

[1] Law also thought that it was the relative quantity of money that mattered, but thought that resources would be unemployed; see section 9.3.

deterring foreigners from lending money in the country concerned and by inducing domestic money holders to hoard money rather than lend it. A reduction in the effective money supply would have the harmful effects listed above (Locke, 1691: 44). Against this, advocates of lower interest rates claimed that lower rates would encourage borrowing to improve land, to expand trade, and so on. Locke replied that at 6 per cent 'the Borrowers already are far more than the Lenders' (Locke, 1691: 125), so cutting the rate would only make matters worse. Borrowing, in other words, was quantity constrained at the controlled interest rate, and the short side of the market governed the quantity borrowed.[1]

Locke had no visible idea that a maldistribution of money between different countries could be self-correcting. He had half of the specie-flow mechanism – a change in the money supply alters prices in the same direction – but not the other half – a change in prices alters the trade balance in the opposite direction, through its effect on competitiveness.

Cantillon's analysis of prices in an open economy looks quite different when it is seen as a response to Locke. To modern readers, the odd thing about Cantillon's treatment of the balance of trade is his insistence that the specie-flow mechanism only works with a long lag, and that it leads to long cycles rather than to equilibrium. Cantillon's starting point was clearly Locke's theory (which he knew, since he referred to *Some Considerations* more than once). He accepted Locke's account of the advantages of a high money stock and a high price level relative to other countries (and developed it in more detail), while at the same time recognizing that these advantages could not last indefinitely (though they might last for decades). Rather than qualifying the specie-flow theory, he added it to a story that had previously contained only the qualifications.

Locke is best known for his monetary theory, but there is a passing comment on rent, in *Some Considerations*, which may conceivably have had as important an influence on Cantillon as all of Locke's other arguments put together. Locke argued that all taxes fall on rent. 'Taxes, however contriv'd, . . . for the most part terminate upon Land' (Locke, 1691: 88). Land taxes, Locke argued, cannot be shifted on to the tenant because the tenant is already paying the maximum rent he can

---

[1] Law had a similar argument; see section 9.3.

afford, and cannot pay more without being forced to abandon the land. Taxes on commodities would be passed on by merchants, who will not trade in a good at all unless they can get their usual profit, while the 'poor Labourer and Handicraftsman just lives from hand to mouth', and cannot take any cut in his living standards. Only the landholder is able to pay, and unable to pass on any increase in costs.[1]

Locke's argument was not very clear – in particular, he did not give any really adequate explanation of the ability of merchants to pass on cost increases – but it can be read as a claim that only the landowner has any truly disposable income, and that the surplus of output over costs accrues to him as rent. These are, of course, crucial elements of Cantillon's model. Cantillon cannot have taken more than the hint of an idea from Locke, since there is no more than a hint of an idea there (and Locke did not develop it any further), but it is a more plausible starting point for Cantillon's theory than Petty's rather incoherent remarks on rent (which Cantillon may well never have seen anyway).

9.3 LAW

John Law and his 'system' played such an important part in Cantillon's life that they must have coloured his thinking.[2] Law only actually published one book setting out his economic ideas, *Money and Trade Considered with a Proposal for Supplying the Nation with Money*, written in 1705 when he was in Scotland. Whether Cantillon knew *Money and Trade Considered* is unclear, but Law's later memoranda, letters, policy proposals, and the like (collected in Law, 1934) follow similar lines. Cantillon must have been familiar with Law's ideas in some form or other. I will concentrate on *Money and Trade Considered*, because it is the fullest statement of Law's views.

Law argued that resources were grossly underutilized in Scotland.

---

[1] Cf. Petty, who did think that taxes on rent would be shifted on to the tenant, and then on to the price of the products of the land (Petty, 1662: 39–40).

[2] On Law's life and relations with Cantillon, see chapter 1; on his economics, see Hamilton (1969), Hutchison (1988: 134–9), Murphy (1991), and Vickers (1959: 111–40).

Numbers of People, the greatest Riches of other Nations, are a burden to us; the Land is not improv'd, the Product is not manufactured; the Fishing and other Advantages for forreign Trade are neglected. (Law, 1705: 152)

Money and Trade Considered deals with Scotland, because that is where Law was, and where he hoped to win support for his proposals. It is clear, however, from remarks in *Money and Trade Considered*, and from later writings dealing with other countries, that he thought most places in Europe, except perhaps the Netherlands, were in the same situation.

Scotland had many advantages for trade; it was well situated, had 'a large Territory', 'plenty of People', mines, fishing grounds, harbours, and so on (Law, 1705: 150–2). Neither land nor labour was scarce.[1] It is clear, from several of Law's examples, that he thought unemployed labour was generally available, with no opportunity cost. For example, he argued that if fifty additional men were employed, producing fifteen shillings worth of extra output each, there would be a gain to the country of fifteen shillings per man, even if they earned twenty five shillings each, and thus made a loss for the employer (Law, 1705: 16).

Deficient demand was not the main reason for the underutilization of resources. Law made this explicit when discussing proposals to encourage exports by (in effect) devaluing the currency to make Scottish exports cheaper.

> It may be alleg'd, we have more Product and Manufacture, than is consum'd or exported; and selling cheaper, would occasion a greater demand for our Goods Abroad. ... Product and Manufacture might be much encreas'd, if we had Money to imploy the People: But I'm of Opinion we have not any great Quantity of Goods, more than what is consum'd or exported. (Law, 1705: 62)

That the problem was lack of output, not lack of demand, is also clear from Law's treatment of the balance of trade. For example, he thought that import restrictions were unlikely to improve the trade balance, because domestically produced goods would be substituted for imports, reducing the amount

---

[1] See the extract quoted above: the land is not improved; numbers of people are a 'burden'.

of goods available for export in line with the reduction of imports (Law, 1705: 76). Again, the problem is clearly a lack of available output, not of demand. More generally, Law thought that there was no shortage of demand for Scotland's exports – the volume of exports was determined by the difference between domestic production and domestic demand.

An increase in the money stock, he claimed, would lead to an increase in output.

> But as this Addition to the Money, will employ the People [who] are now idle, and those now employ'd to more Advantage: So the Product will be encreas'd, and Manufacture advanc'd. If the Consumption of the Nation continue as now, the Export will be greater, and a Ballance due to us. (Law, 1705: 144)

If output (the 'yearly value' of the nation) were increased by £500,000, and if a quarter of the increased income were spent on a greater consumption of home produced goods, a quarter on consumption of imports, and a quarter on building up stocks of imported goods ('Magazines of Forreign Goods'), there would still be an improvement in the balance of trade of a quarter of the increase in output (Law, 1705: 146; there is a similar argument on pp. 16–18). The numbers were intended merely as an example, but the theoretical point is clear: increased demand is the consequence, not the cause, of an increase in output.

How can an increase in the money stock lead to an increase in the supply of goods, independent of any effect on demand? Law was not wholly clear, but the most plausible reading is that he identified money with capital, especially working capital. He repeatedly ascribed the sorry state of Scotland to the lack of money 'to employ the people'. Since this is an essential component of his argument, and since he never spelled out exactly what he meant, it is worth quoting what he did say at some length.

> Domestic trade depends on the Money. A greater Quantity employes more People than a lesser Quantity. A limited Sum can only set a number of People to Work proportion'd to it, and 'tis with little success Laws are made, for Employing the Poor or Idle in Countries where Money is scarce. (Law, 1705: 14–16)

without some Addition to the Money, 'tis not to be suppos'd next years Export can be equal to the last; It will lessen as Money has lessened; a part of the People then imploy'd being now idle; not for want of Inclination to work, or for want of Imployers, but for want of Money to imploy them with. (Law, 1705: 46)

To refuse to expand the money supply by issuing paper money is like a merchant refusing an interest-free loan to expand his 'stock' (Law, 1705: 54).[1] Law did not say explicitly that an increase in the money supply *was* an increase in stock, only that it was in some way *like* an increase in stock, or had the same effects as an increase in stock, but the argument is at least suggestive. In a later work (*Projet d'ètablissement d'une banque à Turin*, 1711–12), Law wrote:

There is not enough metallic money to employ the people; a limited sum can only set to work a number proportional to that sum: the same piece of money cannot serve in different places at the same time. (Law, 1934: 215)

Like the other statements quoted above, it might just be possible to read this in terms of the circulatory functions of money (if there is too little money, the number of transactions is limited, and so employment is limited), but Law never put it that way; he always linked money directly to employment.

One possible interpretation might be that an increase in the money supply would lead to lower interest rates, which would in turn encourage borrowing and investment.[2] Law did indeed claim that an increase in the money stock would lower interest rates (Law, 1705: 26), and would encourage trade, but he also argued that lowering interest rates by law would not help, because it would do nothing to increase the volume of money available (Law, 1705: 26). He thought that there was an excess demand for loans at the existing (controlled) interest rate (following Locke in this), so expansion of

---

[1] On Law's attitude to metallic and paper money, see Cesarano (1990).

[2] Though it might still seem odd to modern theorists to suppose that the increased investment would increase output so quickly that the increased supply of goods would outweigh the increase in demand in the first period, as Law evidently thought.

the money supply would increase the volume of borrowing, and thus the level of output, directly.

Borrowers were quantity constrained:

> Tho' interest ... continued at 6 [per cent] in Scotland; if Money were to be had equal to the Demands at 6, the Advantages we have for Trade ... would enable us to extend Trade. (Law, 1705: 26; cf. Locke, 1691: 125 and *passim*)

That increased investment should increase supply more than demand is comprehensible if, first, Law assumed that investment was primarily investment in working capital, in paying the wage bill (as his repeated references to the need for money 'to employ the People' suggest); if, second, any output lag is ignored (Law said nothing about time lags); and if, third, employing additional people adds more to output than to consumption.[1] In one of Law's examples, he assumed that extra workers would each be paid three pence, while the extra profit per employee would be three pence. The addition to workers' consumption would only be a penny each (since they had been consuming enough to survive before they were employed), so the increased demand would only be one penny per worker and the increased output six pence.

Law was very unclear about the relation between money and capital. It seems that he simply identified them, and that he assumed that printing paper money would represent a direct addition to the capital stock. For example, he constructed an example of an island with a single landowner (Law, 1705: 132– 6).[2] Initially, the island knows nothing of manufacture; the people produce agricultural goods enough for their needs, with an 'overplus' enough to trade with the mainland for manufactured goods. There are 300 poor people with no land, who subsist on charity.

> 'Tis proposed to the Proprietor, that if a Money were establish'd to pay the Wages of Labour, the 300 Poor might be imployed in manufacturing. (Law, 1705: 132)

This would increase the total income of the island. Indeed,

---

[1] If production is to be profitable, the addition to output must evidently exceed the addition to the wage bill.

[2] Cf. Cantillon's isolated estate.

more people might be attracted from the mainland (since on Law's arbitrary numbers, the available 'poor' were not enough to manufacture all the available raw materials and consume all the 'overplus' of food).

The puzzle, however, is why money should be needed at all. If the real resources are there, and if the island could manage with barter as long as its economy was purely agricultural, why could manufacturing not be set up on the same basis? The most plausible explanation is that Law thought of money as needed 'to pay the Wages', in other words, to act as capital. Cantillon's examples of a self-sufficient estate, by contrast, are presented entirely in real terms, with money as a unit of account and as a convenience in carrying out exchanges.

In sum, Law certainly advocated monetary expansion in order to expand output, and he thought that extra money would lead directly to an expansion of output; his argument did not involve the Keynesian notion that monetary expansion would induce extra demand, which would then call forth a response of output.[1] In Law's story, an increase in demand might *follow* an increase in the money supply, but it would be a consequence, not a cause, of the increased output and incomes. Law thought that monetary expansion would permit, or induce, extra investment. It seems that he may have simply identified money with capital, and thus regarded an increase in the money supply as essentially the same thing as an increase in the capital stock.

If this reading is accepted, Law has a more significant place in the history of economics than he has been credited with, since it makes him one of the very first writers to recognize capital scarcity as a major constraint on output. Petty had hinted at capital scarcity in a few isolated passages in his writings, but in other passages he explicitly denied that there was any shortage of 'stock' (1690: 311). Locke and Law have much more in common – it may be that Law was merely re-stating Locke's arguments as he understood them. Law's remarks read as if he identified money with capital, but then some of Locke's arguments come very close to it. The difference may be no more than a minor difference of style. Locke did refer to the possibility of borrowing to improve land or to

---

[1] Cf. Murphy (1986, 1991), who describes Law as a proto-Keynesian, with Cantillon as a proto-monetarist.

go into trade (Locke, 1691: 123), an idea which he attributed to others (unnamed). Cantillon recognized that an individual needed capital to go into business (chapter 4 above), but did not treat capital scarcity as a constraint at the aggregate level.

On the other hand, Law clearly failed to see capital scarcity as a shortage of the necessary stocks of real goods, to be remedied by saving, which is how the classics (and all subsequent writers) saw it, since he thought that it could be dealt with by printing money.[1] His examples imply that he thought of extra employment as leading to increased output and to increased consumption in the same time period, where the classical economists thought that extra consumption would necessarily precede the extra output, so that real saving ('parsimony' in Adam Smith's terminology) is needed to release goods for consumption by the newly employed workers.[2]

Law proposed to increase the money supply in order to stimulate output. There are two obvious lines of criticism. An increase in the money supply may increase prices. If so, the real quantity of money will not increase, and the anticipated benefits of the monetary expansion will prove illusory. Alternatively, in an open economy, an increase in the money supply may lead to a balance of payments deficit and an outflow of money, eliminating the change in the money supply. In an open economy, shortage of money should not be a problem, because prices will fall, increasing the real money supply and also increasing competitiveness and inducing an inflow of money. These arguments against Law's proposals are, of course, implicit in Cantillon's *Essai*, and they have become the stock-in-trade of mainstream economics.

Law provided many of the materials for a defence of his position, but he did not succeed in assembling them into a coherent whole. The effect of an increase in the money supply on the price level is the central issue. If, as Law argued, an increase in the money supply leads to a greater increase in domestic supply than in domestic demand, there would be no reason for prices to rise at all. Indeed, in a closed economy, there could be a virtuous circle, in which an increase in the (real) money supply would lead to a price cut, increasing the

---

[1] Petty, incidentally, distinguished clearly between 'money' and 'stock' (1690: 310–11).

[2] Investment in fixed capital played only a secondary role in all the writings of this period.

real money supply further, and so on. Equally, there could be a vicious circle if the money supply were curtailed. In an open economy, an increase in the money supply would lead to an improvement in the balance of trade (according to Law), a further increase in the money supply, and so on.

Law was not wholly consistent in his treatment of prices or of the determinants of international competitiveness. His basic theory of price was a simple demand and supply theory, stated on the very first page of *Money and Trade Considered*.

> Goods have a Value from the Uses they are apply'd to; and their Value is Greater or Lesser, not so much from their more or less valuable or necessary Uses: As from the greater or lesser Quantity of them in proportion to the Demand for them. (Law, 1705: 2)

If output responds to demand, a change in demand need not affect price.

> Perishable Goods as Corns, etc. encrease or decrease in Quantity as the Demand for them encreases or decreases; so their Value continues equal, or near the same. (Law, 1705: 84).

The value of money need not fall if the money stock increases at the right rate.

> If Money were given to a People in greater Quantity than there was a Demand for, Money would fall in its Value; but if only given equal to the Demand, it will not fall in Value. (Law, 1705: 160)

So far, so good. Monetary policy could work, if prices were sticky downwards, and resources idle (or something of the sort).

Unfortunately, Law completely wrecked this line of argument with his analysis of the value of silver, and hence of silver money. Silver, he said, like everything else, had a value based on demand and supply.

> Silver in Bullion or money changes its Value, from any change in its Quantity, or in the Demand for it. (Law, 1705: 84)

Note, incidentally, that this implies a rejection of any notion that the value of silver is related to its cost of production, as Petty had claimed a few decades earlier, and as Cantillon insisted a couple of decades later.[1]

The value of silver, Law claimed, had fallen drastically over the previous century or more (i.e. goods prices had risen in terms of silver money), and interest rates had fallen, showing that the supply of silver had increased faster than the demand for it. If, however, there was a great shortage of money, as he also claimed, and if the value of money only falls when its quantity exceeds the demand for it, the value of silver money should not have fallen. His argument appears to be inconsistent.

Law had an answer. The value of silver, he said, depends on the demand for it relative to the quantity *in Europe as a whole*. The quantity of money in Europe had been rising, dragging prices up, but Scotland had not benefited from the increase in the money supply, though it had suffered from the price increase.

> The Spaniards bring as great Quantities [of silver] into Europe as they can get wrought out of the Mines. . . . And though none of it come into Brittain, yet it will be of less value in Brittain, as it is in greater Quantity in Europe. (Law, 1705: 96)

> The Value of Goods or Money differs, as the Quantity of them or Demand for them changes in Europe; not as they change in any given country. . . . If Scotland was incapable of any Commerce with other Countries, and was in the state it is now, Money here would buy 10 times the Quantity of Goods it does in England, or more; . . . [but when trade is possible, however much money there is] the Value of Goods would not differ above 30 per Cent from what they were Abroad, because for that difference Goods may be imported or exported. (Law, 1705: 100–2)

The prosperity of any given country depends not on the absolute amount of money it has, but on its share of the

---

[1] It must be admitted, though, that Cantillon, and others, completely neglected any cost-based theory of the value of silver once they started to discuss practical issues.

European total. Once again, Law followed Locke, who had said much the same (Locke, 1696: 15).

This argument does not, however, provide a satisfactory basis for Law's claims, for at least two reasons. First, if output is governed by money supply, as Law thought, why should an increase in the money supply raise prices (reduce the value of money) in Europe as a whole, when it does not do so in each country considered on its own? Law offered no explanation, beyond his general claim that the value of silver is determined by demand and supply. Second, Law was not at all clear about how price changes are transmitted internationally, or about the determinants of costs and wages.

In many of his comments on the effect of price changes on the balance of payments, Law assumed low or zero elasticities of demand, which, on the face of it, conflicts with his implicit claim that price levels are equalized by trade between different parts of Europe. Thus, in his discussion of prohibitions on the export of money, Law claimed that the exchange would move against the country concerned, so the effect would be simply to ensure that they paid more for the same imports (Law, 1705: 34, 40–2).

> Most Goods sent from Scotland are such as Forreigners won't want [i.e. won't do without], tho they payed 10 or 20 per Cent more for them. (Law, 1705: 42)

And again: 'If a Duty were put on such Goods whose Value abroad would bear it, . . . 'tis the Forreigner pays the Duty' (Law, 1705: 44).

Prices, he said, were determined by marking up the cost price or domestic market price in the exporting country. 'Prices are given for Goods, according to their first Cost, Charges, and usual Profit' (Law, 1705: 42). In all of this, there is no recognizable mechanism by which price level changes can be transmitted from one country to another. It might perhaps be argued that the examples quoted in this paragraph deal with small price differentials, and that a differential of 30 per cent crosses some threshold.

On the other hand:

> one Third or more of the Goods exported, could not be rais'd in their Prices Abroad; Because Forreigners might be serv'd cheaper with the same kind of Goods from other

places, or might supply the use of them with Goods of another kind; or might consume less of them. (Law, 1705: 44)

This offers more hope for his account of a Europe-wide price level, though it still lacks an explanation of how price changes for a minority of traded goods can govern the general price level, and hence the value of money (silver).

The key question is: what determines wages? Law said nothing at all on this issue. If all other prices are governed by supply and demand, as Law claimed, why should labour be an exception? If the general price level in Europe is to rise as the stock of silver rises, wages and other costs must clearly rise with it, so there must be some mechanism through which wages adjust. If, however, wages are governed by supply and demand, then the specie-flow mechanism comes into play, to nullify the effects of printing money, but also to make monetary experiments unnecessary.

Suppose Scotland were hampered by a lack of money (capital), as Law thought. The result would be unemployment (in Law's story), but this should bring down wages, making Scottish producers more competitive (in those sectors where competitiveness matters), raising profits, cutting workers consumption, and thus improving the balance of trade. It might be possible to save Law's argument, for example if wages were fixed in real terms, if imported goods entered the wage basket, and if all non-imported wage goods were priced by marking up wage costs. In this case, wages and prices would move together in all countries. Law did not, however, address the issue at all.

The main difference between Cantillon and Law is that Cantillon accepted what came to be called 'the classical dichotomy', between real and monetary events, while Law did not. In Cantillon's story, the allocation of resources is determined by real factors: the available land, the pattern of demand by landowners, conventional (real) wage levels for different grades of workers, and so on. That might seem a surprising claim, since he did identify the wealth of a country with its money stock, in a thoroughly mercantilist fashion, but he thought that the money stock was governed by real factors, such as the productivity and reputation of export trades. Monetary events are either a reflection of real changes, or they have at most a temporary disturbing effect.

Cantillon's very careful discussion of the cases in which an increased money supply and increased prices would be beneficial (essentially, when they were a reflection of real competitive strength), and the cases in which they would not, or at least would not for long (when they were the result of borrowing from abroad or of printing money), must have been intended as a reply to Law's claims.

9.4 CANTILLON AND HIS PREDECESSORS

Cantillon's self-contained, self-confident style, and the sparseness of his (rather offhand) references to his predecessors, make it hard to identify any borrowings with certainty. That he drew on the economic ideas current at the time cannot be doubted, but the surprising thing is how little he took from them, and how thoroughly he made it his own. His theoretical framework was wholly original. Petty cannot really be credited with any of it, and Locke cannot have contributed more than a hint. Cantillon's monetary theory was less strikingly original, but even here he surpassed his only significant mentor, Locke, by a very large margin.

10

Cantillon and his Successors

Cantillon's *Essai* was written sometime around 1730, but remained unpublished until 1755. It was virtually forgotten by the early nineteenth century, and came as a revelation when it was rediscovered by historians of economics very much later. Any role it had in the development of economics came through the influence it had on those who read it in the few decades after its first publication.

It is well known that François Quesnay and his followers, the 'Physiocrats', were very directly influenced by the *Essai*, and that the Physiocrats, in turn, influenced Adam Smith and other classical economists. In addition, James Steuart, whose *Inquiry into the Principles of Political Oeconomy*, published in 1767, was the leading work on economics in Britain for a decade, was undoubtedly influenced by Cantillon. I will, however, argue that Steuart only adopted some rather superficial aspects of Cantillon's theory. In any case, his work was soon eclipsed by Adam Smith's *Wealth of Nations*, so his long term influence was limited. There are also some fairly clear indications that Cantillon influenced Turgot (a much underrated writer who anticipated much of classical economics a full decade before Adam Smith wrote the *Wealth of Nations*), and that Smith himself took at least some of his ideas directly from the *Essai*, as well as those he took from the Physiocrats and from Turgot.

It seems, then, that the most important influence Cantillon had on the development of economic ideas was through his influence on the Physiocrats, on Turgot, and, through them, on Adam Smith and on classical economics. The next two sections deal with the links between Cantillon and Quesnay, and between Cantillon and Steuart. In section 9.3, I will try to assess the extent to which Cantillon's theory contributed to the classical tradition of Smith and his successors. This chapter is not, and does not claim to be, a complete account of the development of economics in the second half of the eighteenth century. That would clearly be too ambitious a task. The focus is strictly on what the writers of this period may have taken from Cantillon.

The emphasis is on theories of population, of distribution, and of resource allocation, the areas where Cantillon made his most distinctive contributions. There is less to say about monetary economics, because it is harder to trace Cantillon's influence on the development of monetary theory. An extensive body of writing on monetary issues had already developed by the second half of the eighteenth century, and almost everything Cantillon said on the subject can be found somewhere else in the literature. Many of his ideas were discovered independently by others in the gap of a quarter of a century between the writing of the *Essai* and its publication. In addition, many of his most interesting and valuable insights had no discernible influence on classical monetary theory. As Bordo (1983) has pointed out, Cantillon's analysis of monetary disequilibrium was lost, and had to be reinvented very much later.

10.1 QUESNAY AND THE PHYSIOCRATS

The 'Physiocrats' were a remarkably cohesive group of economists who were active in France for a fairly short time, from about 1757 to the later 1760s.[1] The leader of this group was François Quesnay, supported by a number of others, including the Marquis de Mirabeau. Turgot is sometimes treated as a Physiocrat (e.g. Meek, 1963: 38), but his work went well beyond the bounds of the rather dogmatic Physiocratic system; I regard him as the first of the classical economists, not the last of the Physiocrats, so I will discuss his work in the third section of this chapter. The word 'Physiocrat' was not coined until 1767 (Vaggi, 1987c); Quesnay's followers were

---

[1] Meek (1963) is still the best general account of the economics of Physiocracy. For an account of the rise of the Physiocratic school, and of the political, social, and intellectual background, see Fox-Genovese (1976). The standard reference in French is the Institut National d'Études Démographiques (1958; cited below as *INED*).

known to their contemporaries simply as *les economistes*, 'the economists', while Adam Smith referred to their work as 'the agricultural system'.

Quesnay was born in 1694, only a decade or so after Cantillon. Like Petty and Locke, he came from a fairly humble background, and first made his mark as a doctor. He became the private physician to Madame de Pompadour, Louis XV's mistress, came to the king's attention, and was granted a title and a landed estate. His contacts in the royal household were very important to him – the Physiocrats, under his guidance, always saw themselves as loyal advisers to the monarchy. Physiocracy peaked in the 1760s, when it attracted a number of adherents and was much discussed. After about 1768 or 1770 it began to lose impetus (Vaggi, 1987b: 22; Meek, 1963: 31). In the last years of his life, Quesnay turned his attention to mathematical questions. He died in 1774.

Quesnay's first publication on a medical topic, the effects of bleeding, dates from 1730, the year in which Cantillon probably wrote the *Essai*, but he did not turn to economics until the mid 1750s, when he was over 60. His first publications on economic questions, then, were written more than twenty years after Cantillon's death, but (significantly) only a year or so after the publication of the *Essai*. His main economic writings were completed in little over a decade, with two main bursts of writing in the later 1750s and in the mid 1760s. I shall concentrate on his first group of writings, those of 1756 to 1759, because the signs of Cantillon's influence are likely to be stronger in the earlier writings.

Quesnay's economic theory was based rather closely on Cantillon's,[1] with one crucial difference. Where Cantillon saw land as the only scarce resource (in the long run), Quesnay insisted that French agriculture was performing far below potential, so the land was far from being fully used. This was probably an advance in realism, but it undermined the coherence of the theoretical system which Quesnay had inherited from Cantillon. As a result, Quesnay's system does not hang together in the way Cantillon's did. It was not until

---

[1] '[I]t is precisely the fundamental features of Quesnay's analytical set-up that are unmistakeably foreshadowed in Cantillon's work' (Schumpeter, 1954: 218). '[I]t would be misleading to describe [Cantillon] as the first Physiocrat (because he was so much more than a Physiocrat)' (Hutchison, 1988: 274).

Turgot, West, and Ricardo that capital scarcity was fully incorporated into a consistent model of the economy (cf. Brewer, 1987, 1988c). Quesnay's debt to Cantillon has, of course, often been noted, though I think it has rarely been given its full weight.

The best known features of Quesnay's economics are, first, the claim that only agriculture is 'productive' while all other economic activities are 'sterile' and, second, his diagrammatic representation of inter-sectoral flows of spending, the *Tableau Economique*. Both seem to come almost direct from Cantillon, though the first rests on a misunderstanding of Cantillon's theory.

Consider first the alleged exclusive productivity of agriculture. The idea is that the products of agricultural labour cover the costs of production, including the workers' subsistence, and also yield rent to the landlord. Non-agricultural production, on the other hand, only covers the costs of production (including the merchants' profit).

> Agricultural work compensates for the costs involved, pays for the manual labour employed in cultivation, provides gains for the husbandman, and in addition produces the revenue of landed property. Those who buy industrial goods pay the costs, the manual labour, and the gain accruing to the merchants; but these goods do not produce any revenue over and above this. (Meek, 1963: 72)[1]

This is clearly taken directly from Cantillon's theory of intrinsic value. Value is governed by the land and labour required in production. Industrial work involves no land, so the value added in industrial activities is confined to the labour cost (including the entrepreneur's 'wage'), while the value of agricultural output includes a rent element as well.

Cantillon did not, of course, draw the conclusion that agriculture ought to be expanded at the expense of other sectors. He assumed that the land was always fully cultivated, but even without that assumption, there is nothing in the logic of his case that would force him to describe industry and trade as unproductive. Cantillon and Quesnay share the same value theory, but not the conclusions that Quesnay drew from it.

---

[1] There are many similar statements elsewhere in the writings of Quesnay and other Physiocrats.

The fact that Quesnay's theory of value is the same as Cantillon's is not enough by itself to establish that Quesnay took it from Cantillon. It might simply be the natural result of a theory in which rent and wages are the main forms of income. Quesnay could, for example, have found rather similar ideas in Petty or Locke.

However, Quesnay coupled the argument set out above with another: 'all the expenses incurred in making industrial goods are simply drawn from the revenue of landed property' (Meek, 1963: 73). Compare this with Cantillon's chapter heading: 'All classes and individuals in a state subsist or are enriched at the expense of the proprietors of the land' (*Essai*: 43). Both argued that agricultural prices include an element corresponding to rent, and both argued that spending by landowners (or spending out of taxes derived ultimately from rents) had a special causal significance: spending out of rent was the cause, while the existence of other categories of income, and of spending out of other incomes, were the effect. No-one else combines these two ideas in this way. It is hard to doubt that Quesnay took this complex of ideas from Cantillon, though they drew very different policy conclusions.[1]

According to Quesnay, trade cannot create wealth (Vaggi, 1987a: 43). This clearly follows from the exclusive productivity of agriculture; trade cannot add to the net product (though it might, presumably, allow one country to capture some of the net product of another). However, Vaggi went on to claim that Quesnay was the first to treat trade as unproductive. Now, Cantillon may not have phrased it in the same way, but the idea is clearly implicit in his theory. In Cantillon's story, the landowners are the only 'independent' class; all other classes derive their incomes directly or indirectly from landlords' spending. The scale of agricultural production depends on the available land, and on how it is used (which depends on the spending choices made by landlords). The scale of industrial production and trade depends ultimately on the demand from landlords and from the agricultural sector. International and internal trade affect the location, but not the overall world level of industrial

---

[1] The whole of the section of the 'maxims of economic government' headed 'industrial work does not increase wealth' (Meek, 1963: 73) strikes an immediately recognizable note to anyone familiar with Cantillon's *Essai*.

activity. In particular, neither domestic nor international trade can affect the level of rent (except to the extent that they may allow particularly remunerative cash crops to be grown in favoured locations near large urban markets).

Cantillon's land theory of value makes the point very clearly: value rests on land, while trade merely redistributes it. A country with a relatively high price level has better terms of trade, so it exchanges the product of a smaller amount of land for the product of a greater amount of land (*Essai*: 225). The state gains from trade, but it does so not because trade creates any value, but by exchanging more value for less. Quesnay's account was not essentially different, though he thought that agricultural exports might allow an expansion of agricultural activity or an increase in agricultural prices. Trade did not itself add to the net product, but it could allow the productive sector, agriculture, to produce a greater surplus. Cantillon did not even allow this much 'productiveness' to trade.

Quesnay's *Tableau Economique*, which is widely regarded as the ancestor of 'modern work on social accounts of sectoral interdependence' (Barna, 1975: 485), was also based very closely on Cantillon's *Essai*. Quesnay, in fact, produced a succession of different versions of 'the' *Tableau*[1] – Meek describes a passage about foreign trade in the article for the *Encyclopédie* on 'men' (*hommes*) of 1757, as 'the germ of the *Tableau*'.

> The cultivator and the manufacturer, who sell to the merchant, similarly turn to account the money they receive from the merchant by regenerating exchangeable products. The proprietor uses the money he receives from his farmer to purchase the foreign commodities which the merchant has imported; and the merchant returns this money to the farmer who sells him the products yielded by his cultivation. The workers who are paid by the manufacturer, by the husbandman, and by all those who employ them, buy produce and commodities for their consumption; and the money is turned back into the cultivation of the land and the production of the manufactured goods which are reproduced. (Meek, 1963: 93)

---

[1] See Vaggi (1987b), and Kuczynski and Meek (1972).

There is, of course, no way of proving that Quesnay took the argument of this passage from Cantillon, but it is remarkably similar to Cantillon's account of the circulation of money (section 6.1 above), published only two years before.

The *Tableau Economique* proper was published in a succession of rather similar editions, all characterized by the famous zigzag lines, in 1758 and 1759. Quesnay's idiosyncratic presentation hides the similarity with Cantillon, which emerges again in the final version of the *Tableau*, the *Analyse du formule arithmétique du Tableau économique* (see Vaggi, 1987b: 25; Meek, 1963: 158). In this final version, the zigzags are replaced by simple flows of expenditure between agriculture (the productive class), industry (the sterile class), and the landowners. The framework is exactly the same as in Cantillon's account of circulation between town, country, and landowners. The numbers are different, that is all.

Even in the confusing zigzag versions of the *Tableau*, the circulation of money is analysed in exactly the same way as in Cantillon's version. The story starts just after the landlords have been paid their rents, so they start with the whole money stock (in the simplified model Quesnay took from Cantillon). The landlords spend the money and it passes from hand to hand, ending up with the farmers, who pay it over as rent, ready for the process to start again.[1] Foley (1973: 139–40) has pointed out that Quesnay's terminology coincides exactly with Cantillon's in a number of places, even when Cantillon used rather unusual phrases. He also notes a 'loss of subtlety, distinction and detail', which is what one expects when comparing a copy with the original.

The *Tableau Economique* represented an idealized economy 'which embodies the main characteristics of the natural order of society. If one wants to identify a specific country with the kingdom described in the *Tableau*, it must be England' (Vaggi, 1987a: 31). Exactly the same can be said of Cantillon's *Essai*, though Cantillon said nothing about 'natural order' (one would not expect him to do so, given his reticent and unpretentious style). There is not a word in the *Essai* about the system of feudal privileges, the restrictions on trade, and the like, which were prevalent in France (and which persisted to some degree even in England) at the time.

If it is true that the best known features of Quesnay's

---

[1] See Eltis (1984: 23) for a particularly clear explanation.

analysis were derived directly from Cantillon, his overall view of the economic system, and of the most urgent issues of policy, was not. The difference emerges unmistakeably at the very start of Quesnay's second career, as an economist and political thinker, in his 1756 entry in the *Encyclopédie* under the heading *Fermiers* (Farmers; Quesnay, 1969: 159–92; Groenewegen, 1983). It is almost entirely descriptive, it contains few of the elements normally identified with Physiocracy, and it has therefore often been ignored.[1] However, Quesnay's description of the state of French farming in *Fermiers* set the agenda for all his subsequent economic writings.

Quesnay identified two distinct methods of cultivation. The first involved the use of horses as motive power, and was practised by relatively prosperous farmers with relatively large farms. It required substantial investments, but gave high returns. The second, typically practised by share-croppers on smaller farms, used oxen instead of horses, required less investment (usually financed, at least in part, by the landowner), but yielded much lower returns (Quesnay, 1969: 159–68).[2] He also mentioned cultivation by hand, using neither horses nor oxen, which would not even fully cover costs (Quesnay, 1969: 181). The land of France appeared to be fully cultivated, so those who did not understand farming assumed that all was well.

Quesnay's references to English farming as an example of good practice (e.g. Quesnay, 1969: 174, 175) show that he was influenced by the remarkable development of agriculture in England in the mid eighteenth century. This may explain why he saw agricultural potential where Cantillon, writing earlier, did not. It may also be that Cantillon's experience of trade and finance, based in the major cities of Europe, simply left him rather badly informed about agriculture. It is, however, rather odd that Cantillon, writing earlier and assuming an essentially static agricultural sector, almost always described a fully capitalist agriculture on English lines (characterized by

---

[1] Meek, for example, did not include any of it in his collection of translations (still the main source of Quesnay's writings for English speakers).

[2] It is not wholly clear that he was right to claim that cultivation with horses was superior to cultivation with oxen (cf. Braudel, 1990: 346–7), but there can be little doubt that better methods of cultivation could have been adopted.

the 'three rents') while Quesnay, despite another quarter-century of agricultural advance, described French agriculture (quite realistically; cf. Meek, 1963: 23–4) as mainly based on share-cropping.

After describing the state of French agriculture, Quesnay performed a rather simple calculation (1969: 171–3). The population of France was thought to be about 16 million. Quesnay took an estimate of per capita consumption, and used it to derive an estimate of the domestic demand for wheat (the staple food, and the main product of agriculture), of 36 million *septiers*. This fell short of his estimate of actual output (42 million *septiers*), and even more dramatically short of his estimate of potential output, using best practice techniques (70 million *septiers*). There was a potential surplus of 26 million, even allowing for population growth (1969: 173). Quesnay could see no possibility of external markets absorbing such a massive amount of grain.

He noted that land varied in quality, so that some land would not repay the investment needed to grow corn by the best techniques. This land might be used as pasture for draught animals, for other incidental purposes, or for other cash crops. He thus recognized the existence of an agricultural margin. He also argued that a country like France, with more than enough land to meet its needs for wheat, should concentrate wheat growing on the best lands, using the best techniques. His calculations showed that quite a small fraction of the land would be enough, leaving the rest free for animal husbandry and for other uses. This argument not only shows a clear recognition of an agricultural margin, but also a recognition that the margin could move in response to economic circumstances. His policy conclusions, at least at the time he wrote *Fermiers*, involved finding profitable uses for land not needed for growing wheat, but he did not use the concept of an agricultural margin as a major element in his theory.[1]

France, then, had the potential to increase agricultural output enormously, but demand was not even enough to absorb the meagre levels of output that Quesnay observed.

---

[1] The link between the agricultural margin and the profit rate was first stated clearly by Quesnay's near contemporary Turgot, and rediscovered by Malthus, West, Torrens, and Ricardo (cf. Brewer, 1987, 1988c).

The resulting low prices led to rural poverty and low rents, which perpetuated the backward systems of production in use. In this context, the significance of the notion that only agriculture is productive (which will be discussed below) becomes clear. If agriculture alone can yield a net product, and if agriculture in France (unlike England) was chronically depressed, the poor condition of France could be explained. The problem was to see how it could be remedied.

Cantillon, by contrast, assumed that population would grow whenever there was an opportunity of earning a living, so the land would always be fully used (albeit for purposes chosen by landowners, which might include devoting land to hunting rather than to the growing of crops). In Cantillon's words, 'a single generation suffices to push the increase of population as far as the produce of land will supply means of subsistence' (*Essai*: 81).

Quesnay implicitly rejected Cantillon's population theory, though he never presented any systematic alternative; in the encyclopedia entry on *Fermiers*, he treated population as essentially given, since he based his calculations on the size of the existing population. He did, it is true, make a rather casual allowance for some increase in population, without any clear explanation, and he sometimes claimed, in other writings, that population would increase if only agriculture could be revived (cf. Eltis, 1984: 10–11). Since he thought that best practice techniques could support a population more than 50 per cent above the current level, he may well have thought that there was no question of so large an increase in population in a time scale short enough to be relevant for policy purposes. Cantillon's arguments about population, especially in the first part of the *Essai*, are designed to explain long run equilibrium, as a background to the discussion of trade and money in the second and third parts of the *Essai* – agriculture is the (essentially) unchanging basis of the economy. Quesnay, by contrast, saw the revival of a depressed agriculture as an urgent priority. In any case, Cantillon seems never to have considered the possibility of so large a discrepancy between actual and potential population.

Mirabeau's account of his first discussion with Quesnay in 1757 (an occasion which is often seen as the birth of the Physiocratic school) throws some light on Quesnay's views (see Meek, 1963: 15; Eltis, 1984: 312–13). Mirabeau had already seen Cantillon's *Essai* long before its publication – he had held on to the manuscript, and probably delayed its publication, for many years. As he later told the tale, Cantillon had convinced him that:

> Wealth is the fruit that comes from the land for the use of men; the labour of man alone possesses the capacity to increase wealth. Thus the more men there are, the more labour there will be; the more labour there is, the more wealth there will be. The way to increase prosperity is therefore: (1) To increase men; (2) through these men, to increase productive labour; (3) through this labour to increase wealth. (Meek, 1963: 17)

Quesnay immediately corrected him.

> My critic did not beat around the bush with me, and told me quite plainly that I had put the cart before the horse, and that Cantillon, as a teacher of the public, was nothing but a fool. . . . My man asked me to do the same honour to men as is done to sheep, since anyone who wants to increase his flock begins by increasing his grazing land. (Meek, 1963: 17)

This is really very odd. Far from showing that Cantillon was a fool, Quesnay's reported response could have come from Cantillon himself. In Cantillon's theory, population depends on the demand for labour, which depends on the available land and on the use made of it. Thus: 'Horses, cattle, sheep can easily be multiplied up to the number that the land will support'. 'Men multiply like mice in a barn if they have unlimited means of subsistence' (*Essai*: 67, 83). Mirabeau seems simply to have misunderstood Cantillon, but if Quesnay really agreed with Mirabeau's interpretation and concluded that Cantillon was a fool, it shows that he too had not fully understood Cantillon. Quesnay, however, went on (in Mirabeau's report) to ask whether man arrived on earth with bread to support him until the crops he grew had matured and been harvested (Meek, 1963: 17). This is a different, and more valid, criticism – Mirabeau (and, by implication, Cantillon) had not allowed for the need to accumulate capital before more people can be employed.

Quesnay's treatment of capital was not, in fact, as sharply different from Cantillon's as might at first appear. Cantillon was well aware of the need for investment in farming, as can be seen from the following extract (already quoted, but worth repeating here).

> If the farmer have enough capital to carry on his enterprise, if he have the needful tools and instruments, horses for ploughing, cattle to make the land pay, etc. he will take for himself after paying all expenses a third of the produce of his farm. But if a competent labourer who lives from day to day on his wages and has no capital, can find someone willing to lend him [funds], he will be able to give the lender all the third rent, or third part of the produce of a farm of which he will become the farmer. . . . However he will think his position improved since he will find his upkeep in the second rent and will become master instead of man. (*Essai*: 201)

Cantillon's description of what a farmer needs, in the first sentence of this extract, is strikingly similar to Quesnay's description of good agricultural practice, in the encyclopedia article on *Fermiers*.

Cantillon, it is true, did not see capital scarcity as a constraint on overall output, where Quesnay evidently did. Even so, the difference can be overstated. The classical economists, starting with Quesnay's near contemporary, Turgot, thought in terms of a secular process of growth and capital accumulation, leading to an eventual, far distant, stationary state. Quesnay did not. His aim was simply to restore France to its former glory, to the population it ought to have, represented by its population a hundred years earlier (Meek, 1963: 84).[1]

Quesnay's vision, then, was not really so different from Cantillon's, since Cantillon thought in terms of (very long run) alternations of prosperity and decay, with no underlying trend in output. They differ, though, in their account of the causes of upswings and downswings. Cantillon thought that the mercantilist policies introduced by Colbert in the mid seventeenth century marked the start of a period of prosperity for France, while Quesnay blamed them for French decline (as

---

[1] Modern historical research suggests that Quesnay was wrong about the facts of population change, but that is beside the point here. What matters is what he believed.

Boisguilbert had done more than half a century earlier). Cantillon assumed that agricultural production was always essentially the same, so Colbert's policies allowed industrial expansion to add to a given level of agricultural activity, while Quesnay thought that Colbert's policies diverted resources from the 'productive' to the 'sterile' sector.

Price theory is another point of similarity between Cantillon and Quesnay, since Quesnay's concept of fundamental price (*prix fondamental*) is essentially the same as Cantillon's concept of intrinsic value. Cantillon's argument was presented, in the example of an isolated estate, in terms of the prices which are needed in order to cover costs, to allow the farmers to maintain a customary standard of living, and to allow them to pay rent (*Essai*: 59–61). Quesnay's fundamental price is just the same (Meek, 1963: 93–4). Vaggi is right to claim that the fundamental price includes rent, but his claim that this was an innovation introduced by Quesnay (1987a: 10) is more doubtful. His justification is that Cantillon's intrinsic value is a measure of physical cost, the land directly and indirectly required to produce each good, not of money cost including rent (Vaggi, 1987a: 89). He appears not to see that the two components of intrinsic value, the land directly required in production and the land needed to support the labour force, correspond directly to rent costs and wage costs. On the other hand, Vaggi may well be right to claim that Quesnay put a stronger emphasis than Cantillon did on the 'circularity' of production, that is on the role of produced means of production, and on the need to replace means of production as they are used up. The difference is only one of emphasis; Cantillon did not entirely ignore the use of produced means of production (even the water-carrier's bucket got a mention), but he may have been a little more casual than Quesnay in his treatment of them.

Quesnay thought that the lack of investment in agriculture was due to low prices. If the price of agricultural produce falls below its fundamental price, the cultivator becomes poor, and output falls. If the price is at a level sufficient to cover costs, good practices are assured, and agriculture will prosper (e.g. Meek, 1963: 85–6). This is one of the weakest elements in Quesnay's argument.

Superficially, it could be argued that this is another example of Quesnay copying Cantillon, since Cantillon had noted that excessive rents might impoverish the farmer and make it less likely that the rent would actually be paid.

> When a farmer has some capital to carry on the management of his farm the proprietor who lets him the farm for a third of the produce will be sure of payment and will be better off by such a bargain than if he let his farm at a higher rate to a beggarly farmer at the risk of losing all his rent. (*Essai*: 123)

Cantillon did not, however, argue that low prices would have a similar effect.

The problem with Quesnay's claim that the poor state of agriculture was due to the market price falling below the fundamental price is that it is relative prices, not the absolute price level, that matter, and he was never clear what he was measuring agricultural prices relative to. He insisted that low prices for agricultural products would not bring any gain to the non-agricultural sector, and high prices would not harm them, because

> the labourers, artisans, manufacturers, etc., get paid for their time and their goods in proportion to the cost of their subsistence. (Meek, 1963: 87)

In this case, how can the price of corn be too low to cover the cost of production? Costs must fall with the price, leaving revenue, in real terms, unchanged.

If there were costs fixed in money terms, such as taxes or rents, the argument might be rescued, but Quesnay did not say so. In any case, this would make the state of depression a temporary phenomenon, which could be remedied by renegotiating fixed money payments. It would also mean that a nation could gain by having a rising money stock, and hence a rising general price level, but Quesnay explicitly denied that increases in the money stock mattered (Meek, 1963: 77).

If, as Quesnay claimed, the population was below the maximum which the land could support, and if, as a result, the demand for food was chronically below the potential supply, the equilibrium price of food would indeed have to be low enough to keep agricultural output in line with demand. But in this case, first, the price must be low relative to other prices, so as to make it more profitable to invest in manufacturing and trade than in agriculture. This is merely the normal way resources are allocated in response to demand. There would then be positive profits to investment in manufacturing (or trade), because the surplus over an (assumed) subsistence wage cannot simply disappear as a result of price changes. Quesnay's assertion that manufacturing is sterile, in the sense that its price only covers costs, would thus be false.

Second, if land is not scarce, because population is low, why should it command a positive rent? Cantillon's analysis of rent makes good sense, because he assumed that land was the only scarce resource. If Quesnay dropped that assumption, he should have dropped the rent theory as well, but he did not. Very simply, if scarcity of labour or capital were the problem, the surplus of output over cost should accrue to wages or to profits, not to rent. In this, as in some other features of his theory, Quesnay's ideas seem to have been closer to Petty than to Cantillon.[1] Quesnay did not, in fact, have any good explanation of the existence of rent at all. As Vaggi notes (1987a: 117–18), he was led into a vicious circularity, explaining the existence of a surplus in agriculture by the high price of agricultural products, high agricultural prices by high demand, and demand by the expenditure of the surplus.[2] Quesnay's theory was a step backward from Cantillon's, since Cantillon's theory did not suffer from the same circularity.

One possible way to rescue Quesnay from the charge of confusion might be to say that output is limited by lack of effective demand. Quesnay, and other Physiocrats, have often been read this way (see Meek, 1963: 313–44), with some reason. For example, Quesnay urged:

> *That the whole of the sum of revenue should come back into the annual circulation, and run through it to the full extent of its course;* and that it should never be formed into monetary fortunes. (Meek, 1963: 233)

Similarly, Quesnay's discussion of international trade in the 'maxims of economic government', which form part of the

---

[1] Quesnay knew Petty's work 'well' (Hutchison, 1988: 274).

[2] Given this circularity, it is perhaps not so surprising that Quesnay could think that a low level of demand could simply reduce the net product in agriculture without benefit to any other sector.

(early) article on 'corn' (*grains*) in the *Encyclopédie*, and the very similar pronouncements in the (later) 'general maxims' (Meek, 1963: 72–87, 231–62), invite an interpretation in terms of effective demand.

The case for free trade, it seems, is that exports provide additional demand. For example:

> If a nation gains a million livres through its labour by selling abroad manufactured commodities which it makes at home, and if it also sells abroad a million livres' worth of its raw produce, both of these products equally represent an addition to its wealth and are equally advantageous to it, provided it has more men than the revenue of the kingdom's land can support. For in that case a certain number of these men can subsist only through the manufactured commodities which they sell abroad. (Meek, 1963: 74)

If the land is fully cultivated, manufactured exports allow an increased population to be supported by food imports. That much is clear, and is what Cantillon said. It is harder to understand how the kingdom can export both manufactured and agricultural products. What, then, is imported? Possibly there are imports of goods, manufactured or not, that are not produced locally, and do not compete with local products. Leaving that problem aside, how can a country export agricultural goods when it has 'more men than the revenue of the kingdom's land can support'? If agricultural output were constrained by the available land, or by capital scarcity, how could any be spared for export? If the limit were set by demand, Quesnay's argument would be a little easier to follow, since export demand could then induce an increase in output by adding to total demand, but it is still hard to find a coherent argument in Quesnay's text.[1]

---

[1] It is also unlikely that his argument was appropriate to the France of his day, since the evidence suggests that France was, on balance, a net importer of food at the time (Braudel, 1990: 371–82). It is true that Quesnay claimed only that France had the potential to become a net exporter on a large scale, not that it actually was a net exporter, but it is hard to claim that lack of demand was the problem, and that free exportation would help, when French consumers had to turn to foreign sources for their food.

More generally, it is worth noticing the frequency with which Quesnay used phrases like the number of men that '*the revenue of the kingdom's land* can support' (in the above extract, emphasis added), rather than the number that *the land* can support. The *Tableau Economique* also implies that the *spending* of the revenue (i.e. of rent) plays a special role in generating employment. It is true that Cantillon said something of the sort, but in Cantillon's story, I have argued, there was no problem of effective demand, and the land was fully used. The pattern of spending by landlords governs the composition of output, and the allocation of land between different uses (and the size of the population that the land supports), but there is no question of land standing idle or being used at less than optimal intensity. It may be used for purposes other than growing food for human beings, of course, but that is because the landowners so choose. All this emerges very clearly from Cantillon's analysis of the isolated estate.

There is at least a hint, in Quesnay, of a different story, in which a depressed agriculture only generates low rents, while the spending of these low rents induces a low level of demand for manufactures and for agricultural products. Agriculture remains depressed, causing a vicious circle, or low level equilibrium. External markets might break this circle, and allow a higher level of output. Again Quesnay never spelled out the argument at all clearly. This aspect of Quesnay's thinking probably derived from Boisguilbert (1966).[1]

In sum, much of Quesnay's economics came almost direct from Cantillon. His price theory and his distribution theory were taken from Cantillon almost unchanged. The special role of agricultural production, of the agricultural surplus, and of demand generated by the spending of agricultural revenue (rent), all come from Cantillon's distribution theory and from his account of the role of landlord's spending, though Quesnay used these ideas in a way that Cantillon would not have countenanced. The *Tableau Economique* is, essentially, a simple restatement of Cantillon's analysis of the circulation of money. The decisive difference between them is that Quesnay saw that French agriculture was very backward, by the standards of England or of the Netherlands, and deduced that there was massive scope for improvement. In practical terms,

---

[1] Boisguilbert's main works were originally published between 1695 and 1707; see also Groenewegen (1987a) and Spengler (1984).

of course, this observation was enormously important, though not especially original (there was a large literature on agricultural improvement in English, if not in French). It is not surprising that Quesnay made little real progress in modifying Cantillon's framework to deal with this issue, since land scarcity was so fundamental to Cantillon's theory.

10.2 STEUART

James Steuart was born in 1713, son of the Lord Advocate of Scotland. The first part of his life was conventionally successful; he passed his bar examinations in 1735, and spent the next five years making a grand tour of Europe, as wealthy young men did at the time. During this tour, however, he met Jacobite exiles at Avignon, and then the Old Pretender himself at Rome, and was converted to the Jacobite cause. Back in Scotland, he supported the rebellion of 1745, and was in Paris as a representative of Prince Charles when the rebellion was defeated at the battle of Culloden. He remained in exile for nearly twenty years, despite many efforts to get a pardon. He lived successively in Paris, Angoulême, Tubingen, Rotterdam, and Antwerp, and also travelled extensively, gathering materials on economic circumstances.

His *Inquiry into the Principles of Political Oeconomy* was started during this period, and completed after he had finally been allowed to return to Scotland in 1763. It was published in 1767, to mixed reviews; many reviewers were put off by the interventionist tone of the book. None the less, it was the main work in the field for nine years, until it was eclipsed by Adam Smith's *Wealth of Nations*. Smith was, of course, strenuously opposed to Steuart's mercantilist interventionism, and did not mention him once in the *Wealth of Nations*. Steuart died in 1780.[1]

There is no direct evidence that Steuart knew Cantillon's work (though he did refer to Philip Cantillon, whose book, *The Analysis of Trade,* was based on Richard Cantillon's *Essai*), but sections of the *Inquiry* read very much as if they were based on Cantillon. He certainly knew French writings, such as Mirabeau's *L'Ami des Hommes*, which were themselves

---

[1] On Steuart's life and work, see Skinner (1966) and Eltis (1987); on his economics see Eltis (1986) and Skinner (1990).

inspired by Cantillon. However, I doubt whether his work did much to perpetuate Cantillon's ideas, since he took over only the more superficial aspects of Cantillon's theory.

There are fundamental differences between them. Cantillon understood the case for the market, and advocated intervention only when there was good reason to think that the market would not achieve the aims of policy. For example, Cantillon recognized that policy makers were concerned with military strength, and therefore with population (as a source of military manpower), but that consumers could not be expected to take this into account in their individual buying choices. Intervention, then, was justified by a sort of market failure. Steuart, by contrast, mistrusted the market (perhaps because he did not understand how it worked), and argued that a state needed a 'statesman' to oversee every aspect of the economy. In addition, Cantillon's model was essentially static and timeless, where Steuart's was a model of a process of development, driven by changing wants.

The first book of Steuart's *Inquiry* is on population and agriculture. Like Cantillon (and others), Steuart maintained that population was endogenous, and was determined by the availability of subsistence.[1]

> I apprehend that in man, as in every other animal, the generative faculty is more than able to repair all losses occasioned by regular diseases; . . . multiplication never can stop but for want of food. (Steuart, 1767: 98; cf. Cantillon, *Essai*: 73, 77, 83, etc.)

Steuart tended to emphasize the effect of mortality rates as a check on population (cf. Steuart, 1767: 33), where Cantillon stressed variations in marriage rates and hence birth rates. Characteristically, Steuart took over this part of Cantillon's theory while changing it into a case for intervention:

> a parish priest might, properly enough, be warranted not to join a couple unless they could make it appear that their

---

[1] Marx accused Malthus of plagiarizing Steuart's population theory; in fact, there were plenty of others, including Cantillon, who Malthus could just as well have taken it from. Marx was, of course, right to stress that there was nothing very original in Malthus's population theory.

children were not likely to become a burden to the parish. (Steuart, 1767: 77–8)

Like Petty and the Physiocrats, but unlike Cantillon, Steuart thought that agriculture, and hence population, in most of Europe, was far below its real potential. At one point (in a discussion of the introduction of new machines), he described a perfect state, an isolated state 'peopled to the utmost extent', which bears some resemblance to the closed economy model of part one of Cantillon's *Essai*, but immediately added that 'the present state of every country in Europe' was 'widely distant from this degree of perfection' (Steuart, 1767: 123). This was, no doubt, a realistic assessment, but in rejecting Cantillon's rather Panglossian approach, he rejected the theoretical framework as well.

He offered (at least) two different explanations for underutilization of the land. First, productivity might be limited by ignorance or by outdated customs. In Scotland, each farm was surrounded by the huts of underemployed cottagers, whose wives and children could be, but were not, employed to spin and weave on a commercial basis. It would take time for them to attain the necessary skill, 'but if the undertaking is supported with patience, these obstacles will be got the better of' (Steuart, 1767: 106; cf. Cantillon, *Essai*: 155).

Steuart's second, more substantial, and more interesting, explanation for the poor performance of agriculture was that demand was lacking. The starting point is the claim, perhaps derived from Petty (direct, or via Cantillon), that one person working in agriculture can produce subsistence for more than one (Steuart, 1767: 34; cf. Cantillon, *Essai*: 87). Cantillon discussed what the non-agricultural population should be employed to do, but did not (apparently) think that there might be any general lack of demand. Steuart, like Petty, took the opposite view. If the people were 'without trade, without the luxurious arts, and without ambition', they would not produce a surplus, because they would have no use for it, and they would 'immediately give over working' (Steuart, 1767: 39). 'A free man who by his industry can procure all the comforts of a simple life, will enjoy his rest, and work no more', if his tastes are correspondingly simple (Steuart, 1767: 155). This is the key to Steuart's theory of economic development; the economy develops as new wants are created, for example by the invention of new commodities which satisfy 'needs' that no-one had previously thought of (cf. Steuart, 1767: 157).

Steuart's argument is simple enough, and is familiar to modern development economists; the problem is not a lack of demand, but of supply, because farmers find leisure more attractive than additional income. It does, however, seem to conflict with Steuart's claim that

> the generative faculty . . . and the love we have for our children, first prompt us to multiply, and then engage us to divide what we have with our little ones, (Steuart, 1767: 33)

so that subsistence is divided and subdivided, until there is no surplus left.

In any case, the argument that farmers will not produce a surplus unless there is something they want to trade it for, though correct enough, did not deal with the normal case in eighteenth century Europe, where the land was not owned by the farmer but by a landlord. Where Cantillon argued that unequal ownership of the land was inevitable, Steuart argued that it was desirable, apparently because wealthy landowners were more likely to spend on luxuries, thus employing the 'industrious poor' (Steuart, 1767: 127). In a quite different context, he argued (as Cantillon had) that equality of wealth would not persist, even if it could be established in a modern, market, society:

> Absolute equality . . . is an absurd supposition, if applied to a human society. Must not frugality amass, and prodigality dissipate? (Steuart, 1767: 317)

What Steuart did not explain clearly is what landlords would do with their rents if they did not spend them in some form or other, and thus why there should be any general lack of demand. Provided the surplus generated in agriculture is spent, there is no problem of demand, as Cantillon explained. The money value of the surplus is spent on non-agricultural products or services, so it accrues as income to the providers of these goods and services, who spend it on food.

Steuart treated rents (in the case of land owned by a class of landowners separate from the cultivators) in very much the same way as Cantillon had before him – the rent is, or should be, what is left of output after deducting the subsistence of the farmer, his family, and the farm workers, the out-of-pocket expenses of cultivation, and a reasonable profit 'according to the custom of every country' (Steuart, 1767: 53). He cited Petty's estimate of the total rent for England, as corrected by Davenant, but his explanation of it was remarkably similar to Cantillon's.[1] Here, as elsewhere in Steuart's work, there are quite strong indications of Cantillon's influence, but it seems that Steuart took over elements of Cantillon's theory without seeing it as a whole. If land was not fully utilized, it is not clear why the surplus output should accrue to the landowner.

Steuart's price theory, too, contains elements which were probably taken from Cantillon, either direct or via the Physiocrats. He distinguished between the 'real value' or 'intrinsic value' of a commodity, essentially its cost of production, and the 'profit upon alienation', or the markup of market price over cost (Steuart, 1767: 159–60). It is not entirely clear whether real value and intrinsic value are the same; Steuart argued that persistent high profits could become the norm, and be 'consolidated, or, as it were, transformed into the intrinsic value of the goods', or 'consolidated with the intrinsic value' (1767: 193, 194; emphasis removed). This may mean that intrinsic value is real value, or cost, plus an accepted or conventional, profit, leaving only unusual or exceptional profits as 'profit on alienation'.[2]

The real value of something depends on the labour needed to produce it, the subsistence costs of the worker, and the value of the materials used. If the materials are themselves produced by labour, their value must, in turn, be reduced to labour and materials costs, and so on. Whatever materials costs remain after this process must presumably be identified with land, or with the spontaneous products of nature (unless

---

[1] He also took over Cantillon's analysis of the location of activities and the significance of transport costs in the vicinity of a town (Steuart, 1767: 134–5; cf. Hebert, 1981: 74).

[2] Steuart also defined 'intrinsic worth' and 'useful value', but these are quite different from 'intrinsic value', in either his own, or Cantillon's, sense of the term, and are mentioned here only to avoid any possible confusion. The intrinsic worth of something is the value of the materials actually incorporated into it, as for example the value of a silver ornament considered merely as a bit of silver, while the 'useful value' is the value added by the workmanship involved in manufacturing it (Steuart, 1767: 312).

the process of tracing materials costs back to labour costs in earlier stages of production ends by eliminating them altogether).

This concept of real, or intrinsic, value clearly has much in common with Cantillon's concept of intrinsic value; it is made up of labour costs, plus something which might be identified with the land required (as in Cantillon), and labour costs are in turn identified with the costs of workers' subsistence (as in Cantillon). However, Steuart's version is a good deal less well defined than Cantillon's. It is not at all clear how costs are to be calculated and added up, unless in money terms, while performing the calculation in money terms introduces an obvious circularity, since the money prices of articles of subsistence should (presumably) be reduced, in turn, to their costs of production. It is also very unclear how, if at all, rents are to be included among costs. It is possible that Steuart did not intend the calculation of real values to extend to agricultural goods, since the other component of price, profit upon alienation, is described as 'the manufacturer's profit' (Steuart, 1767: 160–1). Cantillon's land theory of value avoids all of these problems.

In any case, market price is determined by supply and demand, so the real value does not determine what the price will be, though it does set a lower limit to it. The difference between price and real value is the 'profit upon alienation'. Steuart discussed price determination at some length (e.g. 1767: 172–8, 189–96), in terms somewhat reminiscent of Cantillon (*Essai*: 117–21). However, where Cantillon explained why relative prices tend towards relative intrinsic values, because of the mobility of resources in response to market opportunities, Steuart seems to have ignored the self-correcting workings of the market mechanism, and called instead for intervention to maintain equality of supply and demand at a price which yields an adequate, but not excessive, profit.

Suppose, for example, that increased demand raises prices and profits; 'if, after a short vibration, the supply comes to be increased *by the statesman's care*, no harm will ensue', but if not, the high profit will be treated as normal and incorporated into the 'intrinsic value' (Steuart, 1767: 192–3; emphasis added). The market cannot be trusted. There are echoes here of the Physiocratic notion of the *bon prix*, of a proper price which policy should aim to establish, but the Physiocrats were concerned with agricultural prices, where Steuart seems to have been more interested in manufactured goods' prices. In any case, the Physiocrats wanted to achieve a *bon prix* mainly by removing mistaken state interference, while Steuart, as always, wanted more state supervision of the market.

In his discussions of foreign trade, competitiveness, and the balance of payments, like his theories of rent and prices, Steuart seems to have adopted some of Cantillon's ideas, but without recognizing how they hang together. Compare, for example:

> A sagacious statesman will, at all times, keep a watchful eye upon every branch of foreign commerce.... The matter exported from a country, is what the country loses; the price of the labour exported is what it gains. (Steuart, 1767: 291)

with Cantillon:

> It is by examining the results of each branch of commerce singly that foreign trade can be usefully regulated.... When the state exchanges its labour for the produce of foreign land it seems to have the advantage. (*Essai*: 233, 225)

On closer examination, however, the similarity of these (carefully selected) quotations turns out to be somewhat misleading. Cantillon called for regulation, not because of a general mistrust of markets, but because the policy maker was assumed to have objectives, such as military strength, and hence population size, which individual consumers could not be expected to take into account. In particular, exports of manufactures and imports of raw produce allow the population to expand beyond the size that could be supported by domestic agriculture alone.

Steuart, by contrast, thought that agriculture was performing below potential in all European countries, and that increased demand for agricultural products would stimulate output. This is clearly incompatible with his claim that it was good to export labour (i.e. labour intensive goods) and import 'matter' (primary products); he had a Physiocratic view of agriculture, but he took over Cantillon's (opposite) view of trade. Steuart's reason for the statement cited above is simply a paraphrase of Cantillon's, but it is incompatible with the rest of his argument. It is hard to avoid the conclusion that he was reproducing Cantillon's arguments without understanding their logic.

Steuart, like Cantillon, thought of prosperity and competitive success as essentially temporary. A successful exporter is hard to challenge, so whichever country is on top will stay there for a fair time, but eventually it will be challenged by lower cost competitors. Cantillon's argument was based on the specie-flow mechanism; a positive balance of trade leads to an increased money stock, an increased price level, and an eventual loss of competitiveness. He did not accept the quantity theory of money in its simplest form, and he thought the specie-flow mechanism would only work slowly, and would generate cycles, because of the long time lags involved.

Steuart, by contrast, did not accept that the quantity of money had any systematic effect on the general price level, so he had to reject the specie-flow mechanism, leaving him without any very clear reason why success should not last for ever. He argued, following Cantillon, that an increase in the money supply could only increase prices if it affected demand and supply in the markets for goods (Steuart, 1767: 344; cf. Cantillon, *Essai*: 117). He then argued that additional money need not come into circulation, because it could be 'locked up, or converted into plate' (1767: 344). So it could, of course, but Steuart gave no reason why it should be. As Cantillon explained, extra money brought in as a result of a positive trade balance accrues to merchants and the like as extra income, and they can be expected to spend it, adding to demand and driving up prices, though they can also be expected to hold on to (some of) the money for a while. The price increase may be delayed, but it happens eventually.

Without this line of argument, Steuart could only depict success in international markets as a kind of balancing act, dependent on the skill of the statesman (market forces, remember, cannot be relied on to do a good job without the statesman's help). Eventually, the tight-rope walker is bound to fall. Steuart produced some remarkably contorted arguments to back up his case (cf. 1767, vol I, bk 2, chap. 12). A positive trade balance, in itself, does nothing to raise prices or reduce competitiveness, but simply enriches the country at the expense of its neighbours (Steuart, 1767: 363). Steuart seems to have simply confused the accumulation of money with saving; thus he likened a country to a country gentleman who had to live on the product of his estate, and who would be poorer if he spent more than his income (1767: 362). Adam Smith quite rightly treated this crude form of mercantilism with scorn.

In sum, there is considerable circumstantial evidence that Steuart drew on Cantillon's economics for a number of his ideas, but there are few signs that he understood the underlying theoretical framework of the *Essai*. Cantillon used the example of the isolated estate (*Essai*: 59–65) to show that there was no need for the owner to direct every aspect of production personally. Steuart's central idea was the exact opposite: an economy needed a 'statesman' to watch over it and to intervene, like an overanxious nanny, at every stage.

Tribe (1978: 81, 85) has claimed that economists of the seventeenth and eighteenth centuries conceived of the state as a royal household, to be managed by a 'sovereign' or 'statesman'. This description fits Steuart's *Inquiry* very well (Tribe quotes it as a key example), but it does not do justice to Cantillon at all. Cantillon did, it is true, assume a ruler concerned with prestige and with power, but the main thrust of the argument is to show how rarely the 'statesman' need intervene, and how limited his power really is. Steuart looked backwards, to an older conception of economics; Cantillon, a generation earlier, had pointed the way to the new approach that was to make Steuart's work obsolete only a few years after its publication.

10.3 CLASSICAL ECONOMICS

From the late eighteenth to the mid nineteenth centuries, economic thinking was dominated by a system of thought which is now called 'classical' economics. Adam Smith (1776) and David Ricardo (1817) are the best known members of this school, though Turgot (1766) anticipated all the important features of their theory. The classical economists, of course, went well beyond anything they inherited from Cantillon, but many of the central elements of classical theory have recognizable roots in Cantillon's work.

Cantillon recognized two basic factors of production (or two basic contributions to production): land and labour. There were therefore two basic types of income, in his system, and two elements in costs: wages and rent. The classical economists added capital (or stock) to the list, so there were three types of income and three elements in costs: wages, rent, and profit (or interest).

Cantillon had not wholly ignored the need for capital, but he seems to have implicitly assumed that opportunities to make profits would automatically induce investment, so that capital scarcity need not be allowed for in the basic theory. In the classical story, by contrast, there is scope for very large amounts of investment, but these investment opportunities can only be taken up at a rate governed by the willingness of the population to save and thus to accumulate capital. The result is a very long-lasting process of accumulation and growth. Ultimately, the economy reaches a stationary state, when it has acquired what Smith called its 'full complement of riches'. This stationary state is, essentially, what Cantillon considered as the normal state of an economy; output is constrained by the available land, while landowners capture all the surplus over and above the supply price of labour and capital (subsistence wages for labour, enough returns to cover the wages of management and to compensate for risk).

The argument for free imports of corn, and other agricultural products, as formulated by West, Ricardo, and others, is essentially the same as the argument that Cantillon used to support the encouragement of manufactured exports. If land scarcity constrains economic expansion, imports of land intensive goods can allow further expansion, as Cantillon had claimed. West had a particularly clear statement of the case (1815), as did Torrens (1821), who explicitly discussed the economics of the stationary state, with results strikingly similar to Cantillon's.

Like Cantillon, the classical economists assumed that population responds to the demand for labour, so labour could be treated like an intermediate good. Given time to adjust, any demand for labour would be met at a given real wage. There is a minor complication here: since classical models allowed for a continuous process of capital accumulation and growth, in a way that Cantillon did not, some classical writers allowed for wages to be above the level corresponding to a static demand for labour by the amount needed to induce the necessary growth in the labour force. This adjustment, introduced by Adam Smith, is a natural adaptation of what had by then become the standard wage theory, to take account of economic growth. A further refinement is to allow for a two-way interaction between wages and growth. High growth pulls wages up, but high wages eat into profits and reduce the growth rate.[1] The treatment of wage differentials in Smith and in other classical writings was very similar to Cantillon's.

With wages essentially fixed, the remaining output is divided between profits and rent. The central theoretical problem for the classical economists was to account for the division of the surplus between these two categories of income. Smith never produced a coherent theory of rent or profits, despite the fact that Turgot had already arrived at a solution (1766). Turgot's solution was rediscovered, much later, by Malthus, West, Torrens, and Ricardo (all 1815). Here the classical economists clearly went beyond Cantillon.

The theory of prices used by classical economists was also a natural development of Cantillon's theory. Cantillon's 'intrinsic' values, or long run equilibrium prices, were prices which covered wages and rent at the going rates, with some element of profit included in the 'wages' of entrepreneurial labour. Turgot's 'fundamental values' or Smith's 'natural prices' covered wages and rent, plus interest (Turgot) or profits (Smith). Ricardo, of course, eliminated rent from prices by considering costs on marginal land, but costs and revenues on non-marginal land were still divided between the three elements of wages, rent, and profits. In all classical writings, market prices depend on demand and supply, but any divergence of price from its long run equilibrium value sets up forces which tend to return it towards the equilibrium, as agents respond to profit opportunities. Cantillon's account of the equilibrating mechanisms involved set the pattern for all his successors. What is missing in Cantillon, of course, is any clear notion of the equalization of profit rates – this essential component of the classical theory was developed by Turgot.

Classical monetary theory also has many elements in common with Cantillon, though it seems probable that the classics took their monetary theory mainly from Hume (1752). Hume's economic writings date from the long period in which Cantillon's *Essai* was completed but not yet published, so the presumption must be that the two writers arrived at rather similar views independently, with Locke as a common

---

[1] West set out the factors involved (1815, cf. Brewer, 1988c), but whether Ricardo recognized them clearly is a matter of debate (see e.g. Hicks and Hollander, 1977; Peach, 1986).

ancestor. It is possible that Hume knew Cantillon's work, perhaps through Postlethwayt's (1749, 1751) plagiarism, but there is no way of deciding whether it influenced him, even if he did know it. Hume and Cantillon shared the quantity theory of money and the specie-flow mechanism for balance of payments adjustment. Both explained interest rates in terms of real rather than monetary factors. Hume emphasized equilibrium outcomes, where Cantillon gave reasons why equilibrium might not be reached, or might be long delayed, and reasons why the path to equilibrium might affect the outcome. The classics generally followed Hume rather than Cantillon in their monetary theory (cf. Bordo, 1983).

Many of the central elements of classical economics, then, seem to have roots in Cantillon's theory, modified to deal with the visibly growing economy of England in the late eighteenth and early nineteenth centuries, rather than the apparently static world of the early eighteenth century, the background to Cantillon's work. This does not, of course, show that the classical economists actually took their ideas from Cantillon. Eighteenth and nineteenth century writers did not always acknowledge intellectual debts, so one can rarely be certain how far an idea was taken from the common stock, and how far it was reinvented independently.

Anne Robert Jacques Turgot (1727–81) was, in many ways, the first classical economist (though he is not always recognized as such). He had a distinguished career as an administrator, becoming Intendant of Limoges in 1761, and he wrote about a wide range of subjects. For nearly two years in 1774–6, he was Minister of Finance in the government of Louis XVI. He carried through a number of important reforms, but his attempts to replace the *corvée* with a more general land tax, and to remove the privileges of the guilds, stirred up too much opposition, and he was driven from office. It has often been claimed that the French revolution could have been avoided if Turgot's reforms had been completed. The quality of his economic writings is astonishing, given the limited time he devoted to economics in a very crowded life. Apart from some rather lightweight early works, most date from the decade 1763–73, when he was at Limoges.[1]

---

[1] On his career and his attempts to modernize French policy, see Groenewegen (1987b), or almost any standard work on the *Ancien Régime* in France.

Turgot did not refer to Cantillon in his economic writings. This is not surprising, since most of his economic pieces were short comments and articles, usually written for a specific occasion, and they rarely contained any extensive references at all. As a result, Cantillon's influence can only be traced by looking for similarities of content. Turgot almost certainly knew Cantillon's *Essai*, since it seems to have been published by a bookseller called Guillyn, who was closely associated with the group of intellectuals and economists around Vincent de Gournay. Turgot regarded Gournay as his mentor, at least in economic matters, and was an active member of Gournay's group, which was distinct from the Physiocrats, though not in general opposed to them. Murphy has suggested that the publication of the *Essai* was part of a deliberate programme of publication by Gournay and his followers (Murphy, 1986: 307). Turgot must surely have known a work which was part of that programme.

Turgot's earliest works were written before Cantillon's *Essai* was published, and were presumably not influenced by it. The 'Letter on paper money' of 1749 (Groenewegen, 1977: 1–8), a critique of proposals like Law's, has some ideas reminiscent of Cantillon, but must have been developed independently. The literature on monetary theory was already quite extensive, and Law's system attracted rather similar criticisms from a number of sources. The article on 'Fairs and markets', published in the *Encyclopédie* in 1757, on the other hand, may have been influenced by Cantillon, since it starts with an account of local markets which is strikingly similar to Cantillon's analysis of the functions of market towns (Hebert, 1981). Turgot used it as the basis of a claim that the great fairs were the artificial product of restrictive regulations and special fiscal privileges, which should be abolished.

Turgot's most important economic work, and the one which shows the clearest signs of Cantillon's influence, is his *Reflections on the Formation and Distribution of Wealth* of 1766 (Groenewegen, 1977: 43–95). It is very similar in style and character to Cantillon's *Essai*, and in particular to part one of the *Essai*, which is about the same length. (The English translation of the *Reflections* takes up fifty one pages, that of part one of the *Essai*, fifty four.) Both attempt to explain the basic workings of an economy, in abstract terms, referring to particular cases only as examples of general principles. Both use simple, direct language, and both are divided into short chapters or sections, each making a specific point.

The similarity of content between the two works is closest in the first twenty eight numbered sections in the *Reflections*. In section 29, Turgot started to describe the role of capital in production, which was, of course, where he made a decisive advance over Cantillon. Up to that point, however, his model was strikingly like Cantillon's. Both described a system with three classes, or component parts of society: husbandmen (that is, agricultural workers and farmers), artisans (non-agricultural producers), and landowners. The order of presentation is not quite the same, but the arguments are. Cantillon started with the division into owners and non-owners of land, and then discussed the urban–rural division. Turgot did it the other way round, first arguing that the gains from specialization in working up agricultural products into forms suitable for final consumption lead to a division of the population into husbandmen and artisans, and then dividing the rural population into landlords and others.

According to Turgot, competition between artisans ensures that the price of non-agricultural products is no more than enough to allow the producers to cover their subsistence needs (Groenewegen, 1977: 46). Turgot did not elaborate on his wage theory in the *Reflections*, but in another work, only a year later, he explained:

> High wages, on the one hand enable wage earners to consume more, and to increase their well being: on the other hand, this well being and these high wages offered, encourage population; the fruitfulness of the earth attracts foreigners, multiplies the people; and the increase in people in turn lowers wages through competition. (Groenewegen, 1977: 127)

This is, of course, the standard (classical) theory of wages and population, derived from Cantillon and others.

There is, however, a surplus of output over subsistence, which accrues, at this stage in the argument, to the husbandmen, since they are also the owners of the land.

> Nature does not bargain with [the husbandman] to content himself with what is absolutely necessary. What she grants is neither related to his wants, nor a contractual valuation

of the price of his days of work. It is the physical result of the fertility of the soil, and of the wisdom, far more than the laboriousness, of the means which he has employed to render it fruitful. (Groenewegen, 1977: 46)

At first sight, this may look like a claim that agriculture is uniquely productive because its products are a gift of nature, or something of the sort.[1] It is not. The husbandman grows crops; the artisan works them up into final products. The system generates a surplus because that is how things are. The artisan must sell his product at an agreed price, which will be forced down by competition, but agricultural prices will not be forced down by free entry in the same way, because land is scarce.

The next step was to argue that, once land is scarce, the ownership of land will inevitably become unequal, leading to the emergence of a distinct land owning class. Cantillon set out exactly the same case, at a rather earlier stage in his exposition. The grounds given by the two are almost identical (*Essai*: 5; Groenewegen, 1977: 47–8). The very close similarity in their arguments at this point is among the stronger reasons for suspecting some direct influence of Cantillon on Turgot.

Once ownership of land is concentrated into relatively few hands, the landowner can obtain non-landowners to do the actual work of cultivation. Turgot went through the various possibilities: slavery, personal bondage to the soil (a form of slavery or serfdom), vassalage, share-cropping, and simply renting the land to a farmer. Renting is to be preferred to share-cropping, because it allows the owner 'a more tranquil enjoyment of his revenue, being freed from the care of making advances and keeping an account of the product' (Groenewegen, 1977: 55). Similarly, Cantillon argued that renting (as compared to direct control by the landlord) saves the owner 'care and trouble' (*Essai*: 59). They agreed that renting improved the incentives for the farmer (*Essai*: 61; Groenewegen, 1977: 55), and also transferred risk from the landlord to the farmer, who now had to pay his contracted rent regardless of the success of the harvest (*Essai*: 47–8;

---

[1] Note, incidentally, the hint of the potential significance of technical change, in Turgot's remark that wisdom matters more than laborious work.

Groenewegen, 1977: 55). The earnings of both farmers and farm workers are now determined by competition (in the market for land to rent and in the labour market), and the surplus (depending on the fertility of the land) accrues to the landowner.

At this stage in the exposition, Turgot's model was effectively identical to Cantillon's. There are three classes (or, if you prefer, two classes, landowners and the rest, and two sectors, agriculture and the rest). Land is the only scarce resource, so all the surplus over subsistence accrues to the landowner.

Turgot next introduced the return on capital as a further category of income, and started to diverge from Cantillon. Capital is needed in production, and is scarce, so the owners of capital can choose between employing it themselves (in agriculture, industry, or trade), or lending it out at interest. Mobility of capital between different uses equalizes returns, making due allowance for risk and for other relevant factors. Cantillon had, at most, hinted at some of this. Turgot stated it clearly and explicitly, anticipating the similar, if more long winded, discussion in Adam Smith's *Wealth of Nations* by a decade.

Turgot recognized the significance of the agricultural margin. As capital is accumulated, the interest rate falls, and it becomes worthwhile cultivating lands which would not yield enough profit to justify cultivation at a higher interest rate. Marginal land yields enough to cover costs, including interest. Intra-marginal land yields rent equal to the excess of revenue over costs, including interest and risk discount among the costs. Here, Turgot clearly anticipated Malthus, West, and Ricardo by very nearly half a century.

Turgot's discussion of price, in the *Reflections*, is fairly skeletal; though the implied price theory is clear enough. If wages and profits (or interest) are equalized between different activities, it follows that the equilibrium price must cover labour and capital costs, plus rent (for agricultural products grown on non-marginal land). In a later work, Turgot spelled it out:

> Two types of value may be distinguished: fundamental value and exchange value. The fundamental value is what the thing costs to him who sells it, that is, the raw material cost, the interest of the advances, the wages of labour and

industry. The exchange value is the price that the buyer agrees upon with the seller. . . . It is not in any essential proportion to the fundamental value, but it has a tendency to approach it continually, and can never move away from it permanently. (Groenewegen, 1977: 120n)

The terminology is the same as Quesnay's, but the concept is not, since Quesnay's 'fundamental value' was what the price ought to be, while Turgot, in this extract, makes it clear that the fundamental value is the equilibrium which the market price (exchange value) tends towards. It is a natural development of Cantillon's concept of intrinsic value. Turgot's theory was not, of course, a land theory of value, because the interest on capital invested has to be included in the calculation.

In sum, Turgot and Cantillon were the finest economic theorists of the eighteenth century. Quesnay and Smith were more influential, but neither could match the coherence and clarity shown in Cantillon's *Essai* and Turgot's *Reflections* (cf. Samuelson, 1982: 47). There are very strong indications that Turgot built his model of growth and distribution on the foundations which he inherited from Cantillon.

Adam Smith may not match Cantillon or Turgot considered purely as a theorist, but he is a key figure in the history of economics because of the enormous influence he had on almost all his immediate successors.[1] He knew Cantillon's *Essai*, and referred to it directly in the *Wealth of Nations*, but only once. The editors of the Glasgow edition find another forty places in the *Wealth of Nations* where there is a close enough correspondence between Smith and Cantillon to justify a footnote reference to the relevant passage in the *Essai*, though that may, of course, simply reflect their thoroughness rather than any definite influence. Smith's writing was so discursive that one can find points of comparison with other texts almost too easily. There is, in addition, general agreement that Smith was influenced by the Physiocrats, who were, in turn, very directly influenced by Cantillon. He knew Turgot's *Reflections*, and he had met Turgot and discussed

---

[1] I shall not make any attempt to give a complete account of Smith's economics, or to refer to the massive literature on him. That would require a book, or several books, in itself (see Lightwood, 1984 – a whole book of bibliography, which can still only include a selection of works about Adam Smith).

economics with him. He also knew (and disagreed with) Steuart's work. Even so, it is hard to say whether any of his ideas actually came, directly or indirectly, from Cantillon's *Essai*. I shall examine some of Smith's central ideas to pick out those which might have roots in Cantillon's *Essai*.

Smith's theory of population and wages is a natural starting point. It has a great deal in common with Cantillon, though it has to be said that the line of thought which Smith and Cantillon share[1] was becoming almost a commonplace at the time. Smith's only direct quotation from the *Essai* occurs in this context (Smith, 1776: 85). Like Turgot (and many other contemporary writers), Smith stressed the relation between income and death rates (especially rates of infant mortality), which implies an equilibrium wage close to the physical minimum of subsistence (at least for the lowest paid groups, in a bad year), where Cantillon had stressed birth rather than death rates. In Cantillon's version, the decision to marry and have children (he took the two to be synonymous) depends on (expected) employment opportunities, so the equilibrium wage can be above the bare subsistence level. Smith did, however, note that wages would rise above subsistence in a growing economy, to induce enough population growth to keep the supply of labour in line with the (growing) demand.

Some of the phrases Smith used in his discussion of population and wages are very similar to Cantillon's, suggesting, though not, of course, proving, that there may have been some direct influence. For example, Smith wrote: 'men, like all other animals, naturally multiply in proportion to the means of their subsistence' (Smith, 1776: 162), a turn of phrase that calls to mind Cantillon's: 'Men multiply like mice in a barn if they have unlimited means of subsistence' (*Essai*: 83). Similarly, Smith's analysis of wage differentials (Smith, 1776: 116–28) reads almost as if it were directly modelled on Cantillon's (*Essai*: 19–23).

Smith's treatment of capital and profit, on the other hand, was a major advance over Cantillon's few and sketchy comments on the subject. Capital accumulation plays a central role in Smith's story, even more than in Turgot's. Smith, like Turgot, recognized profit as a distinct component of income and of (opportunity) costs. Unlike Turgot, he did not have

---

[1] Now, oddly, associated with the name of Thomas Malthus, who wrote later still.

any well developed theory of the overall level of the profit rate. There are suggestions that the agricultural margin may play some role, notably in the discussion of colonies, and in the account of the 'natural progress of opulence' – investment is forced out of agriculture into manufacturing for export, and finally into slow yielding and risky investments in shipping and trade, as opportunities for investment in agriculture dry up – but these do not amount to an explicit or well developed theory.

Smith's rent theory is rather complex, and has been the subject of much debate. The important question here is: what links are there with Cantillon? Smith distinguished between different uses of land: growing food for human consumption (with a further division between corn growing and animal husbandry), the production of raw materials, such as timber, and so on. The level of rent on corn land plays a particularly important role in his system, and is explained as follows:

> But land, in almost any situation, produces a greater quantity of food than what is sufficient to maintain all the labour necessary for bringing it to market, in the most liberal way in which that labour is ever maintained. The surplus too is always more than sufficient to replace the stock which employed that labour, together with its profits. Something, therefore, always remains for a rent to the landlord. . . . Land in the neighbourhood of a town, gives greater rent than land equally fertile in a distant part of the country. Though it may cost no more labour to cultivate the one than the other, it must always cost more to bring the produce of the distant land to market. (Smith, 1776: 162–3)

There are very strong echoes of Cantillon, and of his disciples, the Physiocrats, in this. Rent appears as a pure surplus over costs, just as it does in Cantillon's account, though profit at the going rate appears as a deduction rather than being hidden away in the 'wage' paid to farmers, or in the farmer's third of the produce, as it is in Cantillon's version. Rent on other kinds of land depends on relative prices; Cantillon too hinted at this, though he only stated it at all explicitly in his discussion of land near the capital. Smith's analysis of rent in the vicinity of a great city stands in a tradition which goes back to Cantillon, and before him to Petty. Prices are higher near the city, because goods from more distant sources have to bear transport costs, so money rents are also higher (cf. *Essai*: 151–5).

Smith's analysis of 'natural price' (long run equilibrium price, the equivalent of Cantillon's 'intrinsic value'), and of the relation between natural and market price, is another of the main elements of his theory which has very visible antecedents in Cantillon. In Smith's story, of course, capital costs have to be added to labour and land costs, in the calculation of natural prices, but his account of the equalization of returns by mobility between different industries is essentially the same as Cantillon's. Eatwell (1982: 204) says that Cantillon and Turgot had 'partially developed' the concept of natural price, but Smith presented 'the first satisfactory formulation' of it. He gives no justification for this judgement. As far as I can see, Cantillon and Turgot, taken together, had anticipated all of Smith's analysis.

None of this amounts to proof of Cantillon's influence, of course, since there are many examples of unnecessary originality in the history of economics, but it does show how directly Cantillon stood in the main line of descent leading to classical economics, and thus to all subsequent economic theory.

11

Conclusion

Cantillon's *Essai* was an amazing achievement. His analysis of pricing, distribution, and resource allocation in the first part of the *Essai* was the first complete and coherent model of an economic system as an interconnected whole. Even a sketch of such a model would have been a major advance, but Cantillon worked out the implications of his model with a rigour that was hardly matched for a century or more.

If his monetary theory was less strikingly original, it was only because monetary theory had already developed further than other branches of economics. Many of the components of Cantillon's monetary theory can be found somewhere in the earlier literature, but Cantillon made them into a coherent whole. He used the principle that money can only affect prices through its effects on the demand and supply for goods, to produce a coherent account of the dynamics of price changes. The quantity theory of money then emerges as a characteristic of long run equilibrium, with qualifications – a disturbance stemming from a change in real competitiveness, for example, can be expected to have continuing real effects. As with his analysis of a closed, non-monetary economy, it is hard to find an analysis of equal quality until far later.

Cantillon's impact on others, and thus on the development of the subject, is harder to trace than might be expected, given the quality of his work. His reputation as an economist never spread beyond a very limited circle, and his influence was often anonymous or indirect. Despite its high quality (never a guarantee of success), the *Essai* suffered from a number of crushing handicaps. By the time it appeared, fashions had changed, and most of the (few) readers able to appreciate its merits were committed supporters of *laissez-faire* and opponents of the mercantilist policies which Cantillon advocated.

Economists, then as now, were often judged more by their views on policy than by their contribution to the development of the subject. In addition, Cantillon's spare, dry, style may endear him to a modern economist, but it was not the way to win a wide audience. Adam Smith's more prolix but less precise writings were far more successful. Cantillon's most direct and obvious influence was on the Physiocrats, but they misused his work, and made it into a dogmatic and cranky system. Little wonder that the *Essai* sank into obscurity.

Cantillon's influence may not have been acknowledged, but it was essential. It is enough to point to two central elements of classical economics which must have come from the *Essai*. First, and perhaps most important, is Cantillon's concept of long run equilibrium, in which mobility of resources between different activities equalizes factor returns, so that relative prices fluctuate around their equilibrium levels ('intrinsic values' in Cantillon's terms, 'natural prices' in Smith and Ricardo), while any shift in consumer demands induces a corresponding reallocation of resources. Second, there is the notion of an endogenous population, and of an elastic supply of labour at a conventionally determined wage. Neither of these was wholly new, but Cantillon showed how to build a system around them, and the classical economists followed his lead. There can be little doubt that the architecture of the classical system, which dominated economics for a century, was based on Cantillon's *Essai*.

Bibliography

Allen, W. (1987) 'Mercantilism', in J. Eatwell, M. Milgate, and P. Newman (eds) *The New Palgrave: a Dictionary of Economics*, Houndmills: Macmillan.

Aspromourgos, T. (1986) 'Political economy and the social division of labour: the economics of Sir William Petty', *Scottish Journal of Political Economy*, **33**: 28–45.

—— (1988) 'The life of William Petty in relation to his economic writings', *History of Political Economy*, **20**: 337–56.

Bairoch, P. (1985) *De Jéricho à Mexico: Villes et économies dans l'histoire*, Paris: Gallimard.

Barbon, N. (1690) *Discourse of Trade*, London.

—— (1696) *A Discourse Concerning Coining the New Money Lighter*, London.

Barna, T. (1975) 'Quesnay's *Tableau* in modern guise', *Economic Journal*, **85**: 485–96.

Blaug, M. (1979) 'The German hegemony of location theory: a puzzle in the history of economic thought', *History of Political Economy*, **11**: 21–9.

—— (1985) *Economic Theory in Retrospect*, fourth edition, Cambridge University Press.

—— (1991a) (ed.) *Richard Cantillon (1680–1734) and Jacques Turgot (1727–1781)*, Aldershot: Edward Elgar.

—— (1991b) Review of O'Donnell (1990), *History of Economic Thought Newsletter*, **46**: 11–12.

Boisguilbert, P. (1966) *Pierre de Boisguilbert ou la naissance de l'économie politique*, Paris: Institut National d'Études Démographiques.

Bordo, M. (1983) 'Some aspects of the monetary economics of Richard Cantillon', *Journal of Monetary Economics*, **20**: 1–14; reprinted in M. Blaug (ed.) *Richard Cantillon (1680–1734) and Jacques Turgot (1727–1781)*, Aldershot: Edward Elgar, 1991.

—— (1987) 'Law, John', in J. Eatwell, M. Milgate, and P. Newman (eds) *The New Palgrave: a Dictionary of Economics*, Houndmills: Macmillan.

Boss, H. (1990) *Theories of Surplus and Transfer: Parasites and Producers in Economic Thought*, Boston: Unwin Hyman.

Bowley, M. (1973) *Studies in the History of Economic Theory before 1870*, London: Macmillan.

Bowman, M. (1951) 'The consumer in the history of economic doctrine', *American Economic Review*, **41**: 1–18; reprinted in M. Blaug (ed.) *Richard Cantillon (1680–1734) and Jacques Turgot (1727–1781)*, Aldershot: Edward Elgar, 1991.

Braudel, F. (1990) *The Identity of France: Volume Two: People and Production*, English translation by S. Reynolds, London: Collins.

Brems, H. (1978) 'Cantillon versus Marx: the land theory and the labour theory of value', *History of Political Economy*, **10**: 669–78.

—— (1986) *Pioneering Economic Theory, 1630–1980*, Baltimore: Johns Hopkins Press.

Brewer, A. (1987) 'Turgot, founder of classical economics', *Economica*, **54**: 417–28.

—— (1988a) 'Cantillon and the land theory of value', *History of Political Economy*, **20**: 1–14.

—— (1988b) 'Cantillon and mercantilism', *History of Political Economy*, **20**: 447–60.

—— (1988c) 'Edward West and the classical theory of distribution and growth', *Economica*, **55**: 505–16.

Cairnes, J. E. (1873) *Essays in Political Economy: Theoretical and Applied*, New York: Augustus M. Kelley, 1965.

Cantillon, R. (1755) *Essai sur la nature du commerce en général*, English translation by H. Higgs, New York: Augustus M. Kelley, 1964; original written c1730 (cited as *Essai*).

Cesarano, F. (1990) 'Law and Galiano on money and monetary systems', *History of Political Economy*, **22**: 321–40.

Child, J. (undated) *Selected Works, 1668–1697*, Gregg Press.

Coleman, D. (ed.) (1969) *Revisions in Mercantilism*, London: Methuen.

Deane, P. (1989) *The State and the Economic System: An Introduction to the History of Political Economy*, Oxford University Press.

Dunn, J. (1984) *Locke*, Oxford University Press.

Eatwell, J. (1982) 'Competition', in I. Bradley and M. Howard (eds) *Classical and Marxian Political Economy*, London: Macmillan, pp. 203–28.

Ekelund, R. and Hebert, R. (1983) *A History of Economic Theory and Method*, second edition, Singapore: McGraw-Hill International.

Eltis, W. (1984) *The Classical Theory of Economic Growth*, London: Macmillan.

—— (1986) 'Sir James Steuart's corporate state', in R. Black (ed.) *Ideas in Economics*, Houndmills: Macmillan; reprinted in D. Mair (ed.) *The Scottish Contribution to Modern Economic Thought*, Aberdeen University Press, 1990.

—— (1987) 'Steuart, Sir James', in J. Eatwell, M. Milgate, and P. Newman (eds) *The New Palgrave: a Dictionary of Economics*, Houndmills: Macmillan.

Foley, V. (1973) 'An origin of the *Tableau Economique*', *History of Political Economy*, **5**: 121–50.

Fox-Genovese, E. (1976) *The Origins of Physiocracy: Economic Revolution and Social Order in Eighteenth Century France*, Ithaca: Cornell University Press.

Gilbert, F. (1787) *Recherches sur les moyens d'étudier et de perfectionner*

la culture des prairies artificielles en Picardie, Paris.
Goubert, P. (1973) *The Ancien Régime: French Society 1600–1750*, translated by S. Cox, New York: Harper and Row.
Groenewegen, D. (1977) *The Economics of A. R. J. Turgot*, The Hague: Martinus Nijhoff.
—— (1983) *Quesnay: Farmers 1756 and Turgot: Sur la Grande et la Petite Culture*, University of Sydney: Reprints of Economic Classics, series 2, no. 2.
—— (1987a) 'Boisguilbert, Pierre le Pesant, Sieur de', in J. Eatwell, M. Milgate, and P. Newman (eds) *The New Palgrave: a Dictionary of Economics*, Houndmills: Macmillan.
—— (1987b) 'Turgot, Anne Robert Jacques, Baron de L'Aulne', in J. Eatwell, M. Milgate, and P. Newman (eds) *The New Palgrave: a Dictionary of Economics*, Houndmills: Macmillan.
Hamilton, E. (1969) 'The political economy of France at the time of John Law', *History of Political Economy*, **1**: 123–49.
Hebert, R. (1981) 'Richard Cantillon's early contributions to spatial economics', *Economica*, **48**: 71–7; reprinted in M. Blaug (ed.) *Richard Cantillon (1680–1734) and Jacques Turgot (1727–1781)*, Aldershot: Edward Elgar, 1991.
—— (1987) 'In search of economic order: French predecessors of Adam Smith', in S. T. Lowry (ed.) *Pre-Classical Economic Thought*, Boston: Kluwer Academic Publishers.
Heckscher, E. (1931) *Mercantilism*, 2 vols, English translation by M. Shapiro, London: Allen and Unwin, 1934.
Hennings, K. (1987) 'Capital as a factor of production', in J. Eatwell, M. Milgate, and P. Newman (eds) *The New Palgrave: a Dictionary of Economics*, Houndmills: Macmillan.
Herlitz, L. (1961) 'Trends in the development of Physiocratic doctrine', *Scandinavian Economic History Review*, **9**: 107–51.
Hicks, J. R. and Hollander, S. (1977) 'Mr Ricardo and the moderns', *Quarterly Journal of Economics*, **91**: 351–69.
Higgs, H. (1931) 'Life and work of Richard Cantillon', in R. Cantillon, *Essai sur la nature du commerce en général*, H. Higgs (ed.), reprinted New York: Augustus M. Kelley, 1964.
Hollander, S. (1987) *Classical Economics*, Oxford: Basil Blackwell.
Hone, J. (1944) 'Richard Cantillon, economist – biographical note', *Economic Journal*, **54**: 96–100; reprinted in M. Blaug (ed.) *Richard Cantillon (1680–1734) and Jacques Turgot (1727–1781)*, Aldershot: Edward Elgar, 1991.
Hoselitz, B. (1951) 'The early history of entrepreneurial theory', *Explorations in Entrepreneurial History*, **3**: 193–220; reprinted in M. Blaug (ed.) *Richard Cantillon (1680–1734) and Jacques Turgot (1727–1781)*, Aldershot: Edward Elgar, 1991.
Hull, C. H. (1899) *The Economic Writings of Sir William Petty*, 2 vols, Cambridge University Press.
Hume, D. (1752) *Political Discourses*, Edinburgh.

Hyde, H. Montgomery (1969) *John Law: the History of an Honest Adventurer*, London: W. H. Allen

Hyse, R. (1971) 'Richard Cantillon, Financier to Amsterdam, July to November 1720', *Economic Journal*, 81: 812–27.

Hutchison, T. (1988) *Before Adam Smith*, Oxford: Basil Blackwell.

Institut National d'Études Démographiques (1958) *François Quesnay et la Physiocratie*, Paris: Presses Universitaires de France (cited as *INED*).

Jevons, S. (1881) 'Richard Cantillon and the nationality of political economy', *Contemporary Review*, reprinted in R. Cantillon, *Essai sur la nature du commerce en général*, H. Higgs (ed.), reprinted New York: Augustus Kelley, 1964.

Johnson, E.A.J. (1937) *Predecessors of Adam Smith*, New York: Prentice Hall.

Keynes, J. M. (1930) *A Treatise on Money*, 2 vols, London: Macmillan; reprinted as vols V and VI of J. M. Keynes, *Collected Writings*, D. E. Moggridge and E. Johnson (eds), London: Macmillan, 1971.

King, G. (1936) *Two Tracts*, Baltimore: Johns Hopkins Press; written c1697.

Kuczynski, M. and Meek, R. (eds) (1972) *Quesnay's Tableau Economique* with the *Extrait des Economies Royales de M. de Sully* and the *Explication du Tableau Economique*, London: Macmillan.

Ladurie, E. Le Roy (1966) *Les Paysans du Languedoc*, English translation by J. Day, *The Peasants of Languedoc*, Urbana: University of Illinois Press, 1974.

Law, J. (1705) *Money and Trade Considered with a Proposal for Supplying the Nation with Money*, in Law (1934: 2–164).

—— (1934) *Oeuvres Complètes*, 3 vols, P. Harsin (ed.), Paris: Librarie du Recueil Sirey.

Leigh, A. (1974) 'John Locke and the quantity theory of money', *History of Political Economy*, 6: 200–19.

Letwin, W. (1963) *The Origins of Scientific Economics: English Economic Thought 1660–1776*, London: Methuen.

Lightwood, M. (1984) *A Selected Bibliography of Significant Works about Adam Smith*, Basingstoke: Macmillan.

Locke, J. (1691) *Some Considerations of the Consequences of the Lowering of Interest and Raising the Value of Money*, London, reprinted in 1696.

—— (1696) *Several Papers Relating to Money, Interest and Trade, &c.*, London, reprinted New York: Augustus M. Kelley, 1968.

Low, J.M. (1952) 'An Eighteenth Century Controversy on the Theory of Economic Progress', *Manchester School*, 20: 311–30.

—— (1954) 'The rate of interest: British opinion in the eighteenth century', *Manchester School*, 22: 115–38.

Malthus, T.R. (1815) *An Inquiry into the Nature and Progress of Rent, and the Principles by which it is regulated*, London.

Mandeville, B. (1714) *The Fable of the Bees: or, Private Vices, Publick*

Benefits, in P. Harth (ed.), Harmondsworth: Penguin, 1970.

Marx, K. (1963) *Theories of Surplus Value*, Part I, London: Lawrence and Wishart; written 1862–3.

Meek, R. (1963) *The Economics of Physiocracy: Essays and Translations*, Harvard University Press.

Mun, T. (1664) *England's Treasure by Forraign Trade*, London; reprinted Oxford: Basil Blackwell, 1949; written c1621.

Murphy, Antoin E. (1984) 'Richard Cantillon – an Irish banker in Paris', *Hermathena*, **135**: 45–74; reprinted in M. Blaug (ed.) *Richard Cantillon (1680–1734) and Jacques Turgot (1727–1781)*, Aldershot: Edward Elgar, 1991.

—— (1986) *Richard Cantillon: Entrepreneur and Economist*, Oxford: Clarendon Press.

—— (1991) 'John Law: aspects of his monetary and debt management policies', in W. Barber (ed.) *Perspectives in the History of Economic Thought, Volume V: Themes in Pre-Classical, Classical and Marxian Economics*, Aldershot: Edward Elgar.

North, D. (1691) *Discourses upon Trade*, London; reprinted Wakefield: S. R. Publishers and New York: Johnson Reprint Corporation, undated.

O'Donnell, R. (1990) *Adam Smith's Theory of Value and Distribution: a Reappraisal*, London: Macmillan.

Peach, T. (1986) 'David Ricardo's treatment of wages', in R. D. Collison Black (ed.) *Ideas in Economics*, Houndmills: Macmillan.

Perotta, C. (1991) 'Is the mercantilist theory of the favorable balance of trade really erroneous?', *History of Political Economy*, **23**: 301–36.

Petty, W. (1662) *A Treatise of Taxes and Contributions*, in C. H. Hull (ed.) *The Economic Writings of Sir William Petty*, vol. I, Cambridge University Press, 1899, pp. 1–97.

—— (1672) *The Political Anatomy of Ireland*, in C. H. Hull (ed.) *The Economic Writings of Sir William Petty*, vol. I, Cambridge University Press, 1899, pp. 121–231.

—— (1687) *A Treatise of Ireland*, in C. H. Hull (ed.) *The Economic Writings of Sir William Petty*, vol. II, Cambridge University Press, 1899, pp. 545–621.

—— (1690) *Political Arithmetick*, in C. H. Hull (ed.) *The Economic Writings of Sir William Petty*, vol. I, Cambridge University Press, 1899, pp. 233–313; written 1676.

—— (1691) *Verbum Sapienti*, in C. H. Hull (ed.) *The Economic Writings of Sir William Petty*, vol. I, Cambridge University Press, 1899, pp. 99–120; written 1664.

—— (1695) *Sir William Petty's Quantulumcunque Concerning Money*, in C. H. Hull (ed.) *The Economic Writings of Sir William Petty*, vol. II, Cambridge University Press, 1899, pp. 437–48; written 1682.

Postlethwayt, M. (1749) *A Dissertation on the Plan, Use, and Importance of the Universal Dictionary of Trade and Commerce*,

London; reprinted in M. Postlethwayt, *Selected Works*, vol. I, Gregg International, undated.
—— (1751) *Universal Dictionary of Trade and Commerce*, vol. I, London.
—— (1755) *Universal Dictionary of Trade and Commerce*, vol. II, London.
—— (1757) *Great Britain's True System*, London.
Prendergast, R. (1991) 'Cantillon and the emergence of the theory of profit', *History of Political Economy*, **23**: 419–29.
Quesnay, F. (1969) *Oeuvres Economiques et Philosophiques de F. Quesnay, Fondateur du Système Physiocratique*, A. Onken (ed.), New York: Burt Franklin.
Ricardo, D. (1815) *An Essay on the Influence of a Low Price of Corn on the Profits of Stock*, in *The Works and Correspondence of David Ricardo*, vol. IV, P. Sraffa (ed.), Cambridge, 1951.
—— (1817) *On the Principles of Political Economy and Taxation*, in *The Works and Correspondence of David Ricardo*, vol. I, P. Sraffa (ed.), Cambridge, 1951.
Roncaglia, A. (1985) *Petty: the Origins of Political Economy*, University College Cardiff Press.
—— (1987) 'Petty, William', in J. Eatwell, M. Milgate, and P. Newman (eds) *The New Palgrave: a Dictionary of Economics*, Houndmills: Macmillan.
Samuelson, P, (1959) 'A modern treatment of the Ricardian economy: I. the pricing of goods and of labor and land services', *Quarterly Journal of Economics*, **73**: 1–35.
—— (1982) 'Quesnay's *Tableau Economique* as a theorist would formulate it today', in I. Bradley and M. Howard (eds) *Classical and Marxian Political Economy*, London: Macmillan, pp. 45–78.
Schumpeter, J. (1954) *History of Economic Analysis*, London: Allen and Unwin.
Skinner, A. (1966) 'Introduction' to J. Steuart, *An Inquiry into the Principles of Political Oeconomy*, Edinburgh: Oliver and Boyd.
—— (1990) 'Sir James Steuart: Economic Theory and Policy', in D. Mair (ed.) *The Scottish Contribution to Modern Economic Thought*, Aberdeen University Press.
Smith, A. (1776) *An Inquiry into the Nature and Causes of the Wealth of Nations*, R.H. Campbell, A.S. Skinner, and W.B. Todd (eds), Oxford University Press, 1976.
Spengler, J. J. (1942) *French Predecessors of Malthus*, Durham, NC: Duke University Press.
—— (1954) 'Richard Cantillon, first of the moderns', *Journal of Political Economy*, **62**: 281–95, 406–24.
—— (1984) 'Boisguilbert's economic views vis a vis those of contemporary *Réformateurs*', *History of Political Economy*, **16**: 69–88.
Spiegel, H. W. (1983) *The Growth of Economic Thought*, revised edition, Durham, NC: Duke University Press.

Spooner, F. (1972) *The International Economy and Monetary Movements in France, 1493–1725*, Harvard University Press.

Sraffa, P. (1960) *The Production of Commodities by Means of Commodities*, Cambridge University Press.

Steuart, Sir J. (1767) *An Inquiry into the Principles of Political Oeconomy*, A. S. Skinner (ed.), 2 vols, Edinburgh: Oliver and Boyd, 1966.

Stone, L. and Stone, J. C. F. (1986) *An Open Elite? England 1540–1880*, Oxford University Press.

Tarascio, V. (1981) 'Cantillon's theory of population size and distribution', *Atlantic Economic Journal*, **9**: 12–18; reprinted in M. Blaug (ed.) *Richard Cantillon (1680–1734) and Jacques Turgot (1727–1781)*, Aldershot: Edward Elgar, 1991.

Torrens, R. (1815) *An Essay on the External Corn Trade*. London.

—— (1821) *An Essay on the Production of Wealth*, London; facsimile reproduction, New York: Augustus M. Kelley, 1965.

Tribe, K. (1978) *Land, Labour and Economic Discourse*, London: Routledge and Kegan Paul.

Turgot, A. R. J. (1766) *Reflections on the Formation and Distribution of Wealth*, in P. D. Groenewegen, *The Economics of A. R. J. Turgot*, The Hague: Martinus Nijhoff, 1977.

Vaggi, G. (1987a) *The Economics of François Quesnay*, Houndmills: Macmillan.

—— (1987b) 'Quesnay, François', in J. Eatwell, M. Milgate, and P. Newman (eds) *The New Palgrave: a Dictionary of Economics*, Houndmills: Macmillan.

—— (1987c) 'Physiocrats', in J. Eatwell, M. Milgate, and P. Newman (eds) *The New Palgrave: a Dictionary of Economics*, Houndmills: Macmillan.

Vaughn, K. (1980) *John Locke, Economist and Social Scientist*, University of Chicago Press.

—— (1987) 'Locke, John', in J. Eatwell, M. Milgate, and P. Newman (eds) *The New Palgrave: a Dictionary of Economics*, Houndmills: Macmillan.

Vickers, D. (1959) *Studies in the Theory of Money 1690–1776*; reprinted New York: Augustus M. Kelley, 1968.

Viner, J. (1937) *Studies in the Theory of International Trade*, London: Allen and Unwin.

—— (1948) 'Power versus plenty as objectives of foreign policy in the seventeenth and eighteenth centuries', *World Politics*, **1**: 1–29; reprinted in D. Coleman (ed.) *Revisions in Mercantilism*, London: Methuen, 1969, and in Viner (1991).

—— (1968) 'Mercantilist thought', in D. Sills (ed.) *International Encyclopedia of the Social Sciences*, New York: Macmillan, vol. 4, pp. 435–43; reprinted in Viner (1991).

—— (1991) *Essays on the Intellectual History of Economics*, D. Irwin (ed.), Princeton University Press.

BIBLIOGRAPHY

Walsh, V. (1987) 'Cantillon, Richard', in J. Eatwell, M. Milgate, and P. Newman (eds) *The New Palgrave: a Dictionary of Economics*, Houndmills: Macmillan.

—— and Gram, H. (1980) *Classical and Neo-Classical Theories of General Equilibrium*, New York: Oxford University Press.

West, E. (1815) *Essay on the Application of Capital to Land, with observations showing the impolicy of any great restriction of the importation of corn, and that the bounty of 1688 did not lower the price of it*, London; originally credited to 'a fellow of University College, Oxford'.

Index

agriculture 15–16, 32–3, 35, 46, 47–8, 109; role in Cantillon's model 24, 79; Quesnay on 161–3, 165–7, 170–1; Steuart on 177–8; Turgot on 188–9
Allen, W. 106n
artisans, handicraftsmen 22, 23, 42; incomes of 53–4; rural 77
Aspromourgos, T. 125n
augmentation 14, 92–5

Bairoch, P. 33
banknotes 82, 85, 102–3
banks, banking 4–5, 13, 14, 98–104; fractional reserve 102–3; national 103–4
Barbon, N. 124
Barna, T. 163
barter 77, 80
bills of exchange 99, 100–1
birth rates 37–8, 176
Blaug, M. 49, 50, 75, 105, 113
Boisguilbert, P. de 124–5, 174
Bordo, M. 5n, 92, 186
borrowing 56–7; from abroad 90–1, 114
Boss, H. 45, 159
Bowley, M. 132, 133
Bowman, M. 28
Braudel, F. 3, 33, 35, 37, 38, 43, 46, 165n, 173n
Brems, H. 61, 70n
Brewer, A. 70n, 161, 166n, 185n
Brydges, J. (Earl of Carnarvon, Duke of Chandos) 3, 4

Cairnes, J. E. 92
Calverley, Lady M. 138
Cantillon, Chevalier R. 4
Cantillon, P. 175
Cantillon, R. 1–196; on allocation 24–5, 27, 34; on banking 98–104; on capital 11, 34–5, 54–60; and classical economics 183–94; death (murder?) 8–9; on exchange rate(s) 98–104; on incomes and income distribution 49–60; and J. Law 5–8, 146–57; and J. Locke 137–46; life 1–9; model of economy 11, 19–35; on market prices 62–3; as mercantilist 105–6, 118–19; on money 12, 74–97; and W. Petty 125–37; on population 11, 13–14, 36–48, 108–13; and predecessors 15, 123–57; and A. Smith 191–4; and J. Steuart 175–83; and successors 15, 158–94; as theorist 10, 127; on trade policy 105–19; and A. R. J. Turgot 186–91; on value 61–74; on wages 52–4
capital 11, 34–5, 110, 117–18, 129; in classical economics 183–4; and employment 90; Law on 148–52; Quesnay on 168–9; return on 54–60, 63, 190; scarcity of 161; Turgot on 190; *see also* profit(s), interest
Cesarano, F. 149n
Chandos, Duke of *see* Brydges, J.
Charles II 125
Charles, Prince 175
Child, J. 124
circular flow 76
cities 22–4; capital 23–4, 30
classical economics 15, 16, 79, 105–6, 158–9, 169, 183–94; monetary theory 185–6; and population 184–5; prices in 185; profit and rent in 185
coin(s) 82
Colbert, J.-B. 124, 169
Coleman, D. 106n
competitiveness 12, 83–4, 88,

205

INDEX

114, 119, 181–2
consumer sovereignty 28, 107
consumption 27–8; by farmers, merchants 28; needs 67
contraception 46
cost of production 63
currency 93
cycles 90, 117

Davenant, C. 47, 178
Deane, P. 5n
death rates 37–8, 176
demand: deficiency of 147, 172–4; elasticity of 139, 140; and supply 56, 62, 91, 96, 180
Denier, J. 8
diminution 14, 92–5
Dunn, J. 138

Eatwell, J. 194
Ekelund, R. 127
Eltis, W. 164n, 167, 175n
employment 45, 85, 108
entrepreneur(s) 26, 50–2; incomes of 52, 54–60
Essai sur la nature du commerce en général (Cantillon) 1, 5, 9–13, 19, 74, 158, 167–8, 187–8.
estate, isolated or self-sufficient 24–9, 43, 53, 71, 72, 174
exchange: multilateral 100–1; rate(s) 14, 98–104

factors of production 183–4
fairs 187
fancy (preferences) 25, 26, 27–8, 50, 64
farmers, spending by 77
feudal(ism) 21, 164
Foley, V. 164
Fox-Genovese, E. 159n

Gage, J. 7
Gilbert, F. 46
gold 14, 75, 83, 85, 93–4, 100–2; minting of 101–2; value of 95–7

goldsmith(s) 102, 103
Goubert, P. 21n, 40n, 57n
Gournay, V. de 187
government: intervention by 89; spending by 92
Gram, H. 28
Graunt, J. 128
Groenewegen, P. 125n, 165, 174n, 187
Guillyn, P. A. 187

Halley, E. 47
Hamilton, E. 125n, 146n
Haydn, J. 26
Hebert, R. 30n, 125n, 127, 179n
Heckscher, E. 106n
Hennings, K. 57
Herbert, Lady M. 7
Herlitz, L. 61, 118n
Hicks, J. R. 185n
Higgs, H. 1, 26n, 50, 57, 80n, 99, 118
Holland *see* Netherlands
Hollander, S. 54n, 185n
Hoselitz, B. 51
Hull, C. H. 125n
Hume, D. 114, 185–6
Hutchison, T. 124n, 125n, 146n, 160n, 172n
Hyde, H. M. 5n

income(s) 14, 40, 49–60; distribution of 22, 49–50; spending of 77
infant industry 32, 89, 112–13
interest, interest rate(s) 14, 35, 55–7, 58–60; Law on 149–50; Locke on 141–3; and money 91–2, 141–3, 149–50; Petty on 131
investment 48, 149–50

James II 125
Jevons, W. S. 1
Johnson, E. A. J. 109n

Keynes, J. M. 92

Keynesian economics 151
King, G. 47, 124
Kuczynski, M. 163n

labour 19; demand for 43;
  employment of 44, 45; supply
  of 129
Ladurie, E. Le R. 37
laissez-faire 107
land 19–20; allocation of, use of
  24–5, 27, 66, 107; heterogeneous 68–70; ownership of
  13, 20–2, 189; price of 131, 142;
  par with labour (Cantillon) 24,
  65–8, 72–4 (Petty) 126, 132–3,
  137; and population 38–41; as
  scarce resource 11, 14, 34, 66,
  118, 129, 190; theory of value
  11, 61–74, 163
landowner(s), landlord(s) 21–2;
  and allocation 27, 34; as
  consumer(s) 25, 26, 43, 178;
  dominance of 34; incomes of
  49–50; and population 43;
  residence of 22, 23, 78
Law, J. 5–8, 13, 14, 15, 32, 56, 92,
  98, 104, 114, 123–4, 144n, 146–57, 187; on capital 148–52;
  career of 5–6; on interest rates
  149–50; and J. Locke 151–2,
  155; on money 147–57; on
  prices 153, 155–6; on underuse
  of resources 146–7
Leigh, A. 138n
lending 56–7
Letwin, W. 124n
Lightwood, M. 191n
location 29–32; of cities 23–4; of
  manufacturing 31–2; and price
  levels 30–1; of towns 23; and
  transfers of money 98–9; of
  villages 22–3
Locke, J. 15, 75, 80, 83, 95, 123–4,
  134, 137, 137–46, 157, 160, 185;
  career of 137–8; on interest
  rates 141–3; and J. Law 151–2,
  155; on money 137–41, 143–5;

on prices 138–9; on rent 145–6
Louis XIV 3, 5n
Louis XV 160
Louis XVI 186
Louvigny, Chevalier de 8
Low, J. M. 56n, 75n, 114
luxury 88

Malthus, T. 166n, 176n, 185, 190
Mandeville, B. 124
manufacturing 84, 109, 114–15;
  exports 106, 110; location of
  31–2
market: case for 105, 106–7, 176;
  price 14, 61, 62–3, 63–4, 76,
  133, 171, 180; world 117–8
marriages 37–8, 46, 176–7
Marx, K. 15, 39, 63, 140n, 176n
Meek, R. 159n, 160, 161, 163,
  164, 165n, 166, 167, 168, 170,
  171, 172, 173
mercantilism 12–13, 14, 19–20,
  44, 105–6, 113, 115, 134
mining 69, 83
Mirabeau, Marquis de 127, 159,
  167, 175
Mississippi Company 6, 25
money 12, 14, 73, 75–97; abundance of 88, 104, 114, 118; and
  balance of payments 84–91;
  circulation of 33, 76–82, 103,
  104, 164; classical theory of
  185–6; and interest rates 91–2,
  141–2, 149–50; Law on 147–57;
  Locke on 137–41, 143–5; minting of 101–2; Petty on 133–4;
  and price level 83–4, 113–15;
  quantity theory of 12, 75, 82,
  118–9; Quesnay on 171;
  Steuart on 182; supply of 91–2,
  103, 144–5, 149; transfers of
  98–9, 102; value of 140;
  velocity of circulation of
  (Cantillon) 76, 80–2 (Petty) 125
  (Locke) 134; and wealth 106–7,
  118, 139
Mun, T. 124

Murphy, A. 1, 2, 5n, 8, 9, 32, 146n, 151n, 187

Navigation Acts 111–12
neoclassical economics 49–50
Netherlands 3, 111, 112
Neuman, J. von 70
Newton, I. 97, 127
North, D. 124

O'Donnell, R. 49

par: in foreign exchanges 100–2; between land and labour 24, 65–8, 72–4; Petty on 126, 132–3, 137
payments, balance of 14, 84–91, 101–2; *see also* trade, balance of
Peach, T. 185n
Perotta, C. 106n, 109n
Petty, W. 2, 13, 15, 20, 36, 45, 47, 54n, 123, 125–37, 138, 142, 146n, 152n, 157, 160, 172, 177, 178, 193; Cantillon's comments on 126; on capital 129, 151; career of 125; on interest 131; on money 133–4; on par 126, 132–3; on population 126, 128; on prices 131–3; on rent 130–1; on trade policy 134–5
Physiocrats 15, 20, 55, 79, 158, 159–75; Smith and 191, 193; Steuart and 177, 178, 180–1; Turgot and 187
Poland 112
political arithmetic 126–7
Pompadour, Madame de 160
population 11, 13–14, 24, 36–48; classical theories of 184–5; growth of 46–8, 184–5; horses and 43–4, 108; and land 38–41; Malthusian theory of 14, 37, 38; occupational composition of 24, 41–2; in open economy 44, 108–13; Petty on 126, 128; and policy 42–5, 108–13; Quesnay on 167–8, 169; rural

and urban 33–4, 78; and standard of living 40–1, 108–9; Steuart on 176–7
populationism 36
Postlethwayte, M. 9n, 186
Potter, W. 114
preferences (fancy) 25, 26, 27–8, 50, 64
Prendergast, R. 55, 59n
price(s) 26–7; in classical economics 185; fundamental 170; Law on 153, 155–6; level of 83–4, 90, 113–15; Locke on 137–9; market 14, 61, 62–3, 63–4, 76, 133, 171, 180; natural 63, 133, 185, 194; Petty on 131–3; of production 63; Quesnay on 170–1; relative 87; Steuart on 179–81; Turgot on 188, 190–1; *see also* value
production: cost of 63; factors of 183–4
profit(s) 14, 54–60, 179; on alienation 179–80; classical theories of 185

Quesnay, F. 15, 158, 159–75, 190; on agriculture 161–3, 165–7, 170–1; on capital 168–9; career of 160; on international trade 172–3; on money 171; on population 167–8, 169; on prices 170–1; on rent 161–2, 172; *Tableau Economique* 79, 161, 163–4; on value 161–2

rent 14, 49, 71–2; Locke on 145–6; Petty on 130–1; Quesnay on 161–2, 172; spending of 23, 77–8, 80–2, 164, 174; Steuart on 178–9; three rents 39, 77
resources: allocation of 22, 26–7, 34, 87, 156; underuse of 146–7; *see also* land, allocation of
Ricardo, D. 63, 110, 140n, 161, 166n, 183, 184, 185, 190, 196
risk 50, 51, 53–4, 56, 59

Roncaglia, A. 125n

Samuelson, P. 61, 191
Schumpeter, J. 123, 125–6, 128n, 131, 133, 136–7, 160n
Shaftesbury, Earl of 137
ships, shipping 43–4, 111–12
silver 14, 71, 75, 83, 85, 93–4, 100 –2; minting of 101–2; value of 95–7, 132, 138, 153–5
Skinner, A. 175
slave(s), slavery 25, 52–3, 65
Smith, A. 1, 13, 14, 16, 19, 29, 39, 63, 105–7, 110, 111–12, 118, 152, 158, 159, 175, 183, 184, 190, 191–4, 196; on capital and profit 192–3; on population and wages 192; on price 194; on rent 193
society, human 19–22
South Sea Company 6, 7
specie-flow mechanism 12, 14, 75, 86, 105, 113, 182; Locke on 145; *see also* payments, balance of
Spengler, J. J. 1, 37, 125, 127, 174n
Spiegel, H. W. 37
Spooner, F. 35
Sraffa, P. 50, 70
state: revenue 115–6; spending 116
stationary state 184
Steuart, J. 16, 118, 158, 175–83; on agriculture 177–8; career of 175; on economic development 177–8; on foreign trade 181–2; on money 182; on population 176–7; on price 179–81; on rent 178–9; on statesman 176, 180, 183; on value 179–80
Stone, J. C. F. 47n
Stone, L. 47n
supply and demand 56, 62, 91, 96, 180
surplus 22, 49–50, 130

Tableau Economique (Quesnay) 79, 161, 163–4
Tarascio, V. 39, 40
tariff, optimal 115
taxes, incidence of 130, 145–6
technology, transfer of 89
Thunen, J. H. von 31
Torrens, R. 166n, 184, 185
towns 23, 187; *see also* cities
trade: balance of 12, 76, 85, 90, 101, 106, 113–18; 145, 147; foreign 13, 14, 105–19, 172–3, 181–2; policy 14, 89, 105–19, 134–5; terms of 115, 119
transport: costs 29, 30–1, 87, 89, 99, 100; by horses 43–4; by sea 43–4
Tribe, K. 28–9, 51–2, 183
Turgot, A. R. J. 16, 158, 159, 161, 169, 185, 186–91, 192, 194; on agriculture 188–9; on capital 190; career of 186; on ownership of land 189; on prices 188, 190–1; on wages 188

undertaker(s) 26n; *see also* entrepreneur(s)
unemployment 45, 134, 147

Vaggi, G. 159, 160, 163n, 164, 170, 172
value: Cantillon's theory compared with others 161, 170, 179–80, 185, 190; fundamental 185, 190; of gold 95–7; intrinsic 14, 61, 63–4, 75–6; labour theory of 61, 131–2; land theory of 11, 61–74, 163; of metals 69, 95–7; Quesnay on 161–2; real 179–80; of silver 95–7, 132, 138, 153–5; Steuart on 179–80
Vaughn, K. 138n
velocity of circulation 76, 80–2; Petty on 125; Locke on 134, 139; *see also* money, circulation of
Venice 3, 103–4
vent 138–9, 140

Vickers, D. 75n, 138n, 146n
villages 22–4
Viner, J. 106n, 114, 118

wage(s) 14, 27, 52–4, 58;
  differentials in 14, 53–4;
  geographical differences in 28;
  land equivalent of 65–8;
  Turgot on 188
Walsh, V. 2, 28
wealth 19, 106–7, 117, 118, 135, 168; of states 116
West, E. 161, 166n, 184, 185, 190
work, export of 109